THE VIOLENT UNDERPINNINGS OF AMERICAN LIFE

The Violent Underpinnings of American Life

How Violence Maintains Social Order in the US

Liam Downey

NEW YORK UNIVERSITY PRESS

New York

NEW YORK UNIVERSITY PRESS
New York
www.nyupress.org

Library of Congress Cataloging-in-Publication Data
Names: Downey, Liam, 1966–   author.
Title: The violent underpinnings of American life : how violence maintains
social order in the US / Liam Downey.
Description: New York : New York University Press, [2023] |
Includes bibliographical references and index.
Identifiers: LCCN 2022036089 | ISBN 9781479814848 (hardback) |
ISBN 9781479814923 (ebook) | ISBN 9781479814930 (ebook other)
Subjects: LCSH: Violence—United States. | Social control—United States. |
United States—Social conditions.
Classification: LCC HN90.V5 D696 2023 | DDC 303.60973—dc23/eng/20230210
LC record available at https://lccn.loc.gov/2022036089

New York University Press books are printed on acid-free paper, and their binding materials
are chosen for strength and durability. We strive to use environmentally responsible
suppliers and materials to the greatest extent possible in publishing our books.

Manufactured in the United States of America

10 9 8 7 6 5 4 3 2 1

Also available as an eBook

For all the people of the world who have
suffered violence at the hands of others.

CONTENTS

Introduction

Why Violence?

This is the first of two books I am planning on violence and social order. Born out of my motivation as both a sociologist and a citizen of the United States to better understand what kind of society I live in, these books address questions that have motivated all my research. Is the United States a society that values all its citizens? Does it treat all its people and the people of the world as fully and equally human, deserving of human rights, dignity, full and healthy lives, and the chance to develop their abilities, talents, and creativity to their fullest? Or is it a society that violates the rights of its own and other countries' citizens, lacks compassion, and routinely benefits from, even relies on, the harms done to others? And most importantly, at least for the purposes of this book, does it refrain from violence and harm or regularly rely on violence and harm to achieve its goals, guarantee its position in the world, improve its citizens' standards of living, and maintain social order both at home and globally?

These are important questions for any society, but in particular for the United States, which, as the world's most powerful nation, intrudes greatly on the lives of most of the earth's people and environments. These are also important questions for the United States because the United States likes to think of itself as an inherently good and peace-loving nation that harms others and resorts to violence only when absolutely necessary, often in the name of freedom, human rights, and democracy, and only when provoked or threatened by external enemies or deviant populations within its own borders.

Belief in its inherent goodness and peacefulness is not incidental to the United States' self-identity and sense of purpose in the world. Indeed, this belief allows the US government and middle-class Americans to look down on much of the rest of the world and a significant minority of the US population from a position of purported moral superiority, allowing the US government and its middle-class citizens to cloak many morally suspect deeds they carry out or support in a patina of moral righteousness that justifies these deeds in their eyes. This belief also allows the US government and its middle-class citizens to justify their intrusions into the lives of others by portraying these intrusions as purely beneficial to those affected by them.

But what if it turns out that violence—which I define as any action, inaction, or property of the social structure that *severely harms* an individual, community, or society, either physically, emotionally, or psychologically—is so widespread and central to the US social order that US citizens' lifestyles depend on it and it helps maintain social order throughout society (what I refer to as overall social order)? Moreover, what if the US social order and standards of living in the United States, including the living standards of the wealthy and middle-class, are based to a significant degree on violent social relations in other nations, on violence perpetrated in other nations by the United States and US corporations, and on violence that is both perpetrated against and carried out by subordinate groups and average people in the United States?

If these things are true, then the US government, US elites, and middle-class Americans rely on violence for their well-being, and thus cannot define foreign people, groups, and governments or subordinate groups within the United States as morally inferior simply because these people, groups, and governments are violent or because they have been labeled violent. If these things are true, and if mainstream America was to recognize them as true, it would also be much more difficult, if not impossible, for the US government, US elites, and middle-class Americans to justify morally suspect actions, structures, and social relations they rely on or take by referring to their society's basic goodness and inherent moral righteousness. If they are true, it would also mean that US citizens who benefit from violence, either because it helps produce social order or maintain their standard of living, would have to recognize that they have a moral obligation to help those who are harmed by this violence regardless of who carries out the violence or where those who suffer from it live.[1]

At the same time, however, if it turns out that social order in the United States relies on the violent treatment of a large percentage of the US population, and if in addition to this the social order produces widespread alienation, harm, and oppression while generating and perpetuating extreme gender, race, class, and other inequality, then drastically reducing the violence upon which the social order stands could potentially help liberate most Americans from the injustices, inequality, and oppression they experience. The majority of US citizens, even many of those who violently harm others, might therefore benefit greatly from the abolition of violent social relations in the United States and around the world.

Given the stakes involved, it is imperative that we determine the degree to which violence, conceived as a broad and overarching conceptual category, permeates the US social order. We must also determine whether different types of violence and violence occurring in different social arenas and different parts of the world work together and in conjunction with nonviolent factors to produce social order. In addition, if violence does promote overall social order, we must theorize the role violence plays in producing that order and by implication, the inequality, oppression, and alienation created by that order.

There was a time, prior to the mid-twentieth century, when social scientists were comfortable theorizing and investigating the relationship between violence and overall social order. But for a variety of historical and theoretical reasons, this is no longer the case. During the twentieth century, for instance, Marxists came to believe that state violence alone could not account for the persistence of capitalism and thus shifted much of their attention from state violence to Gramscian notions of consent (Gramsci 1971). Similarly, Foucault convinced many social scientists that the basis for social order had shifted from sovereign (state) violence to the ways in which individuals govern themselves and others through bodily discipline, biopower, and discourse (Nealon 2008), while Bourdieu highlighted the role embodied knowledge and habitus play in ordering behavior (Jenkins 1992).

It is my contention, and the main argument of this book, that although these theoretical shifts have provided social scientists with critically important insights into how social order is maintained, they have also led social scientists to unduly minimize the role violence plays in producing social order.[2] The approach I take in this book, therefore, is to argue that violence (broadly conceived) plays a key role in producing social order, and thus inequality, oppression, and alienation, and that it does so both directly and because it is often implicated in and inseparable from consent, discipline, discourse, biopower, habitus, and embodied knowledge (I explain these concepts and provide an in-depth discussion of Gramsci, Foucault, and Bourdieu in chapter 1).

As an example of this, it seems likely that consent to the US social order is produced to a significant degree by the fact that many US citizens are able to partake in a highly materialistic consumer culture predicated on the availability of a wide variety of inexpensive consumer goods. But this is at best a partial explanation of consumption-based consent. In particular, it begs the question of how companies are able to produce goods so inexpensively. One reason companies can do this, of course, is that they and their host countries' governments often treat workers and communities in ways that severely harm them and are thus violent according to my definition of violence. For instance, companies and governments sometimes use police, military, or mercenary forces to put down strikes, force people to leave their homes to make way for mines, or minimize dissent that threatens economic activity. In addition, companies often violate environmental, health, and safety regulations, and they sometimes pay wages that are so low that workers cannot feed themselves and their families. These actions, in turn, reduce production costs, and thus the prices consumers pay for goods and services, and they sometimes even make production possible. But they also produce severe physical and psychological harm—including exposure to highly toxic and hazardous materials, extreme hunger and disease, serious injury, severe emotional damage, and death—among workers, families, and communities. The lower prices these practices generate thus increase consent to the US social order by increasing Americans' ability to consume, but at the cost of inflicting violence on people around the world (Downey, Bonds, and Clark 2010; Global Witness 2016).

Violence is also intimately tied to many discourses and bodily practices (or disciplines) that produce overall social order. For instance, rape, which produces severe physical, psychological, and emotional harm, represents the extreme end of a continuum of patriarchal relations, discourses, and bodily practices that treat women as submissive, inferior bodies that exist to be enjoyed by men. Thus, when women are raped and when society favors rapists rather than those who have been raped, the entire continuum of relations, discourses, and bodily practices that make up the patriarchal order is reinforced and the order is strengthened.

But in addition to reinforcing patriarchal discourses and bodily practices, rape and the social construction of rape also reinforce a neoliberal
discourse that blames subordinate groups for the harms they experience,
and thus women for being raped (Anderson and Doherty 2008), and
that treats people and the earth as bodies or objects to be exploited for
the profitable enjoyment of capitalists. Rape and the social construction
of rape, both of which produce severe physical, emotional, and psychological harm and both of which treat women as sexual objects who exist
to be enjoyed by men (see chapter 3), thus promote overall social order
by reinforcing discourses, bodily practices, and unequal social relations
in multiple social arenas and not just the arena in which they occur.
Moreover, because violence can be so psychologically and emotionally intense and powerful, it is quite likely that the violence inherent
in rape shapes individual subjectivities and identities in ways that are
particularly psychologically and emotionally salient to its victims and
its perpetrators. And this, in turn, likely aligns victims' and perpetrators'
subjectivities and identities with dominant institutional practices and
external social and power relations, thereby further strengthening the
overall social order.

To demonstrate that violence plays a key role in producing and reinforcing overall social order, I develop five broad theoretical claims in
chapter 1 that link consent, discipline, discourse, biopower, habitus, and
embodied knowledge to both violence and social order. I define social
order as existing when social relations are stable *enough*, both within
a society and globally, that elites can regularly achieve their goals and
maintain or increase their advantaged position in society; and as previously noted, I define violence as any action, inaction, or property of the
social structure that severely harms an individual, community, or society, either physically, emotionally, or psychologically.

My overall argument, from which my five theoretical claims are
drawn, is that the US social order is more stable when (1) non-elites
have or are given a material, cultural, or psychological interest in supporting (or consenting to) the social order or some important aspect of
that order; (2) subordinate groups have difficulty organizing themselves
collectively so as to challenge the social order; (3) individual identity
and subjectivity are aligned with dominant institutional practices, external power relations, and objective social relations; (4) dominant dis-

courses and bodily practices, both within and across different arenas of social life, reinforce each other by invoking the same or highly similar discursive elements and symbolic structures; and (5) social, political, economic, and institutional arrangements within and among nations generate stable profits and secure investment opportunities, which are necessary for capital accumulation and the production of affordable consumer goods. Moreover, violence plays a key role in producing each of these outcomes.

I do, of course, make other theoretical arguments in this book, and I also argue that violence sometimes produces social order independently of consent, discipline, discourse, biopower, habitus, and embodied knowledge. But the important point for now is that each of the five theoretical claims I focus on most closely in this book and its projected companion volume links violence in multiple arenas of social life to overall social order *and* to one of the five tenets of my overarching argument, with each claim linked to its own tenet. This allows me to simultaneously test my specific theoretical claims and overarching argument and to show how violent relations in multiple arenas of social life combine to produce overall social order.

In accomplishing these tasks, this book and its projected companion volume extend sociological theory and fill several important gaps in the literature by developing and providing strong empirical support for a new theoretical model that links violence to consent, discipline, discourse, biopower, habitus, embodied knowledge, and social order. Moreover, though the theory I develop in chapter 1 does not directly link violence to inequality, oppression, and alienation, it implicitly links violence to these outcomes because these outcomes are produced by the social order that violence helps create and maintain. The *empirical evidence* provided in this book and the second projected volume also links violence to inequality, oppression, and alienation in multiple social arenas. This book and the projected volume thus extend sociological theory and fill important gaps in the field by providing a new explanation for how violence is linked not just to social order, but also to inequality, oppression, and alienation.

But extending sociological theory, filling key gaps in the literature, and accomplishing the tasks listed in the preceding paragraphs, while critically important to me, are in some sense just a springboard for addressing the kinds of issues that have always interested me: determining what kind of society I live in and whether my country supports the development of healthy people and relationships or damaged people and relationships. Another key goal of this book and the projected volume, then, is to determine just how fundamental violence is to our social order and, more pointedly, how much we rely on violence to live the lives we lead. The evidence is not good. Indeed, as we shall see, violence so permeates our social order that it is something of a miracle that the United States and its citizens are able to ignore both the evidence and their senses and describe themselves as peace-loving.

And yet, it is also perfectly understandable that the US government, US elites, and middle-class Americans do not want to admit that violence permeates the social order, for such an admission would undermine US legitimacy, the legitimacy of our economic, political, and social systems, and the psychological foundation upon which American life rests. It would also force us to recognize our moral obligations to others.

But the costs of denial are extremely high too and include the perpetuation of all the violence and harm that are currently being done to ourselves and others, the continued silencing and oppression of those who are the victims of violence, and our never-ending alienation from ourselves, each other, and the world we live in. For unless we believe that humans' primary trait is a propensity for violence and that violence does not harm the psyches of those who engage in it and are victims of it, then relying on extremely high and sustained levels of violence to maintain our lifestyles and social order is alien to our innate humanity. Treating others violently and being treated violently also alienate us from other people, with those experiencing extreme violence often alienated not just from those who harmed them but from all or most of the people they know. Furthermore, the ability to deny the consequences of our actions and to ignore what is going on in the world requires a rupture between our consciousness and thought on the one hand and our experiences and available evidence on the other that alienates us from both ourselves and the world we live in.[3]

My other main goal in writing about violence and social order, then, is to help remove the blinders that prevent Americans from seeing the violence that both surrounds them and makes their lives possible. This, I hope, will contribute to efforts to reduce violence and alienation in the United States and around the world and help convince readers that dominant groups are not morally superior to groups that are normally associated with violence and that the United States is not morally superior to other nations.

To accomplish the goals and tasks set forth in the preceding pages, I use evidence on sexual violence against women, police and political violence against African Americans, consumption- and profit-related violence, and militarism to test my theoretical claims and demonstrate that violence does indeed play a key role in producing overall social order in the United States. In this book, I investigate sexual violence against women and police and political violence against African Americans. In the projected volume, I examine consumption- and profit-related violence and militarism. This book thus highlights violence that occurs within the United States, while the later book will examine violence that occurs both inside and outside the United States. Nevertheless, both books will highlight the role violence plays in producing overall social order within the United States.

This book is organized as follows. In chapter 1, I present my theoretical argument. I begin by demonstrating that violence is so strongly and intimately associated with the United States' position in the world and with US citizens' lives and lifestyles that it is impossible to separate this nation's power, position, and wealth and citizens' lives and lifestyles from this violence. I then provide detailed justifications of my definitions of violence and social order, present my theory and situate it in the broader literature, and argue that rather than attempting to replace prior theories concerning the production of social order, I see violence as working with factors highlighted by prior theory—factors such as consent, discourse, bodily practices, habitus, biopower, and embodiment—to produce social order.

I turn my attention in chapters 2 and 3 to sexual violence against women. In these chapters I demonstrate three key points: first, that the portrayal of women and girls in popular culture, female bodily practices based on this portrayal, sexual harassment, rape, and society's reaction to rape are all violent practices and that they all display a common set of cultural scripts, symbolic structures, and discursive elements drawn from patriarchal and neoliberal discourse; second, that these violent social practices form a coherent, unified, interdependent, and violent social structure that shapes the behavior, identity, internal consciousness, subjectivity, and interests of women, girls, men, and boys; and third, that because of the foregoing, these violent practices play a key role in promoting overall social order. Most importantly, they (a) strongly reinforce dominant patriarchal and neoliberal discourses that undergird the social order, and thus strengthen key discourses in multiple social arenas; (b) align individual subjectivity and identity with dominant institutional and discursive practices and external social and power relations; and (c) provide many men and some women with psychological, cultural, and material benefits that give them reason to support, or consent to, the social order.

Chapter 4 investigates police violence against African Americans, which promotes overall social order in several key ways: it creates divisions between subordinate groups that make it difficult for them to work collectively to challenge the social order; reinforces dominant discourses in multiple social arenas; aligns White subjectivity and identity with dominant institutional practices and external social and power relations; and promotes the psychological, cultural, and material interests of many Whites. To demonstrate that police violence against African Americans supports overall social order in these ways, I first describe the role police violence plays in the lives of Black Americans and show that this violence occurs and is threatened so regularly that it impinges directly upon the lives of most Black people, restricting their freedoms and rights on a daily basis. I then discuss mass incarceration and its consequences for African Americans, particularly for poor African Americans. I highlight the many ways in which police violence and mass incarceration harm Black people and then tie police violence and mass incarceration to social order in the ways outlined at the beginning of this paragraph.

Chapter 5 is the last empirical chapter of the book. In it, I examine the race and crime rhetoric that US presidents, presidential candidates, and political analysts from the Truman administration in the late 1940s to the Clinton administration in the late 1990s used to support mass incarceration and the violent policing of Black people. I demonstrate that from the late 1940s to the late 1990s the Democratic and Republican Parties both employed racist rhetoric that linked Black people to crime and that in the 1980s and 1990s they both supported highly violent anti-Black policing policies. I further demonstrate that the two parties' racist anti-crime policies and rhetoric became increasingly similar over time and nearly identical in the 1980s and 1990s and that the reason the two parties adopted harsh anti-crime and anti-Black policies and rhetoric was that neither party believed it could win elections without doing so.

I then argue that the history recounted in chapter 5 provides strong support for my theory of violence and social order. On the one hand, by constantly reminding African Americans that the dominant White society viewed them as dangerous, inferior, and uncivilized and by providing the justification needed to make violent anti-Black policing acceptable to Whites, the racially biased anti-crime rhetoric employed by the two parties inflicted severe psychological, emotional, and physical harm on African Americans, and was thus extremely violent. On the other hand, the two parties' racist anti-crime rhetoric played a key role in producing overall social order: it reinforced dominant discourses in multiple social arenas, promoted the psychological, cultural, and material interests of many Whites, aligned White subjectivity and identity with dominant institutional practices and external social and power relations, and created divisions between subordinate groups that made it difficult for them to organize collectively to challenge the social order. It also justified the enactment of racially biased anti-crime policies that produced many of the same order-producing outcomes as did the rhetoric. Moreover, the social divisions created by the two parties' rhetoric and policies still exist today, and not only between Blacks and Whites, as many would expect. These divisions also exist between Whites who take different positions on police violence and racist political rhetoric, imbue these differences with great moral, cultural, and political significance, and fail to see that their political leaders do not differ nearly so much on race, rhetoric, and policing as they would like to think they do.

Chapters 2–5 thus provide strong empirical support for four of the five claims that form the heart of my theoretical argument. In particular, they support those claims that hold that in the United States violence plays a key role in producing overall social order by (a) giving non-elites a material, cultural, or psychological interest in supporting (or consenting to) the social order or some important aspect of that order; (b) making it difficult for subordinate groups to organize themselves collectively so as to challenge the social order; (c) aligning individual identity and subjectivity with dominant institutional practices, external power relations, and objective social relations; and (d) reinforcing dominant discourses and bodily practices in multiple social arenas.

Indeed, there is only one key theoretical claim not tested in this book. However, this claim, which holds that violence promotes social order by producing stable political, economic, and institutional arrangements within and among nations that generate stable profits and secure investment opportunities, will be tested extensively in my next book. Taken collectively, then, the empirical chapters in this and the next book will test all my major theoretical claims, with each of these claims supported by evidence drawn from multiple social and institutional arenas, and thus from some combination of arenas (and relationships) as different from each other as those associated with sexual violence, police violence, political-rhetorical violence, consumption- and profit-related violence, and militarism. Testing multiple sets of claims in multiple empirical chapters also allows me to show how violent actions, inactions, and structures in very different social and institutional arenas work together to promote social order. It should thus be clear that I am able to provide considerably stronger, broader, and deeper empirical support for my theoretical argument than I could if I investigated only one social or institutional arena or if I tested only one theoretical claim in each empirical chapter.

Some readers will have noticed that some of the arguments I plan to make and some of the things I plan to demonstrate in chapters 2–5 have already been argued and demonstrated by others. This is a valid point, as is the point that most of the evidence I draw upon in this book is evidence collected by others. But the fact that I borrow arguments and evidence from others does not detract from what I do in this book. First, many researchers, both quantitative and qualitative, rely on secondary data. Second, though a lot of people have written about sexual, political, and police violence, many of these authors have not used their findings and arguments to explain social order, and of those who have, none have done so in the way that I do. Third, what differentiates my case studies from those of other scholars is that regardless of the specific supporting arguments I make in any case study or chapter, the goal of each case study and chapter is to test my theoretical model and demonstrate that violence in multiple institutional arenas interacts with factors highlighted by Gramsci, Foucault, and Bourdieu in ways not specified by other scholars to produce overall social order. As a result, even when some of my arguments are similar to those made by other researchers, my goal in presenting these arguments is different, as are the theoretical conclusions I draw from both these arguments and the evidence I present. I am also much more likely than other scholars whose arguments overlap mine to emphasize violence as a conceptual category distinct from the specific types of violence I am examining.

Thus, what makes this book and the subsequent volume new and unique is not that every argument and finding I make in them is new and unique, though many of them are, and not that I rely on original data. What makes these books new and unique is that I use the many arguments I make, both borrowed and original, and the very wide variety of evidence I employ to (a) fill several critically important gaps in the literature and (b) provide strong empirical support for a new and unique theoretical argument that has not been developed or tested before. This book and its companion volume are therefore quite new and original, and the fact that I use secondary data and sometimes borrow other people's arguments to test my theory and demonstrate its empirical validity in no way detracts from the books or my ability to achieve the goals I have set for myself in them.

Indeed, this book and its companion volume advance the literature in several important ways. Most importantly, they demonstrate that violence is absolutely central to social life, strongly shaping the kinds of factors that Gramsci, Foucault, and Bourdieu highlighted in their investigations and working both independently and interactively with these factors to promote social order throughout society. These books also demonstrate that sociologists need to make the study of violence (conceptualized in broad, abstract terms) a mainstream sociological concern, investigate the myriad ways in which violence throughout society benefits elites and dominant groups, and highlight the fact that violence is not solely or primarily a characteristic of subordinate groups and the deviant but is instead a key property of the US social system. Finally, these books demonstrate that US citizens have a moral obligation to refashion their social, political, economic, and military relationships to others, both globally and domestically, so as to reduce the great harm and suffering that so strongly shape and so often benefit their lives and the fortunes of their country.

1

Violence and Social Order

In the preceding chapter, I argued that violence is so strongly and intimately associated with the United States' position in the world and with US citizens' lives and lifestyles that it is impossible to separate this nation's power, position, and wealth, citizens' lives and lifestyles, and overall social order from this violence. I did not, however, demonstrate that these things are true. My goals in this chapter are thus threefold: first, to demonstrate that this nation's power and position and US citizens' lives and lifestyles are inseparable from violence occurring both in the United States and around the world; second, to convince readers that to better understand and explain not only social order, but also inequality, oppression, and alienation, social scientists must develop new theories or more fully develop already existing theories that link violence (broadly conceived) to social order; and third, to develop a new theory that makes this link.

I begin by highlighting several important ways in which violence helps produce or is otherwise associated with the United States' power, position, and wealth and with US citizens' lives and lifestyles. I then provide detailed justifications of the definitions of violence and social order that I gave in the book's introduction, set forth my theory, and situate it within the broader literature. I also argue that rather than attempting to replace prior theories concerning the production of social order, I see violence as working with factors highlighted by prior theory—factors such as consent, discourse, bodily practices, and embodiment—to produce social order. I thus provide a new and unique theoretical understanding of how social order is produced that fills important gaps in the literature not by dismissing the insights of prior theory but rather by arguing that the factors highlighted by prior theory do not operate independently of violence.

Because I define violence as any action, inaction, or property of the social structure that severely harms an individual, community, or society, either physically, emotionally, or psychologically, violence as I conceptualize it includes murder; rape; hunger and disease caused by global and national economic structures; and psychological harm produced by the objectification of women and by discourses that define some groups as innately inferior to other groups. It also includes the psychological trauma that undocumented immigrants in the United States often experience as a result of US immigration policy; the physical and psychological harm police stop and search practices inflict on millions of US citizens; explicit and implied threats of physical violence by parents, spouses, soldiers, and governments, which can cause severe emotional and psychological trauma; and the physical and psychological harm that forcibly removing people from their homes can produce. Thus, throughout this chapter and book, whenever I discuss an action, inaction, or property of the social structure that severely harms an individual, community, or society, readers should understand that harm and the factors causing that harm to be violent.

Violence and American Life

To put it bluntly, but not at all hyperbolically, our lives and lifestyles and communities and country are drenched in the blood, suffering, and violence experienced by others. It is in the food we eat, the goods we purchase, the images we see, the discourses we use, the ways we hold our bodies and move through the world, and the ways we think about ourselves and others. It is in the visible and invisible boundaries that define neighborhoods, identities, races, and genders, the web of international relations that shapes our geopolitical position in the world and standards of living, and our relations with authority figures, the state, each other, and people around the world.

Examples of this suffering and violence are easy to come by. In 2015, for instance, 77 percent of the telephones, more than 60 percent of the computers and computer equipment, 37 percent of the apparel and clothing accessories, and 26 percent of the machinery and transport equipment imported into the United States were produced in China (Morrison 2017; UN Comtrade data); and in 2019, US goods imports from China were valued at nearly 50 percent of those of the United States' next four top importers (Mexico, Canada, Japan, and Germany), making China by far the United States' largest importer (US Trade Representative's Office 2022). China, however, relies on a labor system that separates workers from their homes and forces them to work exceptionally long hours, thereby severely harming them, both physically and psychologically (research shows that excessively long work hours can produce anxiety, exhaustion, depression, sleeplessness, and cardiovascular and coronary disease). The Chinese labor system also uses the government's policing power, and thus the threat of direct physical violence, to restrict the movement of workers and prevent the formation of labor unions, thereby lowering the prices of goods imported into the United States (Cheng et al. 2014; Lee 2016; Liu and Tanaka 2002; Verité Research 2004).

Nor are goods from China the only violently produced goods US citizens consume. The global agribusiness industry and Western-dominated international trade and finance institutions have, for instance, worked exceptionally hard over the past several decades to create a global agricultural system that in addition to ensuring agribusiness profits and providing Western consumers with relatively low-price food (Downey 2015), has made hundreds of millions of peasant laborers superfluous (Breman 2010; M. Davis 2007; Levien 2013, 2012). These laborers, who were already quite poor, have thus been pushed even further into poverty and hunger than they already were, increasing their fear, discomfort, and pain (severe poverty and hunger can be both painful and scary), making them more susceptible to death and disease, and harming them psychologically by making it clear to them that their societies and the global economy do not care about them. To make way for export-oriented farming and industry, many of these superfluous laborers have also been forced to leave their homes by the threat of state violence and the coercive power of the market, which, along with forced removal, can be physically and psychologically traumatic; and they have often been given little choice but to migrate to heavily and violently policed urban slums (Breman 2006). Moreover, millions of workers and farmers around the world who produce for the US market are forced to work in unsafe conditions or to live on wages or incomes that do not provide them with adequate food, shelter, and health care, resulting in severe hunger and disease, physical impairment, and death (International Trade Union Confederation 2015).

The extraction of natural resources used to produce and transport the goods and materials that American citizens and businesses rely on every day is also associated with extreme violence. For instance, platinum, palladium, rhodium, rare earth elements, manganese, titanium, copper, coltan, cobalt, and petroleum, which are all critical to the functioning of the US economy and/or military, and which all play a key role in our lives, are collectively associated with a wide range of violent activities. These activities, which are fairly widespread and which are associated with the extraction of many natural resources, include rape, torture, murder, the forced removal of people from their homes and villages by police and military personnel, the destruction of villages, the use and threatened use of armed violence against miners and protestors, and the repression of indigenous and colonized people (Downey 2015; Global Witness 2016). Resource extraction is also often associated with full-scale warfare, including in the Democratic Republic of Congo (DRC), where the extraction of minerals used to produce computers, cell phones, and industrial goods has contributed in significant ways to war and armed conflict, resulting in widespread rape, extensive physical and psychological trauma, and the deaths of between 2.5 and 5.4 million people between the mid-1990s and 2010 (C. Lynch 2010; World Without Genocide 2016).

Not surprisingly, extraction-related violence helps increase corporate profits and the material standard of living of US citizens by increasing the supply, and thus reducing the cost, of natural resources used to produce and transport the goods and services US businesses and consumers rely on daily (Downey 2015).[1] The US government and US military also benefit from these reduced costs, which lower the prices of the critical supplies and finished products they purchase. However, the US government does not rely solely on violence carried out by others to ensure a stable supply of the natural resources needed to maintain US military power, ensure business profits, generate taxes, reduce government spending, and keep US consumers happy. It also provides direct support to those who engage in such violence, and it often engages directly in extraction-related armed violence itself.[2]

The United States, for instance, played an important role, along with China, France, the United Kingdom, and a handful of other countries, in arming and otherwise supporting the militias and governments fighting for control of the DRC's natural resources (Amnesty International

2012; Stearns et al. 2012). To ensure stable supplies of Middle East oil, the United States has also funded and trained extremely violent and repressive police and internal security forces in the region (Kuzmarov 2012), while selling vast quantities of weapons to its regional allies, in particular to Israel, Saudi Arabia, and Egypt (Defense Security Cooperation Agency 2014).

Because the United States plays such a large role in helping Israel, Saudi Arabia, and Egypt maintain their overall military power, it bears strong responsibility for the actions these countries' military forces take, regardless of whether the United States or its citizens support or US weapons are used in any specific military action. Thus, US efforts to secure a globally adequate supply of low-priced oil, which hinges on Middle East oil production (Klare 2004), and the benefits US citizens receive as consumers of low-priced oil and of goods and services produced and transported with low-priced oil cannot be separated from the violence carried out by Israeli, Egyptian, and Saudi military forces. Indeed, without Middle East oil production, oil prices would rise dramatically, creating a global economic crisis that would destroy or seriously undermine the US economy and US consumer society.

The violence carried out by Israeli, Egyptian, and Saudi military forces is not insignificant. For instance, in 2015 a nine-nation coalition led by Saudi Arabia launched an ongoing aerial bombardment campaign against Yemen that could not have been undertaken without US targeting, intelligence, and aircraft maintenance and refueling support (*Democracy Now* 2016a, 2016b; *New York Times* Editorial Board 2016; Walsh and Schmitt 2018). By early 2017 this conflict, which had been broadened to include a naval blockade and ground war, had killed at least ten thousand people, displaced three million others, and put millions at risk of starvation. And by 2019 at least nineteen thousand air raids, employing both US and British jets and bombs, had been carried out, with war deaths possibly having risen to sixty thousand people by that time. The war also significantly increased rates of child malnutrition, such that by December 2016 one Yemeni child was dying every ten minutes (Al Jazeera 2019; Walsh and Schmitt 2018; *Democracy Now* 2016b; *New York Times* Editorial Board 2017).

Egypt's military is also associated with extreme violence. In 2013, for example, military forces under General Abdel Fattah el-Sisi took control of the Egyptian government in a coup that overthrew the nation's president, Mohamed Morsi. Between then and 2017, the military-run government became increasingly repressive, severely curtailing Egyptians' civil and political rights, jailing tens of thousands of political opponents, torturing detainees, raiding thousands of homes in Cairo, sentencing hundreds of opponents to death, and in August 2013 killing at least 817 and probably more than 1,000 civilians at a protest encampment in Rab'a al-Adawiya Square in Cairo (Hessler 2017; Human Rights Watch 2017; Mepham 2016; Shenker 2016).

The Israeli military also regularly employs violence to achieve its goals, often but by no means always against the Palestinians. Indeed, regardless of whether one supports or opposes Israeli policy, it is impossible to argue that Israel does not employ extremely high levels of violence in its conflicts with the Palestinians and others. For instance, since Israel's founding, its security forces have detained hundreds of thousands of Palestinians, many of them children and many without trial, with one estimate placing the total number of Palestinians detained or imprisoned since 1948 at 800,000 (Institute for Palestine Studies 2017; Khalidi 2014). The Israeli military has also "subjected Palestinian detainees, including children, to torture and other ill-treatment" (Amnesty International 2017, 203), and through its blockade of the Gaza Strip has decimated the Gazan economy and dramatically increased food insecurity such that in 2012, 57 percent of Gazan households were food insecure (*Democracy Now* 2017; United Nations OCHA OPT 2014). Moreover, during its 2014 invasion of Gaza—which relied on aircraft, weapons, replacement parts, and ammunition provided by the US government (Gottinger and Klippentstein 2014)—Israel "killed 2,145 Palestinians (578 of them children [and most of them civilians]), injured over 11,000 people, and demolished more than 17,000 homes" (Saif 2015), with 500,000 Palestinians, or 28 percent of Gaza's population, displaced at the height of the conflict (United Nations Human Rights Council 2015).[3]

The two US-led wars with Iraq, which were carried out to maintain US access to and control over Middle East oil, and the economic sanctions that the United States had the United Nations impose on Iraq in between these two wars, also produced widespread death and destruction (Klare 2004; Downey 2015). During the first Gulf War, the United States destroyed Iraq's civilian, industrial, medical, and public health infrastructures (Clark 1992) and killed tens of thousands of Iraqis, with casualty estimates ranging from roughly twenty-two thousand to well over a hundred thousand Iraqi soldiers and civilians killed (BBC News 2003; *Frontline*, n.d.; Keaney and Cohen 1993). The destruction of Iraqi infrastructure and the imposition of sanctions that prevented the rebuilding of this infrastructure also resulted in widespread suffering, with estimates of children's deaths due to these factors ranging from the tens of thousands to the hundreds of thousands (Ascherio et al. 1992; Crossette 1995; Pilger 2000; Reiff 2003).

The US-led invasion of Iraq in 2003 also caused much devastation, with estimates of civilian deaths due to the war ranging from just under 175,000 to nearly 1 million (Iraq Body Count 2017; IPPNW et al. 2015). Not all these deaths resulted from the direct actions of US military personnel, and many of the people who died were killed by other Iraqis. But these 175,000–1,000,000 people would not have died or would not have died the way they did if the United States had not started this unprovoked war, making the United States more responsible than any other party for these deaths. In addition, many Iraqis experienced severe psychological trauma from the violence and chaos of the war and, for millions of Iraqis, from being forced to flee their homes and former lives (Downey 2015).

Of course, violence associated with American life does not occur solely outside the United States. For instance, the US agriculture industry, which provides much of the food US citizens eat, depends heavily on undocumented migrant workers from Mexico (US Department of Agriculture 2016), whose low-wage labor and presence in the United States are required if Americans are to maintain their material standard of living and farmers and agribusiness are to maintain their profits. Farmers and agribusiness are able to control undocumented Mexican workers and pay them low wages largely because of state violence, in particular the militarization of the US-Mexico border and the imprisonment and deportation of hundreds of thousands of undocumented Mexican migrants each year (Gonzalez-Barrera and Krogstad 2016; US Immigration and Customs Enforcement 2017).[4] The militarized border, in turn, forces undocumented migrants to enter the United States through extremely hot and dry deserts that claim hundreds of migrant lives each year. The US Border Patrol conservatively estimates, for example, that 6,029 migrants died crossing the US-Mexico border between October 1997 and September 2013 (Martínez et al. 2014).

US citizens are also subjected to much violence. More than 25 million women, or 21.3 percent of all women, in the United States have been raped in their lifetimes and 43.6 percent have experienced other forms of sexual violence (Sharon Smith et al. 2018). Consistent with this, a 2015 survey of 150,000 students at twenty-seven US colleges and universities found that since entering college "27.2 percent of female college seniors . . . had experienced some kind of unwanted sexual contact— anything from touching to rape" (Pérez-Peña 2015, A17).

Child abuse in the United States is also widespread. In 2020, 627,000 of the more than 7.1 million children referred to child protective services had been maltreated, with 75 percent of the maltreated children experiencing neglect, 17.5 percent experiencing physical abuse, 9.3 percent experiencing sexual abuse, and 6.1 percent experiencing psychological abuse (American SPCC 2022). These forms of maltreatment all produce severe physical, emotional, and psychological harm, which is particularly concerning given that one study found that 10 percent of all children in the United States were maltreated in 2008 (Finkelhor et al. 2009) and that in 2010, nearly 16 percent of surveyed adults in ten states and Washington, DC, had experienced physical abuse as children (Centers for Disease Control 2016).

The United States also has the highest per capita inmate population in the world (Walmsley 2013), with poor people, African Americans, and Hispanics overrepresented in prisons; Black and Latino drivers and pedestrians significantly more likely than non-Hispanic Whites to be stopped by the police and to be treated violently when they are stopped; and low-income minority communities experiencing an exceptionally heavy and violent police presence (see chapter 4). Indeed, police violence and racial bias in policing are so severe in the United States that between January 2015 and April 2022, 5,945 people were shot by the police, with Black people two and a half times more likely than White people to be killed in police shootings (*Washington Post* 2022).

The physical violence and threat of physical violence directed at women, immigrants, African Americans, Latinos, poor people, and children are not only physically harmful, however. They can also produce severe psychological and emotional trauma and harm (P. Butler 2017;

McLeod et al. 2020; Gonzales 2016; Kearl 2014; van der Kolk 2014), as can many seemingly nonviolent social practices and discourses that are ubiquitous throughout society. The harsh policies directed at immigrants living in the United States, for example, promote severe anxiety, stress, and trauma among immigrants and their children (Gonzales 2016); and sexist, racist, and xenophobic discourses tell those to whom they are directed that society considers them to be less than fully human, as do many of the physically violent practices and policies discussed in the preceding pages. Recognizing that others consider you to be less than fully human can, as I argue later in the book, cause serious psychological and emotional harm, as can coming to accept and internalize messages that tell you that you are unworthy, less than human, and deserving of the bad and violent things that happen to you.

Dominant discourses also produce social practices that though seemingly nonviolent, actually cause severe psychological, emotional, and physical harm, both by reinforcing the violent discourses upon which they are based and by leading people to harm themselves and others. One example of this is the sexualized portrayal of women and girls in the popular media. This portrayal, which is strongly shaped by dominant patriarchal discourses, leads many women and girls to objectify and surveil themselves in ways that cause serious psychological and physical harm and to engage in beauty practices that do the same (Moradi and Huang 2008; Szymanski and Henning 2007). These beauty practices and this self-objectification, in turn, reinforce violent patriarchal discourses, including those that justify rape. They also lead many men to believe that women are sexual objects, there to be sexually harassed, sexually humiliated, and raped. Moreover, the violent consequences of seemingly nonviolent discourses and practices are not confined to gender and sexuality, but instead are associated with all of society's dominant discourses.

It is thus abundantly clear that violence permeates American life, both by being strongly associated with activities in the United States and around the world that make that life possible and by being so highly ubiquitous. The question is, how central is this violence to the US social order? Is it merely a by-product, albeit an important one, of that order? Or does it play a key role, along with other, nonviolent factors, in producing social order? And if violence in the United States and around the world does play a key role in producing social order in the United States, how do different forms of violence operating in different locations, institutions, and social arenas work together and with nonviolent factors to produce order? Indeed, is it even possible to connect such varied and disparate forms and cases of violence as those discussed in this section into a theoretically compelling and empirically supported whole?

My claim in this book is that developing such a theoretical argument is both possible and necessary, at least if we want to more fully understand how social order is produced, inequality maintained, and human suffering perpetuated. I recognize, of course, that many scholars have linked violence to social order and that much social science literature investigates specific forms of violence operating in specific social arenas. What I offer here is thus an alternative approach to the study of violence and social order, one that I believe illuminates aspects of violence and social order that have received somewhat less attention in the past.

I also recognize that violence sometimes undermines social order, as occurs when police violence engenders riots and rebellions. But just because violence sometimes undermines social order does not mean that it does not also regularly promote order. Thus, in the remainder of this chapter, I set forth an empirically testable theoretical argument that explains how violence interacts with factors first highlighted by Antonio Gramsci, Michel Foucault, and Pierre Bourdieu to promote and perpetuate inequality, suffering, and order. I begin by defining the terms "social order" and "violence."

Defining Social Order

There are many ways to think about and define social order. However, in this book I am specifically interested in the role violence plays in producing a social order that benefits elites, defined as those individuals positioned most advantageously in their nation's (or the world's) four most important power networks: economic power networks, political power networks, military power networks, and ideological power networks (Mann 1986). I therefore define social order as existing in a society when social relations are stable *enough* within that society that elites can regularly (though not necessarily always) achieve their goals and maintain or increase their advantaged position within the society.

For global economic elites and elites in the United States, the world's hegemonic nation, social order also extends globally to include not just reliance on, but the active production of, social, political, and economic relations within and among nations that allow these elites to simultaneously meet their global and national goals and reproduce their global and national power.

I could, of course, define social order in terms of dominant groups rather than elites. However, I employ an elite-based definition for four reasons. First, I am more interested in explaining social order throughout society (*overall social order*) than social order tied solely to specific arenas of social life, such as gender, race/ethnicity, and class, which a focus on dominant groups (men, Whites, capitalists) would force me to do. Second, because maintaining stable gender, race, and class relations is a critical prerequisite for maintaining the stability of the overall social order, social order in these arenas benefits not only dominant groups in each of these domains, but elites as well, who benefit more from the stability of the overall social order than does anyone else. Thus, an elite-based definition allows for the study of overall social order and social order in each of these arenas, while a dominant group definition does not.

Third, most dominant group members are not members of the elite and would potentially be better served by radically changing the structural arrangements that provide elites with their advantaged position and power. Overall social order, *which is the focus of this book*, thus relies significantly on non-elite dominant group members (most men, most Whites) consenting to their subordination at the hands of elites, further justifying my use of an elite-based definition. Fourth, I am interested in the role violence both inside and outside the United States plays in promoting overall social order within the United States. It is certainly likely that some order-producing violence that occurs outside the United States promotes social order in specific social arenas within the United States. For instance, US military action against non-European nations likely reinforces the US gender and race/ethnic orders by reinforcing dominant US patriarchal and race/ethnic discourses. But order-producing violence outside the United States normally produces social order inside the United States without directly strengthening social order in specific arenas of US social life. Thus, defining social order in terms of dominant groups would prevent me from fully exploring the role violence outside the United States plays in producing overall social order within the United States.

Defining Violence

As previously noted, I define violence as any action, inaction, or property of the social structure that severely harms an individual, community, or society, either physically, emotionally, or psychologically. In defining violence in this way, I am staking out very specific positions on two key questions that all scholars of violence must answer. First, is violence solely a physical phenomenon or can we also speak of psychological and emotional violence? Second, does violence occur only when individuals, groups, and organizations intentionally harm others, or can the unintended consequences of actions and decisions, the failure to act, and the way that organizations, institutions, communities, societies, and cultural orders are structured also be violent?

Scholars have offered many different answers to these questions. It is therefore important that I explain why I have answered them the way I do.

Physical, Psychological, and Emotional Violence

Some scholars argue that violence is indeed a purely physical phenomenon, resulting solely from specific instances of physical force and producing only physical harm (Bufacchi 2007).[5] This is a fairly problematic position to take. Most people, for example, would consider a situation in which a husband yells loudly and regularly at his wife and children without ever physically abusing or threatening to physically abuse them to be a violent situation, particularly if the husband is simultaneously telling them that they are in some way worthless, stupid, pathetic, or unworthy of his love. One could certainly argue that yelling is a physical act or that yelling is generally associated with an aggressive physical posture that can be physically threatening. But yelling is not the kind of physical force that proponents of physical definitions of violence are really talking about, and how one perceives the physicality of others, and the effect that specific words have on those being verbally abused, are to a large degree cultural and psychological, rather than physical, phenomena. In any case, whether one is a child being yelled at by a parent or a woman being yelled at by a husband, the yelling does not involve actual physical contact except possibly for the force of the air being expelled through the vocal cords. This strongly suggests that violence does not have to be physical.

The *experience* of violence and the trauma that often results from that experience are never purely physical either. People subjected to violence generally experience pain and fear, which are psychological states. When people experience pain and fear, for instance, that experience is processed and felt in the brain. The brain also attaches *emotional* meaning to pain that strongly affects how we experience it and how much we believe it hurts (Hamilton 2015; O'Mara 2015). Moreover, fear and terror change the way the brain functions, sometimes temporarily and other times permanently, leading people to remember only fragmentary, minor, or meaningless details of violent and traumatic events, to forget the sequence in which violent and traumatic events unfolded, and to sometimes uncontrollably replay portions of these events in their minds over and over again for years (Scaer 2014; van der Kolk 2014). Hopper and Lisak (2014) note, for instance, that

in states of high stress, fear, or terror, like combat and sexual assault, the prefrontal cortex is impaired—sometimes even effectively shut down—by a surge of stress chemicals. . . . Inevitably, at some point during a traumatic experience, fear kicks in. When it does, it is no longer the prefrontal cortex running the show, but the brain's fear circuitry—especially the amygdala. Once the fear circuitry takes over, it—not the prefrontal cortex—controls where attention goes. It could be the sound of incoming mortars or the cold facial expression of a predatory rapist or the grip of his hand on one's neck. Or, the fear circuitry can direct attention away from the horrible sensations of sexual assault by focusing attention on otherwise meaningless details. Either way, what gets attention tends to be fragmentary sensations, not the many different elements of the unfolding assault. And what gets attention is what is most likely to get encoded into memory. . . . The brain's fear circuitry also alters the functioning of a third key brain area, the hippocampus. The hippocampus encodes experiences into short-term memory and can store them as long-term memories. Fear impairs the ability of the hippocampus to encode and store "contextual information," like the layout of the room where the rape happened. Fear also impairs its ability to encode time sequencing information, like whether the perpetrator ripped off a shirt before or after saying "you want this."

Violence thus cannot be as easily separated from psychology, memory, and emotion as proponents of physical definitions of violence would like us to believe.

Victims of violence do not only experience pain and fear, of course. Joanna Connors and Patricia Francisco, for example, describe having out-of-body experiences while being raped:

> I did not believe that out-of-body experiences were real. And yet: at 4:30 p.m. on a hot July afternoon, on a college campus in Cleveland, Ohio, I slipped away from my body and rose, up and up, until I was hovering somewhere in the air. . . . I looked down on the stage of a small theater, where I was on my knees in front of a man who held a long, rusty blade to my neck and was ordering me to . . . (Connors 2016, 3)

> As if from above, I could see my body, blood, the bed. I sensed my own spirit lingering to witness the dying. . . . Time was altered, becoming deep and broad, my consciousness radically inflated like a parachute, slowing down time by expanding my use of it, giving me access to many levels of perception and interpretation at once. (Francisco 1999, 17)

And writing about her sense of self while being raped, Karyn Freedman (2014, 15–16) states, "The feeling that came over me then was one of sheer invisibility. I realized that who I was, my personality, my character, my identity, were totally irrelevant to him and completely subsumed by his." In other words, for Freedman, her rape was not just an assault on her body, it was also an assault on her very being.

It is quite clear, then, that violence is experienced both physically and psychologically. Moreover, for those who experience violence, the prolonged trauma that often follows can involve shame, humiliation, self-blame, anxiety, flashbacks, depression, loss of emotion, lack of self-worth, an inability to trust others, a sense that the world is no longer predictable, and a belief that one no longer has a place in the world

(Enns 2006; K. Freedman 2014; Frewen and Lanius 2015; van der Kolk 2014). As one survivor of rape, speaking of both rape- and non-rape-related trauma, notes,

> Survivors of trauma frequently remark that they are not the same people they were before they were traumatized. . . . I was attacked for no reason. I had ventured outside the human community, landed beyond the moral universe, beyond the realm of predictable events and comprehensible actions, and I didn't know how to get back. . . . [Trauma] not only shatters one's fundamental assumptions about the world and one's safety in it, but it also severs the sustaining connection between the self and the rest of humanity. Victims of human-inflicted trauma are reduced to mere objects by their tormentors: their subjectivity is rendered useless and viewed as worthless. As Herman observes, "The traumatic event thus destroys the belief that one can be oneself in relation to others." . . . Without this belief, I argue, one can no longer be oneself even to oneself, since the self exists fundamentally in relation to others. (Brison 2002, ix–x, 38, 40)

It is thus apparent that violence has both immediate and long-term psychological effects and that the physical and psychological experiences of violence are so intertwined that what we typically think of as physical violence may be better conceived of as being simultaneously physical *and* psychological and thus may not be best described as physical violence but rather as physical/psychological violence. It is also apparent that physical/psychological violence can drastically alter subjectivity and identity and produce feelings of alienation and isolation.

That we cannot define violence in solely physical terms is further supported by the fact that the brain is both a physical and a psychological organ. Thus, when we are violently attacked, the pain, fear, out-of-body sensations, time distortions, and other sensations and states we experience psychologically are the product of chemical and electrical activity in the brain brought on by the attack (Hamilton 2015; Hopper and Lisak 2014; O'Mara 2015; van der Kolk 2014). This is also true of prolonged psychological trauma, which occurs when immediate changes in brain activity brought on by violence produce long-term physical and functional changes in the brain (Frewen and Lanius 2015; van der Kolk 2014).

In other words, violent attacks on the body are simultaneously violent attacks on the brain that produce physical and psychological change and often damage in the brain and the mind.

Some might argue that the fact that the brain is a physical organ means that all violence is physical. I disagree. Instead, I would argue that the psychological is simultaneously physical and that what we normally think of as physical violence is also psychological, both because we perceive and experience it psychologically and because it produces physical and psychological changes and damage in the brain and mind. Moreover, if physical violence is simultaneously psychological and if the psychological is simultaneously physical, then any action, inaction, or property of the social structure that severely harms people, communities, and societies emotionally or psychologically is violent, a point that is further supported by the fact that long-term psychological harm can produce physical changes and problems not just in the brain, but in the body as well (van der Kolk 2014).

Thus, aggressively yelling at women and children, forcing people to leave their homes to make way for a mine, regularly employing discourses that tell subordinate groups they are inferior, undeserving, and less than fully human, and culturally portraying subordinate groups in ways that constantly highlight their sexuality and physicality and regularly downplay their rational minds are all examples of violent actions or structures that can produce severe emotional, psychological, and physical harm.

Does Intent Matter?

Many scholars argue that violence occurs only when individuals, groups, and organizations intentionally harm others (Bufacchi 2007). In this view, the unintended consequences of actions and decisions, the failure to act, and the way that organizations, institutions, communities, societies, and cultures are structured can never be said to be violent. One of the key justifications for this view is that violence is immoral and that those who act violently deserve censure and punishment. We must therefore be very careful to distinguish between those who intend to harm others and situations in which the harm is accidental and unintended or in which the social structure prevents individuals, groups, and organizations from preventing the harm from occurring.

Countering this position, other scholars argue that violence can be said to occur not only when there is an intent to harm but also when there is no intent to harm but the harm is foreseeable and avoidable. This, they argue, is because foreseeability and avoidability make the actor morally culpable (Bufacchi 2007). While I agree with the general thrust of this statement, I would argue that it is problematic to tie one's definition of violence to foreseeability and avoidability because it is too easy to argue that an individual, group, organization, community, government, or society was unable to foresee some outcome, avoid some action, or change some structure, particularly when it is in an actor's interests to make such claims.

The inability to foresee an outcome, for example, is often the product of ignorance, faulty reasoning, hasty decision making, a conscious or unconscious desire to not know the consequences of one's actions or lifestyle, or the fact that foreseeing the outcome or admitting that you foresaw the outcome goes against your interests or makes you morally or legally culpable. However, ignorance, faulty reasoning, and hasty decision making can usually be corrected with just a little work and patience, desires can be changed, and the desires and interests referenced in the preceding sentence are simply selfish. I would therefore argue that none of these provide a sufficient basis to absolve one of blame or to argue that a serious physical, psychological, or emotional harm was accidental, particularly if one benefits in some way from the action, inaction, or structure that caused the harm.

Determining whether an action, a failure to act, or a failure to change a social or organizational structure is avoidable is similarly problematic. Many people would argue, for instance, that the average US citizen has very little political power, and therefore virtually no power as an individual to change US policy or US and global social structures. This does not mean, however, that as collective actors US citizens cannot create significant change. Similarly, just because political or social change seems improbable does not mean it is impossible. As a student in one of my classes once pointed out, it was very unlikely in 1950 that observers would have predicted how successful the civil rights movement would be in the 1960s. Thus, just because an individual, group, community, organization, society, or outside observer believes that an action or inaction is unavoidable, that there are no alternative behaviors or courses of action that can be realistically pursued, or that social or structural change is impossible does not mean that these beliefs are, in fact, valid indicators of what is possible; nor does it mean that that individual, group, community, organization, society, or outside observer took the time to realistically assess alternative options. It may even be the case that what an actor or outside observer claims to believe is not what they truly believe or that they believe what they believe because it is in their interests to do so.

Intent is similarly problematic. How are we to know what an actor's intent is and why should intent matter if some action, inaction, or property of the social structure produces severe physical, emotional, or psychological harm? Indeed, it strikes me that the reason laypeople and scholars care so much about violence has little to do with intent, which in most cases cannot be determined, and much more to do with the physical, emotional, and psychological harm that violence causes. More importantly, the intent argument is often employed to hide or justify the fact that a social group has benefitted from a situation or structure for a long period of time (often decades or centuries), either while harming other groups or precisely because they are harming other groups. Is it really reasonable to argue, then, that violence can occur only if groups benefitting from some situation or structure actually *want* to harm those who are being hurt? If I operate a factory that poisons nearby residents for forty years, am I not morally culpable even if I have chosen not to read the scientific studies demonstrating the poisoning and even if I would prefer not to poison these residents? At what point does my preference (to not poison residents) simply become an excuse and a way of hiding my intent? Or to put it somewhat differently, when does my intent to make profits not also become an intent to harm? And why is it not an intent to harm if after forty years I am unwilling to change my behavior?

Given the difficulties associated with determining intent, foreseeability, and avoidability, and given the empirical problems associated with defining violence solely in physical terms, I believe that it is quite justifiable to define violence as I do: as any action, inaction, or property of the social structure that severely harms an individual, community, or society, either physically, emotionally, or psychologically.

I recognize, of course, that the term "severe" is somewhat ambiguous. But I have chosen to include it in my definition because violence is often defined in such a way as to include outcomes that seem relatively trivial. Galtung's (1969, 168) influential definition of violence provides a clear example of this. Galtung argues that "violence is present when human beings are being influenced so that their actual somatic and mental realizations are below their potential realizations." Galtung's definition has been influential because it allows researchers to persuasively argue that social and cultural structures can be violent (Galtung 1969, 1990). However, it defines as violent not only major impediments to human potential but fairly minor ones as well. For example, though it is true that I am not as good a guitar player as I would be if the social structure did not force me to work a regular full-time job, I do not consider my reduced potential as a guitarist to be a violent imposition on my life. I therefore argue that definitions of violence such as Galtung's and mine need to include qualifiers such as the term "severe" so as to not encompass outcomes that are trivial or socially inconsequential.

Finally, some might argue that despite including the term "severe," my definition of violence is still too broad and still covers too many different social phenomena. On the one hand, this is my point. Violence is pervasive in society and therefore needs to be accounted for in theories of social life. On the other hand, even if one does find my definition too broad, what it and the various arguments I make in this book all point to are the very high levels of physical, emotional, and psychological pain, suffering, and harm that many people and communities in the United States and around the world experience on a daily basis. Some may not want to call this violence. But as I argue throughout this book, regardless of what we call it, it does play a key role in producing overall social order in the United States. It must therefore be accounted for in theories of social life.

The Literature on Violence and Social Order

There have been several different responses since the mid-twentieth century to the question of whether violence and overall social order are linked. By far the most common response has been to investigate violence without reference to social order. Social scientists have, of course, studied many different types of violence, and some of the best theory and research on violence highlight the role violence plays in maintaining social order in specific social arenas (see, for instance, M. Alexander 2010; MacKinnon 1989). But most researchers who study violence study very specific types of violence or violence operating in very specific social arenas and social relationships (Belknap 2010; Burt, Sweeten, and Simons 2014; Randall Collins 2008; Collins, Menard, and Pyrooz 2018; Klare 2001, 2004; Mardorossian 2014; Menjívar and Abrego 2012; Pyrooz and Decker 2019; see Jackman 2002 for an important and extended discussion of this point). So even when they do tie violence to social order, they generally do so in a manner that orients their discussion of social order to the social arena—race relations, gender relations, and so on— that is the immediate focus of their analysis.

Another important response has been for scholars to argue, as I do, that violent actions, inactions, or structures in multiple social arenas work together and with nonviolent factors to produce overall social order. However, the very few scholars who have taken this approach have either (a) employed definitions of violence that are so broad (much broader than mine) that virtually every social activity is defined as violent (Salmi 1993); (b) stated or developed philosophical or theoretical arguments that they do not test empirically (Iadicola and Shupe 2003; Murchadha 2006); (c) listed one act of violence after another without truly demonstrating how these acts of violence work to promote social order (Iadicola and Shupe 2003; Salmi 1993 in some chapters but not others); or (d) failed to actually explain how different types of violence work together and with nonviolent factors to produce social order (Iadicola and Shupe 2003; Murchadha 2006; Salmi 1993).[6] This book avoids these problems by employing a narrower definition of violence than does Salmi, by rigorously testing the theoretical arguments set forth in it, and by demonstrating, both empirically *and* theoretically, how diverse forms of violence operating in multiple social arenas work together *and with nonviolent factors* to promote overall social order.

A third important response to the question of whether violence and overall social order are linked has been to argue that violence in a very specific social arena or set of arenas plays a key role in producing social order throughout society. Cedric Robinson (2000) and others (Kojola and Pellow 2020; Pulido 2017; Vargas 2008) argue, for instance, that capitalism has always been racialized, relying on racial difference, and thus difference-producing racial violence, for its reproduction, while others argue that society is fundamentally gendered (Dworkin 1981; MacKinnon 1989; A. Rich 1980) or founded on intersecting axes of inequality, most importantly gender, race, sexuality, and class (Crenshaw 1991; Taylor 2017). From these latter perspectives, two separate conclusions about violence and social order emerge: first, that violence that reproduces the gender order simultaneously produces overall social order, and second, that order-producing violence is always simultaneously gendered, raced, sexed, and classed, thereby promoting overall social order rather than social order in a single institutional arena.

In a different vein, scholars of settler colonialism argue that anti-Indigenous violence plays a key order-producing role in societies that were founded through permanent colonial settlement. Not only was this violence central to the formation of these societies, they argue, it continues to play a critical order-producing role today by fundamentally shaping these societies' cultures, legitimation myths, and legal and political systems as well as the internal consciousness and identity of these societies' residents, propelling them into a future profoundly shaped and ordered by historical and ongoing violence (Hixson 2013; Slotkin 1973; Veracini 2010; Whyte 2018, 2017). Furthermore, this order-producing violence was and is fundamentally gendered and sexualized, leading the dominant society to view Indigenous bodies and lands as inherently violable and producing acceptance of domination, hierarchy, and difference among both colonizers and colonized, thereby legitimizing the racial, gender, and colonial orders (A. Smith 2005).

In yet another vein, William Blum (2014) argues that the United States maintains its global hegemony by employing military violence and assassination to eviscerate all external resistance to its empire, while James Scott (1998) argues that authoritarian governments sometimes engage in extremely violent social engineering projects so as to make specific populations and geographic regions more legible to the state, thereby increasing state control of these people and regions. And finally, David Nibert (2013) argues that social order and the inequality and violence associated with social order are the result of institutionalized violence against non-human animals.

It is not my intent to criticize these critically important studies, all of which were written to achieve very specific goals and all of which highlight the role specific forms of violence in specific social arenas play in producing overall social order. I do, however, wish to make clear how my book differs from these prior studies. Because the goals of these studies are generally quite different from my goals in this book, and because the authors of these studies were usually not primarily interested in exploring the link between violence and overall social order, they do not all clearly define what they mean by violence. For instance, it is sometimes difficult, when reading these studies, to know whether they consider psychological and emotional violence to be within their purview, to know what types of physical violence they are referring to, or for those studies that discuss racial violence, to know whether their arguments are restricted solely to police violence against racial and ethnic minorities. In addition, these studies do not always fully explain or demonstrate how the violence implicit in the issues they discuss is related to social order, and many of these studies do not demonstrate just how ubiquitous violence is in our everyday lives or how much we rely on violence to live the lives we lead. Finally, these studies often focus on only a single or a few types of violence or on violence occurring in a single institutional arena.

I address these gaps in the literature, at least some of which occur in each of the studies I reviewed, by clearly defining what I mean by violence, fully explaining and demonstrating how the violence I highlight in this book produces overall social order, highlighting multiple forms of violence occurring in multiple social arenas, and demonstrating just how much we rely on violence to live the lives we lead. Put differently, while the third category of studies I have reviewed, when taken collectively, do all or nearly all of the things I just mentioned, very few, if any, do every single one of them. Moreover, unlike any of these "third-category" studies, this book treats violence as a broad, conceptual category and develops a unique theoretical argument to explain how violence, so conceived, interacts with factors highlighted by Gramsci, Foucault, and Bourdieu to produce overall social order. Theoretically, it also treats violence as both a positive, productive power and a negative, destructive power (I explain this distinction later in this chapter).

It is certainly the case that some of the third-category studies I reviewed connect violence to issues Gramsci, Foucault, and Bourdieu highlighted in their research, such as consent, discourse, bodily practices, and embodiment, and that some discuss specific forms of violence in ways that suggest that violence might be a productive power. It is also true that I highlight many highly specific forms of violence in this book. However, none of the research I reviewed that links violence in specific social arenas to overall social order portrays specific forms of violence as manifestations of violence broadly conceived, none develops a theoretical argument that explicitly ties violence, so conceived, to Gramsci, Foucault, and Bourdieu, and none highlights the importance of defining violence as a productive power. This book thus provides new and important insights regarding the relationship between violence, consent, discourse, bodily practices, embodiment, and social order that are not found in prior research. Moreover, though I am very interested in this book in demonstrating how specific forms of violence produce overall social order, I always use the forms of violence I highlight to demonstrate that violence, broadly conceived, produces social order in ways that are consistent with my unique theoretical argument. Thus, though this book is similar in certain respects to the critically important research reviewed in this section, it also differs from this research in several key ways.

Why Violence and Social Order Are Not Linked in Most Theory and Research

Though the important body of social science research I just reviewed links violence to overall social order, most violence research does not make this link. There are, I believe, several reasons for this. First, social scientists tend to favor clever, sophisticated explanations of social life and generally view violence as a rather blunt and unsophisticated weapon and means of social control. Second, many social scientists argue that the routine use of violence by the state undermines both the legitimacy of the state and the effectiveness of state violence as a mechanism for producing order. Third, despite recognizing that violence is multifaceted and employed in many different social arenas by many different actors, researchers and theorists tend to restrict their attention to state violence whenever the question of violence and social order arises, which for the reasons just mentioned, they see as being relatively ineffective. Fourth, and most importantly, the mid-twentieth century saw the rise of three theoretical traditions, based to a significant degree on the work of Antonio Gramsci, Michel Foucault, and Pierre Bourdieu, that attempted to explain social order by shifting attention away from centralized state violence toward more dispersed and seemingly nonviolent mechanisms of social control.

In the remainder of this section, I therefore summarize several of Gramsci's, Foucault's, and Bourdieu's most important theoretical arguments concerning the production of social order. My main goal in doing this is to demonstrate several ways in which these theorists' ideas overlap so that I can use these areas of overlap as the basis of the theoretical argument I develop in the following section. Because not all readers are familiar with Gramsci, Foucault, and Bourdieu, I include details of their arguments that are not directly referenced later in the book. However, without these details, those who are unfamiliar with these theorists will not understand the key points I am trying to make. I also include details that are not directly referenced in subsequent chapters when doing so justifies arguments I make about these theorists that some readers might disagree with. These details, as well as those necessary to demonstrate theoretical overlap, are thus included in the discussion that follows.

The Three Theorists

As anyone who has read Gramsci, Foucault, and Bourdieu knows, they are very different theorists. Nevertheless, there are some important parallels in their work that have guided much subsequent theory and research, parallels that reflect their embeddedness in similar European intellectual traditions and their attempts to come to terms with similar historical phenomena. For instance, all three theorists rejected, either explicitly or implicitly, the idea that under normal circumstances violence plays a decisive role in maintaining social order in modern, liberal-democratic societies.[7] They also all viewed power as being relatively dispersed throughout society and not just centered in a single organization or institution among a single group of elite actors; and despite arguing that power is dispersed throughout society in socially significant ways, they somewhat surprisingly (at least to me) did not make similar claims or, in the case of Bourdieu (see the next paragraph), similarly convincing causal claims for violence. Their arguments regarding social order also highlighted factors internal to societies rather than factors both internal and external to them, and they all believed that social order is based to a significant degree on the creation of subjects who implicitly consent to the social order because their subjectivity and identity are aligned with that order. Finally, in highlighting the central role consent plays in producing social order and in strongly contrasting violence with consent, Gramsci and Foucault strongly suggested that violence is a purely negative and coercive power and not at all productive of consent, subjectivity, and identity, while Bourdieu suggested the same for physical violence and perhaps for certain other forms of violence too. Of the three, Foucault most clearly differentiated between productive power, which maintains social order by "positively" forming subjectivity and identity and increasing the capacities of individuals, and negative power, which maintains order through coercion and force, breaking down or destroying individuals' subjectivities, identities, and capacities rather than building them up. But all three theorists made this important distinction, either explicitly or implicitly.

In making the claims set forth in the preceding paragraph, I am not arguing that Gramsci, Foucault, and Bourdieu ignored violence. Indeed, they all discussed violence in their work: Gramsci argued that at critical junctures state violence can play a key role in maintaining capitalist relations; Foucault argued that despite declining in importance over time, state violence still matters in modern societies; and Bourdieu highlighted a relatively dispersed form of violence, symbolic violence. However, for Gramsci, state violence is of critical importance only during times of crisis when nonviolent mechanisms that normally produce order have failed; for Foucault, violence tends to promote order only when more important, routine, and nonviolent exercises of power have failed;[8] and Bourdieu never explains what is violent about symbolic violence. Bourdieu also fails to clearly distinguish between domination and symbolic violence, both of which he seems to define in identical ways as the acceptance by subordinate groups of the limits imposed on them by dominant symbolic structures and their use of these structures to understand their place in the world.[9]

Violence thus plays a much less central role in Gramsci's and Foucault's work than do other factors, while symbolic violence seems to be an imprecise and less than useful concept for thinking about the relationship between violence and social order. But even if I am being too critical of Bourdieu's concept, it is important to keep in mind that symbolic violence is just one of several types of violence that can potentially be linked to social order. Moreover, as conceived by Bourdieu, symbolic violence is a key consequence of consent rather than a factor producing consent, and it is precisely this latter property of violence, that it can produce both coercion *and* consent, be both productive *and* destructive, positive *and* negative (in a Foucauldian sense), that, along with a few other key arguments and concepts, I am most interested in highlighting in this book.

It is also difficult to determine what role, if any, Bourdieu thought symbolic violence plays in producing subjectivity and identity. Bourdieu clearly argues that domination shapes subjectivity and identity, but since he does not explain what is violent about symbolic violence or how symbolic violence differs from domination, it is not clear whether the violence he associates with domination has any effect on subjectivity and identity and if it does, what effect it has. In other words, it is not clear whether it is the violent or nonviolent aspect of domination, or both, that produces subjectivity and identity. Moreover, because symbolic violence results solely from consent and is produced simultaneously with domination, and thus social order, it is not clear whether symbolic violence plays a role in producing social order or whether it is simply associated with social order. I would therefore argue that like Foucault and Gramsci, Bourdieu does not conceive of violence as being productive of consent, subjectivity, identity, and social order, or at the very least that he does not explain how violence might produce these things.

In a less critical vein, it is important to note that Gramsci, Foucault, and Bourdieu did not all use the term "consent" or think about their arguments in terms of consent, that their arguments concerning subjectivity and identity differed greatly from each other and were not equally well specified, and that their views on the importance of state violence were by no means identical. Nevertheless, their arguments regarding these issues are similar enough in general terms, and their influence over the social sciences is broad enough, that they have directly or indirectly convinced most social scientists, even those who in most respects fundamentally disagree with one another, to dismiss or minimize the role violence plays in producing social order.

Antonio Gramsci

Gramsci (1971), for example, argued that capitalism's ability to survive revolutionary challenges by early twentieth-century workers' movements resulted precisely from the fact that capitalists rely on state violence to maintain their power and position only when other, nonviolent, mechanisms fail. More to the point, he argued that capitalist social order is based primarily on the consent of subordinate groups. This consent is generated in a variety of overlapping and mutually reinforcing ways, some involving subordinate groups' material interests and others involving the production of what can be termed "capitalist subjectivity." Material interests for Gramsci are primarily economic, and are thus organized in the market, while capitalist subjectivity is produced primarily in civil society. Gramsci defines civil society as the arena outside the market where culture, ideas, ideologies, subjectivities, and identities are produced, disseminated, and contested. At times, Gramsci treats civil society as separate from the state, but at other times he provides an expansive view of the state that includes not just the government and politics but civil society as well. But regardless of whether civil society is part of or separate from the state, in advanced capitalist societies it is the primary arena in which class struggle occurs (Gramsci 1971). Finally, for Gramsci, consent is sometimes consciously given, but is often better thought of as involving the absence of dissent, a situation in which subordinate groups, by continuing to participate in the social order, act as though they support it whether they consciously do or not (Przeworski 1985).

One way that capitalist societies generate consent is by convincing subordinate classes that capitalist interests are really universal, or hegemonic, interests such that what is good for capitalists is good for all classes. This is accomplished in part because in capitalist societies everyone does, in fact, depend on capitalist profits and investment for jobs and government revenue and in part because intellectuals, publishing houses, news organizations, schools, and other organizations and associations in civil society create and disseminate ideas and ideologies that regularly and repeatedly proclaim the universality of capitalist interests. The fact that in capitalist societies everyone depends on capitalist profits and that capitalism would collapse without profits also means that profit generation is central to the preservation of capitalist social order (Fontana 2008; Gramsci 1971; J. O'Connor 1973, 1996; Przeworski 1985).

Consent is also produced in capitalist societies, Gramsci argues, when capitalists make compromises with and concessions to other classes, either on their own initiative, through government pressure, or through the resolution of inter- and intra-class conflicts in democratic institutions. These compromises and concessions generate consent because they support subordinate classes' material interests, and resolving conflicts in democratic institutions builds consent by (a) limiting conflict to a narrow range of issues that do not threaten fundamental capitalist interests and (b) demonstrating to the public (accurately or not) that all social groups can influence important political and economic decisions.

Finally, for Gramsci the development of capitalist subjectivity among individuals and social groups occurs at two levels. On the one hand, pro-capitalist civil society actors (intellectuals, publishing houses, news organizations, schools, and so forth) disseminate a set of pro-capitalist ideologies and cultural values that are widely adopted among members of the capitalist and subordinate classes. These values and ideologies are relatively consciously held and generate widespread support for the social order.

Gramsci also argues, however, that civil society creates capitalist subjectivity at a much deeper and less conscious level than this (Fontana 2008; K. Smith 2008). This aspect of Gramsci's work is not often recognized, but is critical to his argument. He notes, for instance, that any class that wants to become society's leading, or hegemonic, class must

> create a new civilization, a new type of man and citizen . . . [and] construct . . . a complex and well-articulated civil society, in which the individual can govern himself [and others] without his self-government thereby entering into conflict with political society—but rather becoming its normal continuation, its organic complement. (Gramsci 1971, 268; also see 266)

Under capitalism, he argues, this involved the creation of a new type of worker who repressed his or her sexual and other instinctual drives in favor of a stable family life and "new and rigid habits of order, exactitude, and precision" (Gramsci 1971, 1992a, 235).

Consistent with the idea that Gramsci conceptualized capitalist sub-jectivity as operating at two levels, Gramsci defined ideology not just in terms of a set of ideas created by intellectuals that justify a specific set of social relations, but also as an overall "conception of the world . . . , a total and molecular (individual) . . . way of thinking and acting" (Gramsci 1971, 267). In this latter sense, ideology unconsciously shapes how people think and act and is unconsciously absorbed by people as they grow up and go about their everyday lives. It is even embedded in the languages people speak and "in art, . . . law, . . . economic activity and . . . all manifestations of individual and collective life" (Gramsci 1971, 328).

It is quite clear, then, that for Gramsci, consent is based not only on the satisfaction of material interests, the operation of democratic insti-tutions, and the relatively conscious acceptance of dominant values and ideologies. It is also based in the development of a much more deeply and unconsciously rooted capitalist subjectivity that creates workers and citizens who at the level of language, discourse, action, temperament, attitudes, adjustment to work, sexual behavior, conceptions of self, self-discipline, and the disciplining of others support capitalist social rela-tions (Gramsci 1971, 1992a, 1992b).

But just as capitalists and their defenders in civil society can develop and foster capitalist subjectivity, it is also possible, Gramsci argued, for subordinate classes to develop their own ideological conceptions of the world. Indeed, they must do so, he claimed, if they are to successfully challenge capitalist hegemony, first in the realm of civil society and then in the state and economy. However, one of Gramsci's key points is that this is exceedingly difficult for subordinate classes to do. Moreover, the moment consent breaks down, the capitalist state will employ armed violence to restore order. State violence thus plays an important role in Gramsci's theory, but it does so only as a last resort and only in the ab-sence of consent. Under normal circumstances, it is consent that is the main guarantor of social order and state violence, conceived of only as a coercive and never a productive power, that lies in the background.

Michel Foucault

Like Gramsci, Michel Foucault was also interested in power, subjectivity, and social order. Foucault argued that in medieval Europe, power was concentrated in the hands of the sovereign and enforced through government violence. However, with the rise of the modern state, the development, starting in the eighteenth century, of new techniques of bodily discipline, and ever-greater knowledge of population processes, markets, and the human body, power became highly dispersed and focused on the non-violent regulation of the human body and mind. Indeed, for Foucault, power in modern societies is so dispersed that it can no longer be said to be something that any person, group, or organization possesses. Instead, it must be conceived of as something that is performed in each and every human interaction and that delves so deeply into human consciousness that it shapes individual subjectivity and identity, unconsciously guiding the way people think, act, move, and perceive themselves and producing social order by getting people to monitor their own and other people's behavior (Dean 1999; Foucault 1977, 1990; Mills 2003).

Foucault identified several overlapping dimensions of power, three of which I will discuss here: disciplinary power, biopower, and discourse. Turning our attention first to disciplinary power, Foucault argued that in the eighteenth and nineteenth centuries, institutions such as prisons, schools, hospitals, clinics, universities, and the army began to exert control through discipline:

> Discipline . . . is internalized by each individual: it consists of a concern
> with time-keeping, self-control over one's posture and bodily functions,
> concentration, sublimation of immediate desires and emotions—all of
> those elements are the effects of disciplinary pressure and at the same
> time they are all actions which produce the individual as subjected to a
> set of procedures which come from outside of themselves but whose aim
> is the disciplining of the self by the self. (Mills 2003, 43)

The internalization of discipline is achieved in large part, Foucault argued, because modern institutions engage in constant surveillance of those whose behavior they wish to regulate: employees, students, clients, inmates, and so on. This constant surveillance leads regulated individuals to continually monitor their own and others' thought processes, movements, bodies, emotions, desires, and behaviors, thereby shaping regulated individuals' subjectivity and identity and guaranteeing that their thoughts, bodies, movements, and behavior conform to the goals of the institution and the norms of the broader society. In this sense, Foucauldian discipline can be viewed as producing unconsciously given consent to the social order by aligning individual subjectivity and identity with broad social norms, goals, and structures.

Ever-increasing knowledge of population processes, markets, and the human body further increases disciplinary pressure on individuals, Foucault argued, because researchers, professionals, and government agencies use this knowledge, which he called *biopower*, to establish widely adhered to norms of proper conduct that like disciplinary power are "enforced" largely through self-monitoring. For instance, medical researchers and government agencies regularly establish norms of physical fitness and acceptable body weight that structure subjectivity and identity and lead people to monitor their own and other people's body shapes and fitness regimens.

Like biopower and discipline, discourse also shapes subjectivity, identity, and self-monitoring practices. Discourse refers to the kinds of statements that people speaking a common language make as well as to the rules that determine what kinds of statements they make. But for Foucault, discourses are also

> ways of constituting knowledge, together with the social practices, forms of subjectivity and power relations which inhere in such knowledges. . . . Discourses are more than ways of thinking and producing meaning. They constitute the "nature" of the body, [the] unconscious and conscious mind and [the] emotional life of the subjects which they seek to govern. Neither the body nor thoughts and feelings have meaning outside of their discursive articulation, but the ways in which discourses constitute the minds and bodies of individuals is always part of a wider network of power relations, often with institutional bases . . . in the law, for example, or in medicine, social welfare, education, [gender relations] and . . . the organization of the family and work. (Weedon 1997, 105)

For Foucault, then, discourses structure our attitudes, values, beliefs, knowledge, thoughts, actions, and bodily practices, including how we present ourselves, how we hold our bodies, and how we move through the world. They also structure how we discipline ourselves and others and how we perceive ourselves and the world. They thus align our subjectivity, identity, and bodies with institutional practices and external social and power relations, thereby playing a key role in producing social order (Foucault 1972, 1981; Lessa 2006; Mills 2003).

Taken as a whole, Foucault's arguments regarding disciplinary power, biopower, and discourse are quite powerful. In demonstrating that these aspects of power produce a modern form of subjectivity and identity and a modern type of citizen/subject who implicitly and unconsciously "consents" to the social order by internalizing particular ways of thinking, knowing, perceiving, acting, moving, feeling, and experiencing, Foucault provides social scientists with a much deeper understanding of how social order is produced. His arguments also suggest quite strongly that identity, subjectivity, and social order are produced in part by the *repeated performance* of specific discursive utterances and actions, which through constant repetition increase the psychological centrality and emotional salience of the discourses they derive from and reinforce actors' unconscious acceptance of the unequal power relations and biased institutional arrangements inherent in these discourses (J. Butler 1990; Reed 2013).

Pierre Bourdieu

As is true of Foucault and Gramsci, Pierre Bourdieu provides researchers with a unique approach to understanding subjectivity, power, and social order. Basing his work in a theory of practical action, Bourdieu argues that society is made up of multiple social fields within which individuals and institutions compete for scarce resources. Each field is defined by its key resource and each has its own particular logic, culture, set of hierarchically structured positions, and relations of domination and subordination. In addition, each field produces a set of culturally defined interests that motivate action, and each has modes of acceptable and unacceptable action.

Bourdieu further argues that within each field, people's actions and decisions are determined much less by rational calculation than by what he calls *habitus*, a subtle and largely unconscious cultural "understanding" of the field and its rules that has been internalized by each individual in the field. More specifically, the habitus is a set of dispositions and generative schemes that while not representing an objective map of the field are "objectively adjusted to the particular conditions in which [they are] constituted" (Bourdieu 1977, 95), thus promoting social actions that are consistent with the inequalities and cultural logic of the field.

For Bourdieu, dispositions are not just attitudes or beliefs. Instead, they include "a spectrum of cognitive and affective factors: thinking and feeling, to use Bourdieu's own formulation, everything from classificatory categories to [opinions, tastes, inclinations,] sense of honour" and an intuitive feel for the rules of social life that "dispose" individuals to behave in certain ways and not others and to take certain social actions and not others (Jenkins 1992, 76).

Generative schemes, on the other hand, are a type of classificatory category: they are matched pairs of opposed and hierarchical terms such as "old and new," "front and back," "man and woman" that order the social world, produce meaning for its inhabitants, and guide perception, thinking, and action (Bourdieu and Boltanski 1976, 39). Dispositions and generative schemes are learned early in life through socialization and experience and are durable and transposable, which means that they tend to persist over time and can often be applied in multiple social fields.

According to Bourdieu, generative schemes and dispositions are internalized both cognitively and by the body (though Bourdieu seems to define cognitive incorporation as a form of embodiment too) and as such, guide our thoughts, feelings, beliefs, attitudes, actions, decisions, and physicality, including how we hold our bodies, how we move, and the gestures we make. Moreover, they do this at a level deeper than consciousness and will and, therefore, cannot "be suspended by a simple effort of will, founded on a liberatory awakening of consciousness" (Bourdieu 2001, 39). They thus form the basis of our identity, subjectivity, and physicality. And because they are objectively adjusted to social fields that are hierarchically ordered and are derived from people's experiences of what is both possible and probable, they lead people to think, act, feel, move, and behave in ways that maintain inequality, domination, and social order, not only in specific social fields but in society more broadly.

Habitus thus produces social order, according to Bourdieu, because it is aligned closely with objective social relations, forms the basis of people's identity and subjectivity, and unconsciously shapes people's cognition, beliefs, perceptions, bodies, emotions, passions, sentiments, and movements. Or to put it somewhat differently, habitus creates subjects who implicitly consent to the social order because their habitus-formed subjectivity, identity, and physicality are aligned with that order.

Theorizing the Link between Violence and Social Order

Bourdieu's, Foucault's, and Gramsci's brilliant analyses of social and political life have taught us much about how social order is produced and maintained in modern capitalist societies. Most importantly, at least for the purposes of this book, their analyses all demonstrate that social order is based to a significant degree on the creation of subjects who consent to the social order because their subjectivity, identity, and interests are aligned with that order. Consent, according to these analyses, can be explicit or implicit, can be conceived of as positive consent or somewhat more negatively as a lack of dissent, and can be "located" at a level of consciousness where it can be intentionally withdrawn or at a deeper, unconscious or bodily level that cannot easily be touched or changed by consciousness-raising efforts. It can also be based on material *and* non-material interests and desires.

Bourdieu's, Foucault's, and Gramsci's analyses also highlight the important role dispersed power plays in producing social order; and Bourdieu and Foucault in particular demonstrate the centrality of the body as an object upon which dispersed power is exerted so as to produce subjectivity, identity, consent, and social order.

Somewhat surprisingly, however, Bourdieu, Foucault, and Gramsci do not seem to have recognized the possibility that just as dispersed power can be exerted on bodies and minds in ways that produce subjectivity, identity, consent, and social order, so too can dispersed violence produce these same outcomes, as can centralized violence. Put differently, Foucault and Gramsci, like most other theorists, seem to have associated violence solely with coercive power and not at all with productive power, while Bourdieu (a) associated physical violence solely with coercive power and (b) viewed symbolic violence as an important effect of productive power without explaining whether or how symbolic violence could be productive.

Bourdieu, Foucault, and Gramsci also paid insufficient attention to the role that state violence, violence occurring outside a nation's borders, and the threat of violence play in producing social order within a nation. In the remainder of this chapter, I therefore develop a theoretical argument that explains how dispersed violence, centralized violence, threatened violence, and violence around the world, both independently and in conjunction with factors highlighted by Gramsci, Foucault, and Bourdieu, produce social order throughout society. But before doing so, I want to remind readers that I do not regard my theoretical argument as being in any way incompatible with the theoretical arguments set forth by Gramsci, Foucault, and Bourdieu. Nor should it in any way be taken as a challenge to their arguments.

Violence and Social Order

Earlier I argued that social order exists in a society when social, political, and economic relations are stable enough within that society that elites can regularly achieve their goals and maintain or increase their advantaged position within society. I further argued that for global economic elites and elites in the United States, social order also extends globally to include not just reliance on, but the active production of, social, political, and economic relations within and among nations that allow these elites to simultaneously meet their global and national goals and reproduce their global and national power.

Based on this definition and the arguments set forth by Foucault, Bourdieu, and Gramsci, one might reasonably conclude that in modern capitalist societies social order is most likely to be achieved when (a) non-elites have or are given a material, cultural, or psychological interest in supporting the social order or some important aspect of that order; (b) subordinate groups have difficulty organizing themselves collectively to challenge the social order; (c) individual identity and subjectivity are aligned with dominant institutional practices, external power relations, and objective social relations; and (d) dominant discourses and bodily practices, both within and across different arenas of social life, reinforce each other by regularly invoking the same or highly similar discursive elements and symbolic structures, thereby (i) deeply and durably embedding these elements and structures in people's minds and (ii) aligning people's subjectivities and identities with dominant institutional practices and external social and power relations. Finally, social order is also more likely to be achieved when (e) social, political, economic, and institutional arrangements within and among nations generate stable profits and secure investment opportunities, which (i) are necessary for the preservation of the capitalist order and (ii) benefit not only capitalist elites, but political, military, and many cultural elites too.

Violence, working both independently and in conjunction with non-violent factors, can play an important role in achieving each of these five outcomes (outcomes *a*–*e*). To illustrate that this is so and to help readers better understand the causal pathways that I believe link violence to these outcomes, I first provide a detailed set of substantive examples that explain how violence likely produces each outcome. I then explain why violence is also likely to be particularly emotionally salient to people and thus particularly effective in achieving these five outcomes and overall social order. Finally, I formalize my argument in abstract, generalizable terms and conclude the chapter with a brief discussion of how I will empirically evaluate it.

Before I proceed, however, it is important to note that though I do not formulate a set of hypotheses derived from the substantive examples I present, one of the key ways I will empirically evaluate my theoretical argument is by demonstrating that many of the causal pathways highlighted in these examples operate in the way I argue they do.

THE CAUSAL PATHWAYS

To begin, let me assert that one of the key bases of consent in the United States is the availability of plentiful, affordable consumer goods, which provide most non-elites in the United States with a material interest in supporting the capitalist order (outcome *a*). The abundant availability of consumer goods is also a key source of capitalist profits and economic stability (outcome *e*), and thus of government tax revenue and

US military power. The availability of consumer goods therefore benefits a wide range of economic, political, and military elites, as well as those cultural elites whose power and privilege are based on the sale of affordable products in the marketplace.

The ability to secure profits and provide non-elites with plentiful, affordable consumer goods is, of course, dependent on a wide range of nonviolent institutional arrangements (Bunker and Ciccantell 2005; Fligstein 2001). But it is likely also associated with violence. Armed violence in the United States and other nations, for example, may be used or threatened against workers demanding better wages and working conditions or against people protesting resource extraction activities, thereby keeping costs down, resource supplies plentiful, profits high, and US prices low. Companies and countries that export goods to the United States may also keep profits high and prices low by flouting labor laws, creating weak labor laws, exposing workers to harmful working conditions, or paying workers such low wages that they cannot fend off hunger and disease, all of which, if extreme enough, are forms of violence as I define it. Governments may also use violence or the threat of violence against workers or immigrants to shape labor markets in ways that reduce production costs and increase profits, as occurs in China and at the US/Mexico border.

Corporate profits and low consumer prices are also supported by US military power, which in conjunction with the military and police power of other nations and nonviolent economic, political, and institutional mechanisms is used to maintain corporate access to investment opportunities and inexpensive natural resources (Downey 2015; Klare 2004, 2001). US military power is also a key source of US geopolitical power, which is used to promote stable economic, political, and institutional arrangements around the world that help preserve corporate profits and investment opportunities, government tax revenue, an abundant supply of inexpensive consumer goods, and US global hegemony (Cypher 2016; Klare 2001).

Thus, maintaining and deploying a strong US military is not only in the interests of US elites. To some degree it is in the economic, or material, interests of US citizens.[10] To the degree that the US military helps promote a stable world order, it may also support the economic interests of citizens and elites in other nations. As such, the US military, which controls more potential violence than any other organization in the world, likely plays an important role in maintaining corporate profits and investment opportunities and producing consent to the US and global social orders and, thus, in promoting overall social order. This is likely also true for the other forms of violence I have discussed so far in this section, all of which provide non-elites in the United States with a material interest in supporting the social order while helping maintain corporate profits and investment opportunities (outcomes *a* and *e*).

At the same time, however, there are many reasons why US citizens and the people and governments of other nations might resent the US military. It eats up a very large share of the US budget, is one of the world's worst polluters, is responsible over the last fifty years for millions of deaths and widespread suffering around the world, including among US citizens, and interferes with the aspirations of many nations and national leaders around the world (Downey 2015; Foster, Holleman, and McChesney 2008). The United States may therefore attempt to increase support for, or at least acceptance of, US military power both inside and outside the nation by creating economic and military dependence on its military among foreign countries, foreign military and political leaders, and US citizens, businesses, and universities (outcome *a*). More specifically, it may promote consent to the US and global social orders by (a) hiring large numbers of people, many of whom have few other economic opportunities and few other ways of gaining social status; (b) locating military bases in states and counties throughout the United States; (c) distributing military contracts to businesses and universities throughout the United States; (d) selling ships, planes, tanks, and other weapons and military equipment to nations around the world; (e) training other nations' military and security forces; and (f) building close ties between the US military and the militaries of other nations.

In addition to promoting consent (outcome *a*), these activities also facilitate the use and threatened use of armed violence by the United States and its allies. Military research conducted in the United States and weapons built by US companies have, for instance, been used by the United States to devastate Vietnam, Laos, Afghanistan, and Iraq. US military equipment and US-trained forces have also been used by our allies to kill, injure, and repress people around the world, particularly in oil- and mineral-rich regions vital to US economic, military, and geopolitical power such as the Middle East and Africa, but also in Asia and Latin America (Branch 2011; Hessler 2017; United Nations Human Rights Council 2015). US military power and the military power of our allies thus promote social order directly and coercively by attempting to order the world in ways consistent with US and elite interests (sometimes successfully, sometimes not).

Violence does not only support elites' and non-elites' material interests, however. It likely also promotes the psychological and cultural interests of at least some subordinate groups. W. E. B. Du Bois (1935) and David Roediger (1991) argue, for instance, that one reason White working- and middle-class Americans have historically supported racism, racial inequality, and physical racial violence is that these violent discourses, structures, actions, and outcomes provide Whites with psychological and symbolic "wages" that lead them to accept a social order that otherwise harms them. Such wages include increased status and respect and feeling better about themselves, important constitutive elements of identity and subjectivity and non-trivial emotions and markers of distinction in a society they often find alienating and that often treats them poorly. Thus, the violence inherent in racism, racial inequality, and physical racial violence likely produce wages of whiteness that promote social order by (a) giving Whites a psychological and cultural interest in maintaining that order and (b) forming White identities and subjectivities that are aligned with, and thus supportive of, dominant institutional practices and external social and power relations (outcomes *a* and *c*).

In a similar way, physical, psychological, and emotional violence against women likely fosters male consent to the overall social order by providing men with psychological and symbolic wages that align their subjectivity and identity with dominant institutional practices and external social and power relations and that make their subordination and alienation in other realms of life more bearable (outcomes *a* and *c*). As many feminists (and Bourdieu) have argued, and as I highlight in chapters 2 and 3, violence against women can also align female subjectivities and identities with external social structures and power relations, thereby providing even greater support for the social order.

Warfare may also provide subordinate groups with important psychological and cultural benefits (outcome *a*). During wartime, the enemy is generally portrayed as culturally inferior and evil, which may provide citizens with a sense of psychological and cultural superiority. Adding to this sense of superiority, US citizens are usually told that they are going to war to make the world a better place for other people, thereby highlighting the idea that the United States is morally righteous and that other societies cannot take care of their own citizens as well as the United States can. These feelings of superiority, in turn, likely promote consent to the social order, which is further strengthened by regular calls for closing ranks against enemies of the nation, both internal and external, and by the kinds of nationalistic identities and subjectivities usually formed during wartime.

Social order may also be strengthened when subordinate groups have difficulty organizing themselves collectively to challenge elite interests (outcome *b*). Difficulty organizing to challenge elite interests can occur for many reasons. Armed violence and threatened violence against protestors, activists, and activist organizations may scare away potential activists and make organizing dangerous and difficult. Violence may also intentionally or unintentionally divide non-elites from each other, thereby weakening the capacity of subordinate groups to organize collectively. For instance, heavy policing of Black neighborhoods, police violence against Black people, the use of psychologically harmful racial discourses that denigrate African Americans and elevate Whites, and politicians' use of "tough on crime" rhetoric that portrays African Americans as violent and less than human likely reinforce Whites' negative images of Black people, while simultaneously increasing African Americans' sense of living in a racist society that does not care about them. These images and perceptions, in turn, probably strengthen divisions between Black and White people that make it difficult or impossible for them to organize collectively.

Violence, regardless of where, when, and under what circumstances it occurs, may also make organizing difficult by traumatizing those who experience it, producing particularly intense forms of subjectivity and identity that make interaction socially and psychologically difficult for those who have been traumatized (outcome *b*). Not everyone who experiences severe violence is traumatized, and among those who are, the consequences vary in form, severity, and duration. Nevertheless, traumatized individuals often experience flashbacks, emotional numbing, loss of agency, alienation from themselves and others, higher than average rates of drug and alcohol abuse, an inability to trust others and plan for the future, and extreme depression and anxiety, among other symptoms (Frewen and Lanius 2015; van der Kolk 2014). One might reasonably expect that people with such symptoms have more trouble working cooperatively with others to achieve common goals than do people without such symptoms, which, if there are enough traumatized people in a society, might weaken the ability of subordinate groups to challenge the social order.

Finally, violence may sometimes represent an extreme form of bodily practice and discourse that promotes social order by reinforcing dominant discourses and bodily practices both inside and outside the social arena in which the violence occurs, thereby reinforcing dominant discourses and bodily practices in *multiple* social arenas (outcome *d*). Sexual violence against women and society's acceptance of this violence, for example, may help maintain patriarchal *and* capitalist social relations by embodying in extreme form gender and neoliberal discourses that support the objectification of others (women, workers, and the earth), using others to satisfy one's desires, and blaming subordinate groups and those who experience harm for their subordination and harm. In a similar vein, if police and politicians are able to justify (to a White audience) the use of violence against African Americans by portraying African Americans as physically dangerous, irrational, and unable to control their impulses, or if police violence promotes physically aggressive behavior on the part of those against whom it is regularly directed, then police violence against African Americans and the justifications this violence requires likely reinforce race, gender, *and* class inequality, all of which are justified by discourses that equate the dominant group with the rational mind and everyone else with the body, irrationality, emotion, and lack of control.

However, it is not only acts of extreme physical violence that promote social order by reinforcing dominant discourses in multiple social arenas. The sexualized portrayal of women and girls in popular culture, for example, and the use of patriarchal myths to justify rape are both violent practices (see chapters 2 and 3) that reinforce nearly identical discursive elements as does sexual violence: they associate women and girls with the body, objectify women and girls, tell men and boys that women and girls are there to satisfy their desires, and in the case of rape myths, blame women and girls for being raped. They thus provide discursive support not only for extreme sexual violence but for gender and neoliberal discourse and inequality too (outcome *d*).

Violent myths, discourses, and practices can also promote social order by aligning subjectivity and identity with dominant institutional practices and external social and power relations (outcome *c*). For instance, when popular culture tells a woman how she should look and behave, the ridicule and negative comments she receives if she does not look or behave as she "should" and the ways in which she is treated when she does achieve society's beauty and behavioral ideals may lead her to objectify herself in ways that are extremely harmful, and thus violent (see chapters 2 and 3). And this violence, by increasing the psychological and emotional salience of the discursive rules upon which society's beauty ideals and her self-objectification are based, likely increases the chances that she will internalize these rules and that both these rules and self-objectification will come to form an important part of her subjectivity and identity, aligning them closely with dominant patriarchal practices and power relations.

Violent racial discourses and practices can also align non-elite subjectivity and identity with dominant institutional practices and external social and power relations. Police violence against Black people and racially biased policing, for example, are justified using highly violent and emotional discourses that denigrate and dehumanize African Americans and tell non-elite Whites that they are better than Blacks (see chapter 5). Racially biased policing has also placed millions of African Americans in prison, thereby falsely suggesting to Whites that African Americans really are violent and criminally inclined, and thus dangerous to Whites, and reducing the number of people that Whites have to compete with for housing, quality schooling, and jobs. As a result, racially biased policing, police violence against Black people, and the violent discourses used to justify these practices likely make Whites feel better about themselves by increasing their economic, educational, and housing opportunities and making them feel superior to Black people. And all this, in turn, likely increases Whites' support of the overall social order by supporting Whites' psychological and material interests and aligning White subjectivity and identity with dominant criminal justice practices and external social and power relations (outcomes *a* and *c*).

Thus, violence, in its myriad physical, psychological, discursive, and emotional forms, can create consent to the overall social order among its victims, perpetrators, and beneficiaries by producing psychologically intense experiences that profoundly shape subjectivity and identity, aligning them in highly emotional ways with dominant institutional practices and external social and power relations. Moreover, violence is particularly likely to do these things when the different forms of violence operating in a particular social arena, such as gender relations or race relations, reinforce the same sets of discursive rules and these rules operate in multiple social arenas.

VIOLENCE, EMOTION, AND SOCIAL ORDER

Before formalizing my theoretical argument, I would like to explain why violence is likely to be particularly emotionally salient to people and thus particularly effective in producing overall social order. I would also like to tie violence more closely to gender, race, sexuality, and aggression, which, broadly speaking, are the subjects of the next four chapters. Specifically, I would like to argue that integral to the functioning and importance of violence in the production of social order are the deeply held meanings and psychologically charged nature of gender, race, sexuality, and aggression. Isaac Reed and Julia Adams (2011, 266–67) note, for example, that social actors have

> not only purposes and experiences, but also unconscious energies [and] repressed memories, drives and desires . . . that are [both] transposed onto [and derived from] social relations and the symbols that mediate them . . . [and that] are formed in their concrete [causal] effectiveness by the[ir] already emotionally laden, energized symbolic [and depth psychological] meanings. . . . These meanings follow a logic that is unconscious, over-determined, and fantastical. . . . Social life is [thus] pushed forward by dynamic links among sexuality, aggression, [race, gender,] and power that, in individuals, occur in the unconscious, and at the collective level, play themselves out in symbols and rituals. To interpret culture causally under this rubric, then, involves analyzing the unconscious sources of action as they are worked out in actual, and imagined and fantasized, human relations.

If Reed and Adams are correct, then violence, as an extreme form of aggression, is intimately tied up with race, gender, power, and sexuality, not just at the social level but also at the level of the unconscious. Moreover, the charged psychological meanings and emotions attached to race, gender, sexuality, aggression, and the body are not just *formed* by the symbolic/cultural order but also give emotionally charged meaning *to* that order and *push it forward*, particularly when played out in ceremonial rituals and the ritualized repetition of everyday life. This has five important implications: first, that actual and fantasized aggression and violence likely play a key role in constituting and affirming the symbolic/ cultural order and, thus, the overall social order; second, that racial, gender, and sexual violence will often deepen the psychological and social salience of, and thus individual and social support for, society's gender and racial discourses and the symbolic, cultural, and material orders supported by these discourses; third, that violence in other social arenas, such as international relations and the market economy, will deepen the psychological and social salience of discourses in those arenas as well; fourth, that violence, particularly when tied to race, gender, sexuality, and nation (which is often conceptualized in racial/ethnic terms), will play a critically important role both in forming identity and subjectivity and aligning them with external social and power relations; and fifth, that dispersed forms of violence woven into the ritualized repetition of everyday life are likely to be particularly effective in shaping and producing the kinds of order-producing factors that Gramsci, Foucault, and Bourdieu highlighted in their theory and research. Reed and Adams's argument thus provides a key explanation for why violence is likely to play an important and unique role in the production and causal effectiveness of discourse, identity, subjectivity, interests, generative schemes, bodily practices, dispositions, group boundaries, and consent, and thus in the production and maintenance of overall social order.

Reed and Adams's argument also suggests that political conflicts over gender, racial, and sexual violence and political conflicts and contests, including electoral campaigns, in which specific subordinate groups are portrayed as violent are likely to be deeply psychologically salient. Indeed, they are likely to be so psychologically salient that they may regularly divert public attention away from economic and political issues that potentially threaten the power and advantaged position of elites.

This is not to say that these conflicts and this violence are less important than issues elites care about, but rather that by diverting public attention away from issues that could potentially threaten elite interests, conflicts over gender, racial, and sexual violence may help promote overall social order by reducing the likelihood that elite interests will be challenged. Moreover, if these conflicts are resolved in such a way, either in the electoral, legislative, judicial, or public arenas, that the perpetrators of gender, racial, and sexual violence tend to avoid legal punishment, *then the withholding of this punishment*, which is really a withholding of state violence (no one would accept legal punishment without the threat of state violence), helps support overall social order by supporting the patriarchal and racial orders.

This raises two important issues: first, that withholding violence may sometimes be as important as the use of violence in maintaining social order—or, to put it differently and perhaps more accurately, that the balance between what is and is not treated violently (including what is and is not punished violently) may play a key role in determining whether social order is produced and maintained; and second, that withholding punishment for certain forms of violence may make those forms of violence appear to be less pervasive and serious than they really are, thereby promoting support for the social order by obscuring both the violence and the inequality of which it is a part and by making the social order appear to be more benign, just, and moral than it really is. Making violence that supports elite or dominant-group interests difficult to see or invisible, whether by withholding punishment, failing to cover it in the news media or educational curricula, blaming it on the victims of the violence, or employing some other tactic, may thus play an important role in producing social order. This is particularly likely to be the case in a nation such as the United States that prides itself on its fairness and moral righteousness and that tends to highlight and exaggerate violence carried out by enemies of the state and those outside the mainstream.

Summarizing and Formalizing the Argument

In the preceding sections I argued that violence plays a key role in producing social order, but that it does not do so in one way or all by itself and that it is not directed solely from centralized power centers. Instead,

I argued that multiple forms of violence work together and with a wide range of nonviolent factors (such as subjectivity, identity, and distrust of government) to produce social order, with order-producing violence sometimes centralized and perpetrated at the behest of elites and at other times dispersed and carried out either at the behest of elites or by non-elites pursuing personal goals that on the surface appear to have little or nothing to do with overall social order (examples of dispersed violence include sexual violence, self-objectification, daily encounters between police officers and African Americans, the sexualized portrayal of women and African Americans in popular culture, and subtle racist behavior).

In this context, arguing that violent and nonviolent factors "work together" means two things: first, that violent and nonviolent factors sometimes interact to produce social order; and second, that they sometimes work independently of each other but in such a way that they are simultaneously pushing society in the same basic direction, toward social order. As a result, social order can be best thought of as the complex product of interacting mechanisms *and* overdetermination.

These arguments are illustrated in figures 1.1 and 1.2, which are divided into three regions, with social order at the center, the five proximate causes of social order (profits, non-elite interests, and so on) placed in the ring immediately surrounding social order, factors shaping these proximate causes located outside this ring, and arrows included to denote causal direction.

Figure 1.1 illustrates my claim (made earlier in the chapter) that violent and nonviolent factors work independently and interactively to produce social order by (a) making it difficult for non-elites to organize collectively to challenge the social order and (b) producing consent through discourse, bodily practices, profit generation, subjectivity, identity, and partially meeting non-elites' psychological, cultural, and material interests. Figure 1.1 also shows that the five proximate causes of social order can influence each other. It shows, for instance, that discourse affects social order directly but also by shaping non-elites' subjectivity, identity, and interests and by making it more or less difficult for non-elites to organize collectively (though all the proximate causes can influence each other, the figure traces out only some of the causal links between them). Finally, because the five proximate causes of social order are often properly thought of as being nonviolent, figure 1.1 also indicates that violence both shapes *and* interacts with a set of nonviolent proximate causes to produce social order. In other words, figure 1.1 indicates that violent and nonviolent factors both shape and interact with each other in the outer *and* the middle rings of figure 1.1.

At the same time, however, the five proximate causes are often properly conceptualized as being violent in their own right. Violence, after all, is often an extreme form of bodily practice. Moreover, the overall effects of discourse can be extremely harmful to individuals, telling them, for instance, that they are worthless, undeserving, less than fully human, or unable to maintain proper standards of thought, beauty, behavior, and responsibility. Discourses are also regularly used to justify

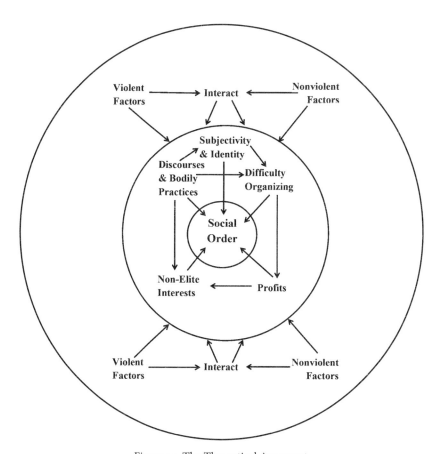

Figure 1.1. The Theoretical Argument

levels of inequality, poverty, and destitution that can cause extreme physical and psychological harm and are often employed to justify direct acts of physical and psychological violence. As is true of bodily practices, many discourses are therefore inherently violent. Nevertheless, the five proximate causes are also often nonviolent, both working with and shaped by violent factors in ways that promote social order. It is thus important to keep in mind that the five proximate causes can be either violent or nonviolent, depending on the specific social context in which they are found.

Figure 1.2 adds to figure 1.1 two forms of violence discussed in the preceding sections, tracing out the causal pathways that I argue connect social order to these forms of violence and demonstrating how specific forms of violence are situated within my larger theoretical argument and how violence interacts with nonviolent factors—such as "distrust in government" and "divisions between non-elites"—to produce social order. Figure 1.2 thus traces out my argument that sexual violence (in the left-hand portion of the diagram) produces social order in at least four ways: it produces a level of trauma that makes it difficult for many of those who experience it to engage in collective action; it reinforces a gender discourse that legitimizes patriarchy and an economic discourse that legitimizes capitalism; it plays an important role in aligning female and male subjectivity and identity with dominant institutional practices and external social and power relations; and in its ritualized repetition in everyday life and in a legal system that rarely punishes it, it provides many men with a psychological "wage" that partially meets their psychological interests and makes the social order more bearable for them.

Figure 1.2 also shows that racial violence (placed at the top of the diagram) helps produce social order in ways that are both theoretically similar to and different from how sexual violence produces social order. This, of course, is true of the many different forms of violence that I highlight in this book, both in relation to sexual violence and to each other, and it highlights one of the things that make this book distinctive: the book demonstrates that though different forms of violence produce social order in ways that are often unique, they more regularly produce social order in ways that are theoretically similar to each other. This, of course, is a key

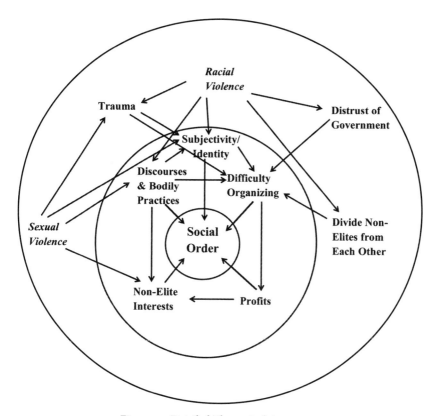

Figure 1.2. Detailed Theoretical Argument

reason why it is important to conceptualize violence as a broad conceptual category distinct from the many specific forms that violence can take.

Finally, figure 1.2 demonstrates that the theoretical claims I made earlier in the chapter about how specific forms of violence produce overall social order can be thought of as *causal pathways* that, on the one hand, connect violence as a broad conceptual category to the five proximate causes of social order and, on the other, connect the outer ring of figure 1.1 to its middle ring. As noted previously, I do not provide a formal list of hypotheses drawn from these theoretical claims. Nevertheless, the empirical chapters that follow do test many of these claims, thereby demonstrating that the specific causal pathways delineated in the preceding sections of the chapter operate as I have argued they do.[11]

Evaluating the Theoretical Model

In the chapters that follow, I present a series of case studies that illustrate the validity of my theoretical argument across a variety of empirical settings, test the theoretical claims I made earlier in the chapter, and demonstrate that we cannot fully explain inequality, oppression, alienation, and social order without investigating the role violence plays in producing these outcomes.[12] These case studies, which are summarized in the introduction, also demonstrate the great degree to which the United States' power, position, and wealth and US citizens' lives and lifestyles are linked to, shaped, and made possible by violence throughout US society and around the world. They thus demonstrate that violence is intimately woven into our everyday experiences and absolutely central to social life, working both independently and interactively with the kinds of factors highlighted by Gramsci, Foucault, and Bourdieu to promote social order throughout society.

The question still remains, however, of how I will empirically evaluate my theoretical argument. When I first began working on this book, I quickly realized that Gramsci, Bourdieu, Foucault, and others had already done an important part of this work for me. Specifically, I realized that these scholars had already shown that social order is stronger when non-elites have a material, cultural, or psychological interest in supporting the social order, when non-elites have trouble organizing themselves collectively, and when non-elite subjectivity and identity are aligned with dominant institutional practices and external social and power relations. They had also already shown that social order is more stable when institutional arrangements ensure stable business profits and secure investment opportunities, when people routinely accept and adopt dominant discourses and bodily practices, and when dominant discourses and bodily practices in specific institutional arenas are aligned with each other.

I therefore decided that my methodological strategy in this and the projected book would be to accept these prior findings as given and focus my attention on demonstrating that violent factors work both independently and with nonviolent factors to produce the proximate causes of social order listed in the preceding paragraph. Or to put it in a language consistent with figures 1.1 and 1.2, I decided to test the theoretical claims I make that take us from the outer to the middle rings (or sections) of the two figures but not from the middle ring of each figure to social order because these latter claims have already been tested and strongly supported by prior research (for instance, see Bartky 1988, 1990; Bourdieu 1984, 1990, 2001; Bourdieu and Boltanski 1976; Bordo 2003; Burawoy 1979; Domhoff 1990; Downey 2015; Ferree 2012; Fligstein 2001; Fontana 2008; Foucault 1977, 1981, 1982, 1990; Gordon, Edwards, and Reich 1982; Harvey 2014; Jenkins 1992; Kimeldorf 1988; Mills 2003; Nealon 2008; Oksala 2012; Paschel 2016; Przeworski 1985; J. O'Connor 1996; K. Smith 2008; Zinn 1980).

Some readers may object to this approach. But I adopt it for three key reasons. First, it allows me to focus my attention more squarely than I otherwise could on (a) the theoretical claims that connect the outer and middle rings of figures 1.1 and 1.2 and (b) my argument that violence both interacts with *and is productive of* consent, discipline, discourse, biopower, habitus, identity, subjectivity, and embodied knowledge. These are the key innovations of my theoretical argument and what I therefore most need to demonstrate empirically. Second, it means I do not need to spend time proving what Foucault, Bourdieu, Gramsci, and subsequent scholars have already proven and what I therefore do not need to prove. Third, because adopting this approach minimizes the time I must spend repeating work other scholars have already done, I am able to cover significantly more empirical ground than I otherwise could. This is important because it means I can apply my theoretical argument to a fairly broad range of social and institutional settings and demonstrate that my theory is more generally applicable than I otherwise could. This methodological approach thus provides me with several important advantages that I would not otherwise have, allowing me to better achieve the key goals I have set for myself in this and the preceding chapter. I therefore adopt it throughout the book.

Finally, I would like to note that to fully substantiate my theoretical argument and fully test my theoretical claims, the empirical chapters in this book delve both deeply and broadly into issues related to sexual violence against women and police and political violence against African Americans. Because of this, it may seem at times that I have strayed far from my theoretical argument and that I am making points related solely to gender, patriarchy, or race and not at all to overall social order.

In a few cases this will, in fact, be true, and I will have taken advantage of an opportunity that has presented itself to discuss an important social or political issue that is not directly related to overall social order. Indeed, it would be remiss of me not to do so.

But the key reason I delve deeply and broadly into the substantive issues highlighted in the empirical chapters is that I cannot test my theoretical claims without doing so. That I do not constantly link the evidence I present in the empirical chapters to my theoretical argument is thus not because the evidence has no bearing on my theoretical argument. Instead, it is because I do not want to constantly repeat myself by too frequently making this link. Nevertheless, because my main goal in this book is to demonstrate that violence plays a key role in producing overall social order, I will always tie the evidence I present in it back to violence and social order. There will often be long stretches where I do not discuss my theoretical argument or overall social order. But in the end, I always come back to these topics and always demonstrate that the evidence I present strongly supports the theory I have developed.

2

Sexualized Violence against Women

In late 2017 and early 2018 it became apparent to the general public that sexual harassment and abuse in US workplaces were incredibly widespread, with highly publicized charges of workplace harassment and abuse being levelled against a wide range of celebrities, businessmen, and politicians, including Harvey Weinstein, Donald Trump, Al Franken, Roy Moore, Roger Ailes, Bill O'Reilly, various managers, investors, and board members in the technology industry, and the doctor for the US women's gymnastics team, who was accused of molesting over a hundred female gymnasts. As accusations against prominent men proliferated, increasingly vocal disagreements arose not only among politicians, pundits, and members of the general public but also among feminist scholars and activists regarding how harmful, violent, and intrusive much of the alleged behavior really was, whether much of the alleged behavior was really harassment, and whether the constant litany of accusations reinforced sexist images of women as passive, non-agentic, and unable to take care of themselves. In addition, though the mainstream media focused considerable attention on workplace sexual harassment, they largely ignored widespread male violence against women and the structured and mutually supportive relationship that exists between this violence, less extreme gender practices, sexual harassment, and rape. It also ignored the key role that sexual harassment, rape, and other violence against women play in supporting patriarchal social relations, broad patterns of gender inequality, and overall social order.[1]

I address these issues in this and the following chapter by empirically demonstrating three key points: first, that the portrayal of women and girls in popular culture, female bodily practices based on this portrayal, sexual harassment, rape, and society's reaction to rape are all violent and all display a common set of cultural scripts drawn from patriarchal and neoliberal discourse; second, that these social practices form a unified, interdependent, and violent social structure that guides the behavior, internal consciousness, subjectivity, and identity of women, men, girls, and boys; and third, that because of the foregoing, these violent practices play a key role in promoting overall social order, which they do by (a) regularly and ritualistically reinforcing dominant patriarchal and neoliberal discourses and thus dominant discourses in multiple social arenas, (b) aligning individual behavior, subjectivity, and identity with these discourses and thus, with dominant institutional practices and external social and power relations, (c) meeting the cultural, psychological, and material interests of key subordinate groups, and (d) shaping and producing subjectivity, identity, interests, and consent.

In addition to demonstrating these important points, I take a strong position on several of the issues raised in this chapter's opening paragraph. In particular, I argue that sexual harassment is violent both in itself and because it supports other forms of sexual violence such as rape. I further argue that one of the key problems with mainstream discussions of workplace sexual harassment and rape is that by discussing harassment and rape as if they are largely separate from and independent of each other and other sexist practices, these discussions ignore how sexual harassment, rape, and other sexist practices strongly reinforce each other, both violently and discursively.

This is a critically important point because, as I have already indicated (and will demonstrate below), it means that harassment, rape, and the other gendered practices highlighted in this and the following chapter are all important structural features of a highly interconnected patriarchal social order that is extremely violent and harmful to women. As a result, one cannot adequately address the issues embedded in the disagreements listed above or fully explain how patriarchy and overall social order are continually reproduced without conceptualizing sexual harassment, rape, and these other gendered practices as interdependent components of a coherent, unified, and violent social structure that (a) strongly shapes women's and men's behavior, consciousness, subjectivity, and identity and (b) limits women's and girls' agency more severely and completely than it limits men's and boys' agency.

Furthermore, because gender differences in agency are produced by patriarchal social structures that harm women and girls and benefit men and boys, highlighting women's and girls' limited agency should be taken as an indictment of these social structures and not of women and girls. I understand that in a neoliberal and patriarchal society, highlighting women's and girls' limited agency is, according to the discursive logics of these two systems of inequality, akin to blaming women and girls for their subordinate social position. But it is impossible to overcome inequality and oppression if social movements must always celebrate the agency of the oppressed and as a result, can never highlight inequality and oppression or the limited agency inequality and oppression impose on subordinate groups. Moreover, it is not as though men's and boys' agency is limitless. Social structures limit everyone's agency, but in ways that benefit dominant groups more than subordinate groups and that limit subordinate group agency more than dominant group agency.

In addition to engaging in these debates, I make two controversial decisions in this and the subsequent chapter. I use the terms "rape victim" and "rape survivor" rather than just the term "rape survivor," and for the most part I do not differentiate between the experiences of women of different races, ethnicities, classes, and sexual orientations or attend to how discourses of sexual violence differ for women whose identity is formed by different combinations, or intersections, of race, ethnicity, sexual orientation, and class. This latter decision is controversial because women who occupy different intersectional positions in the social structure do not have the same interests and experiences or face perfectly identical forms of oppression and violence (Brah and Phoenix 2004; Crenshaw 1989, 1991; Yuval-Davis 2006). One could therefore reasonably argue that what I really examine in this and the following chapter is sexual violence that White heterosexual men perpetrate against White heterosexual women.

This may be true. But even if it is, I still demonstrate that this violence promotes social order in the ways that I theorize it does, which is the main goal of this and the subsequent chapter. Moreover, I fully believe that the arguments I make in these two chapters can be elaborated and reformulated to account for the ways sexual violence perpetrated and experienced by members of different races, ethnicities, genders, and sexual orientations produce, shape, and align subjectivity, identity, interests, consent, behavior, and discourse, thereby promoting social order. That I do not do so here is not because I think it is unimportant to do so but because this book highlights the role that multiple forms of violence operating in multiple social arenas play in producing social order, limiting the space I can devote to sexual violence.

Finally, many feminists argue that portraying women and girls as victims rather than survivors of sexual harassment and rape is highly problematic because it reinforces a key patriarchal stereotype, that women lack agency and are only able to follow men's lead. Though I understand the source of this concern, it is, I believe, misguided. First, female victims of sexual harassment and rape are not victims because of a lack of agency but because of their disadvantaged position in the patriarchal social structure. The term "victim" captures this disadvantage much better than the term "survivor." Second, solely using the term "survivor" can lead people to forget that sexual attacks have perpetrators who are responsible for these attacks. It also helps obscure the role the social order plays in making sexual violence against women such a commonplace occurrence.

Third, our society expects women and teenage girls to strongly police the sexual boundaries between themselves and men and as a result, generally holds women and girls who have been raped or sexually violated to be responsible for their rape and violation. Thus, while patriarchal discourse normally describes women and girls as lacking agency, once a woman or girl accuses a man of sexually attacking her, she is usually accused in turn of improperly policing her sexual boundaries and leading the man on in some way, thereby becoming the agent of the alleged sexual act. It is also often assumed that she could have resisted her attacker if she had wanted to do so. In the case of sexual violence, then, portraying women and girls as highly agentic is problematic because our society believes that agentic women and girls do not get raped or sexually violated. Instead, they get what they want or deserve (Stringer 2013 presents a particularly insightful and forceful version of this argument).

Given the foregoing and the fact that rape victims are also survivors, I use the terms "rape victim" and "rape survivor" interchangeably in this and the following chapter.

* * *

This and the following chapter are organized as follows. In this chapter, I demonstrate that the portrayal of women and girls in popular culture and female bodily practices based on this portrayal promote social order by violently reinforcing dominant discourses in multiple social arenas. To demonstrate that this is true, I first provide a detailed discussion of patriarchal and neoliberal discourse that identifies the symbolic elements underlying each. I then demonstrate that representations of women and girls found in popular culture and female bodily practices based on these representations are violent. Finally, I show that the symbolic elements underlying these representations and practices are identical to those underlying patriarchal and neoliberal discourse, thereby reinforcing both of these dominant discourses.

In the following chapter (chapter 3), I demonstrate that sexual harassment, rape, and society's reaction to rape also reinforce patriarchal and neoliberal discourse. In addition, I demonstrate that the violent practices and portrayals highlighted in both this and the following chapter form a unified, interdependent, and violent social structure that generates consent to the overall social order by meeting the cultural, psychological, and material interests of key subordinate groups and aligning subordinate group subjectivity and identity with dominant institutional practices and external social and power relations.

As we shall see, many feminists and gender scholars argue that women are now highly agentic and that because of this agency and concomitant increases in gender equality, women (a) no longer experience patriarchal oppression and (b) find the media representations and bodily practices highlighted in this chapter to be liberating and fulfilling. In order to substantiate my argument and protect it from criticism, I directly engage with the arguments these scholars make so as to demonstrate that these arguments are not convincing. As a result, I spend a significant amount of time in this chapter and the next demonstrating that patriarchy still exists, that women and girls are not as agentic as these arguments suggest they are, and that the practices and portrayals I highlight are violent and oppressive. It may seem odd at this point in time to have to demonstrate that patriarchy still exists, but many scholars and activists argue that it does not, and these arguments have to be addressed.

Finally, I would like to point out that though prior research has shown that sexual and gender violence reinforce dominant gender discourses, it has not yet been demonstrated that they also reinforce neoliberal discourse. Thus, in demonstrating that this is true, this and the following chapter make an additional important contribution to the literature.

Patriarchal and Neoliberal Discourse

The first step in determining whether sexual violence against women reinforces dominant patriarchal and capitalist discourses is to identify the content and general structure of these discourses. I thus begin this section by discussing the general structure that dominant discourses take as well as why they differ from each other and change over time (this general discussion is important for arguments I make later in this chapter and in the next chapter). I then discuss neoliberal and patriarchal discourse, which provides a springboard for my discussion, in subsequent sections, of the gendered bodily practices I highlight in this and the following chapter.

In the United States, patriarchal, capitalist, and racial discourses all identify the dominant group, whether it is men, capitalists, or Whites, with the mind, rationality, self-control, discipline, civilization, culture, and the ability to plan for the future. They simultaneously identify subordinate groups with the body, irrationality, emotion, nature, lack of self-control, and an inability to plan for the future. Moreover, they view the mind and its associated traits positively and the body and its associated traits negatively (Bordo 2003; Grosz 1994; Lloyd 1993; Prokhovnik 1999; Takaki 1993; also see Mikkola 2022).

But these discourses, despite their common conceptual origin in this mind/body dichotomy, are also quite different from each other. This is because gender, race, and class relations have intertwined but distinct histories; because gender, race, and class inequality are linked but unique systems of stratification that have specific discursive and justificatory needs; and because the mind/body dichotomy is highly flexible and can be applied in very different ways depending upon the system of inequality it is helping to justify and the specific material conditions that it shapes and that shape it. This flexibility also means that the specific forms gender, race, and capitalist discourses take vary over time as material conditions change and as gender, race, and class inequality and their relationships to each other evolve. Yet, at their heart, these discourses and their associated bodily practices are all based to a significant degree on the same basic set of mind/body distinctions.

For instance, prior to the Civil War, when slavery was the labor system and form of racial inequality that had to be justified, racial discourse held that African Americans were childlike, simpleminded, and unable to take care of themselves. Slave owners thus described slavery as being good for African Americans because without it, they argued, African Americans would be unable to fend for themselves. However, when slavery ended and freed slaves could potentially compete with Whites for jobs and other scarce resources, racial discourse evolved to describe African Americans not as innocent and childlike but instead as physically threatening, sexually aggressive, lacking self-control, and dangerous if not properly controlled (Takaki 1993). Then, in the 1950s and 1960s, lack of family values was added to this discursive image of African Americans to explain and justify new forms of educational, residential, and economic inequality (Moynihan 1965a). It is thus clear that these discourses, though clearly different from each other, each associated African Americans with the body, irrationality, and lack of adult control and responsibility.

Capitalist discourses have also varied over time, both shaped by and helping to shape material conditions. For instance, the dominant capitalist discourse of the New Deal era held in part that government institutions have an important interventionist role to play in supporting economic activity and mitigating some of the worst abuses of capitalist markets. But this discourse gave way in the 1970s and 1980s to a neoliberal capitalist discourse that in response to changing market dynamics and increased threats to corporate profits favored individual responsibility over government intervention, resulting in policies that increased corporate profits and inequality.

But before describing this discourse, I would like to make three points. First, discourses tend to contradict themselves and to set up double standards, with internal contradictions and double standards generally benefitting dominant groups. Second, while neoliberal discourse is clearly different from earlier capitalist discourses, it has much in common with and shares many of the same discursive elements as these earlier discourses. This is important to recognize because the same is true of much of the discourse surrounding rape, patriarchy, and sexual violence. As a result, many of the elements of these discourses that currently support neoliberalism supported earlier capitalist discourses too.

Third, all social arenas are shaped by multiple discourses, though within each arena one discourse is usually much more dominant than the others. In addition, discourses from one arena often guide action in another, and within any arena multiple discourses of the same kind (multiple gender discourses, multiple economic discourses, and so forth) may operate, though again only one discourse will be dominant. Neoliberalism is thus the dominant but by no means the only economic discourse in the United States and the world today. Moreover, its legitimacy and strength are potentially challenged not only by other economic discourses but by some non-economic ones as well. Indeed, one of the reasons I would argue that social order relies on consistency across social fields between dominant discourses is that such consistency is one of the best defenses against discursive and other challenges.

Neoliberal Discourse

The most important way in which neoliberal discourse differs from earlier capitalist discourses is that it extends market values and market rationality throughout society. Specifically, it holds that in all arenas of social life individuals, groups, and organizations are responsible for taking care of themselves through rational, self-disciplined action. They are also responsible for living with the consequences of not properly taking care of themselves. The discourse further holds that all individual, organizational, institutional, and government action should be "conducted according to a [cost/benefit] calculus of utility, benefit, or satisfaction [as measured] against a micro-economic grid of scarcity, supply and demand, and moral value-neutrality" (Brown 2003). The government should thus use utilitarian economic logic rather than any other guiding principle when developing and enforcing public policy; and in all arenas of social life, individuals, organizations, and institutions should be judged and held accountable according to how well their behavior accords with self-disciplined, utilitarian economic rationality and how well they take care of themselves (Bay-Cheng 2015; Brown 2003; Lemke 2001; Guthman and DuPuis 2006; Rose and Miller 1992). This argument is summed up nicely by Wendy Brown (2003):

> Neo-liberalism normatively constructs and interpellates individuals as entrepreneurial actors in *every sphere of life*. It figures individuals as rational, calculating creatures whose moral autonomy is measured by their capac-

ity for "self-care"—the ability to provide for their own needs and service their own ambitions. In making the individual fully responsible for her/himself, neo-liberalism equates moral responsibility with rational action; it relieves the discrepancy between economic and moral behavior by configuring morality entirely as a matter of rational deliberation about costs, benefits, and consequences. In so doing, it also carries responsibility for the self to new heights: the rationally calculating individual bears full responsibility for the consequences of his or her action no matter how severe the constraints on this action, e.g., lack of skills, education, and childcare in a period of high unemployment and limited welfare benefits. Correspondingly, a "mismanaged life" becomes a new mode of depoliticizing social and economic [inequality] and at the same time reduces political citizenship to an unprecedented degree of passivity and political complacency. The model neo-liberal citizen is one who strategizes for her/himself among various social, political and economic options, not one who strives with others to alter or organize these options. (emphasis added)

Neoliberalism thus has several important implications for how people understand social life, sexual violence, individual failure, and harm that are relevant for this chapter. First, it describes a world full of atomized, self-centered individuals who, if appropriately rational and competent, can meet their needs on their own and therefore have no interest in or need to work collectively with others to achieve common goals such as challenging the social order. Second, moral autonomy is given only to those who can take care of themselves. All others can be disregarded, punished, or treated as children, who, lacking rational utilitarian competency (as demonstrated by their inability to care for themselves), take on the status of immoral non-autonomous agents who need to be monitored by others, particularly the state, and who are responsible for, and thus deserve, whatever harms and failures befall them. Third, neoliberalism's insistent claim that the chief purpose of individual action is to aggressively and assertively pursue self-centered goals and ambitions in the end becomes a clarion call for the constant and "energetic pursuit of personal fulfillment" (Rose and Miller 1992, 201), for constantly striving to meet one's desires in a world full of desire.

Since under neoliberalism, the moral act, both inside and outside the market, is to achieve one's desires by outcompeting others, using a personal cost/benefit test that disregards the value of others and what they want, and since neoliberal capitalism like all forms of capitalism is based on the exploitation of workers and the natural world, neoliberal discourse also supports using others and the natural world to satisfy one's desires. Moreover, because those who lose out in life's grand competition fail due to their own irrationality (their weakness of mind), thereby losing autonomy and moral worth, it is acceptable under neoliberalism to treat others and the natural world as mindless objects that we can use and harm to achieve our goals. Finally, because those who fail are morally worthless and responsible for their own failures, we can disregard their pain and suffering and the inequality that arises from their failures and our successes.

Identifying neoliberalism's discursive logic is not the same, of course, as demonstrating its degree of influence over social life. Thus, over the past two decades scholars have devoted considerable attention to investigating the extent to which and ways in which neoliberal discourse has permeated non-economic social arenas and been internalized by people in these arenas. These scholars have demonstrated, for instance, that neoliberal discourse shapes public health policy and discourse (Ayo 2012; LeBesco 2011), the provision of public services (Brown and Baker 2012), environmental activism (Harrison 2014, 2015), the way people think and talk about body weight (Guthman and DuPuis 2006; LeBesco 2011), how people monitor their bodies (Guthman and DuPuis 2006; Germov and Williams 1999), and the techniques people use to maintain socially acceptable body weight and form (Luna 2019).

Scholars have also demonstrated that neoliberal discourse shapes women's sexuality (Bay-Cheng 2015), women's reproductive decision making (Katz and Tirone 2015), societal discourses regarding rape, sexual agency and sexual victimhood (Anderson and Doherty 2008; Bay-Cheng 2015; Gill 2008; Stringer 2013), and rape law, rape trial discourse, and rape trial jury verdicts (Gotell 2008, 2010; Stringer 2013). Little attention has been paid, however, to the ways in which neoliberal discourse and discourses and bodily practices surrounding gender, sexuality, and sexual violence reinforce each other, in particular to the role that sexual violence and gender violence play in reinforcing not only dominant gender discourses (a subject that has been studied and theorized) but dominant capitalist discourses too (a subject that has not been studied before).

However, before I can address these topics, I must outline the main tenets of patriarchal discourse and describe the masculine and feminine traits and behaviors defined as normal and acceptable by this discourse.

Patriarchal Discourse

Theories of patriarchy focus on a wide variety of factors, including pornography (Dworkin 1981; MacKinnon 1989), compulsory heterosexuality (A. Rich 1980; MacKinnon 1982), and the relationship between patriarchy and capitalism (Hartmann 1976; Walby 1986). These approaches to patriarchy are all important. But given the purposes of this chapter, I restrict my attention to a different group of theories, those that highlight cultural belief systems and the feminine and masculine traits defined as appropriate by the discursive structures underlying these belief systems.

According to these theories, all societies have multiple masculinities and femininities, with each society having a dominant or hegemonic masculinity that is defined in opposition to a dominant and hegemonic femininity. Each society also has a set of subordinate femininities and masculinities that are defined in relation to the dominant femininity and masculinity (Connell 2000, 2005; Schippers 2007). Summarizing R. W. Connell, who initially developed the concept of hegemonic masculinity, Mimi Schippers (2007, 86–87) notes that Connell defined masculinity as

> an identifiable set of practices that . . . are taken up and enacted collectively by groups, communities, and societies. Through their recurring enactment over time and space, these practices structure the production and distribution of resources, the distribution of power in the form of authority, cathexis, by which Connell means the social arena of desire and sexuality, and symbolism or the production of meaning and value. . . . Connell [thus] . . . defines hegemonic masculinity as "the configuration of gender practice which embodies the currently accepted answer to the problem of the legitimacy of patriarchy, which guarantees . . . the dominant position of men and subordination of women."

Defining hegemonic masculinity and femininity as specific sets of practices is problematic, however, because if the practices that make up hegemonic femininity and masculinity vary within societies, across societies, and over time, as research shows they do (Connell 2005; Pascoe 2012), then there is no clear logic to these practices or to the relationship between hegemonic femininity and hegemonic masculinity other than that which is highly situationally specific. This, of course, makes hegemonic masculinity and femininity less than useful concepts for developing explanations of patriarchy and overall social order.

Schippers (2007) offers a solution to this problem. Drawing on the work of multiple scholars, she argues that instead of thinking of hegemonic femininity and masculinity as sets of practices, it would be more productive to conceptualize them as constituting a system of paired symbols, or symbolic meanings, that "define the relationship between women and men as complementary and hierarchical . . . [and that] provide the legitimating rationale for . . . ensuring the ascendancy and dominance of men." The importance of these paired and hierarchical symbols and meanings, then, is not that they describe the actual characteristics of women and men, but that they provide meaning to thought and action and "a rationale for social practice." Thus, for Schippers (2007, 92),

> Practice . . . is not masculinity and femininity as Connell suggests; social practice, in all its forms . . . is the mechanism by which masculinities and femininities, as part of a vast network of gender meanings, come to organize social life. Masculinities and femininities provide a legitimating rationale not just for embodiment and behavior by individuals but also for how to coordinate, evaluate, and regulate social practices, and therein lies their hegemonic significance.

The question, then, is, what are these paired symbols and meanings, and how do they define femininity and masculinity? Using literary, cultural, linguistic, and historical analysis, feminists spent considerable time in the 1960s, 1970s, and 1980s identifying these symbols and meanings and demonstrating that in many cases they can be traced back to the European Enlightenment and in some cases back to ancient Greece (Bordo 2003; Heckman 1994; Millett 1971). They are therefore deeply embedded in Western thought and action.

For instance, citing Luce Irigaray (1985) and Genevieve Lloyd (1984) among others, Susan Heckman (1994) notes that since at least the ancient Greeks, women in the Western world have been associated with ir-rationality and men with rationality. Susan Bordo (2003) similarly draws on earlier scholarship to demonstrate that since the ancient Greeks, Western women have been associated with the body and men with the mind. This, Heckman and Bordo note, is problematic because Western societies view the rational mind positively and the body and irrational-ity negatively, thus placing women in a subordinate position vis-à-vis men. Moreover, these discursive symbols are matched with other hier-archically ordered and value-laden symbols that inform social practice, further legitimizing and entrenching women's subordination.

The rational mind, for example, is defined in Western discourse as the chief characteristic that separates humans from animals, allowing humans to set and achieve goals; exert their wills and have free will; dispassionately plan for the future; create technology; control their bod-ies, emotions, and passions; seek out knowledge; develop civilization; dominate and control the natural world; achieve autonomy, indepen-dence, and separation from others; and move closer to God and truth. Furthermore, Western thought places the mind in symbolic opposition not only to animals and the body but also to the natural world, all of which, since Descartes and the Enlightenment, have been conceptual-ized as mere machines or objects subject to rational control and violent and nonviolent domination.

Western patriarchal discourse thus views men, but not women, as active, effective, autonomous, and fully human subjects who use their rational minds to control their bodies, emotions, and passions, set and achieve goals, seek knowledge, truth, and God, and develop culture and civilization. Men are therefore viewed as being dispassionate, assertive, calculating, and emotionally detached, and because of their detach-ment, autonomy, and separation from others, as being self-centered, disinclined to attend to the needs and desires of others, and potentially violent. Moreover, because the human body and natural world are con-sidered to be objects rather than subjects, men have the legitimate right to control and dominate the natural world and their own and others' bodies in order to meet their purposes, while women, who are associ-ated with the body and thus the natural world, are by dint of these as-sociations made to be controlled, used, and dominated, nonviolently if possible, violently if necessary.

Because femininity and masculinity and their associated symbols are defined in opposition to one another, Western discourse considers women to be not only body but also to be passive, ineffective, gentle, emotional, sensual, intuitive, overly attached to others, weak-willed, driven by feelings and emotion rather than rational logic, not fully human, and only partially autonomous. They are thus, according to this discourse, unable to achieve goals, seek knowledge and truth, develop culture and civilization, or control their bodies and passions. Lacking full autonomy and closely attached to others, they are also supposedly other-oriented rather than self-centered, receptive to and ready to take care of the needs and desires of others, and submissive and compliant rather than dominant, aggressive, and violent (Bartky 1990; Bordo 2003; Heckman 1994; Millett 1971; Worrell 2001).

Moreover, the body has additional negative connotations in Western thought, connotations that because of the body's association with women are likewise associated with women. It represents, according to Susan Bordo (2003), uncontrolled appetite, deception, temptation, and in Christianity, sin. It imprisons the soul and distances both the soul and the rational mind, and thus the true self, from God, knowledge, truth, and the light. It is, to use Bordo's words, "a drag on self-realization" and thus a source of alienation. It lures men to irrational (sexual) desire and is the source of man's moral downfall.[2]

The symbolic images and personality traits attached to femininity and masculinity are, of course, fantastical, discursive constructions that do not accurately describe women or men as individuals or social groups. But that is not their purpose. Instead, they guide and legitimize individual, organizational, and institutional thought and behavior (practice) by identifying two socially accepted genders and specifying their moral worth and proper relationship to each other. They indicate, for instance, what women and men should want from each other, how they should think and behave, what they can expect from each other, and how they should treat, view, and think about each other. Moreover, the symbolic images and meanings associated with femininity and masculinity are durable, persisting in many cases for thousands of years. They are thus deeply embedded in our culture and in each and every one of us, often overriding, at a deep unconscious level, what we consciously think we believe.

Because these images and meanings have persisted for so long and because discourse interacts with material conditions to shape social practices in specific places and times, the symbolic structure underlying femininity and masculinity has given rise to a wide variety of social practices that vary not only over time but also across and within societies. As a result, sudden or drastic changes in gender practices do not necessarily indicate any change in the symbolic structure underlying patriarchal social relations and hegemonic femininity and masculinity. Indeed, rather than assuming that such changes indicate a weakening or strengthening of patriarchy, we must ask whether new gender practices reinforce or undermine patriarchy's underlying symbolic structure.

In the following two sections, I summarize research findings from the past twenty to thirty years on the sexualized images of women and girls in the US media and on the bodily appearance practices of adolescent girls and young women in the United States. Some scholars argue that these images and practices, along with reduced levels of gender inequality, have undermined the symbolic structure that historically fortified patriarchy. I disagree and present my own and other scholars' arguments for why these images and practices are violent, why they continue to reinforce traditional patriarchal symbolic structures, and why they support neoliberal discourse. Specifically, I argue that rather than undermining patriarchy and neoliberalism, these images and practices strengthen them by violently reinforcing the symbolic structures that underlie them.

I also argue that one of the reasons these images and practices reinforce both patriarchal and neoliberal discourse, and thus overall social order, is that these two discourses share many symbolic elements with each other. They each associate their dominant group with the mind, aggression, rationality, and violence and their subordinate group with the body, passivity, irrationality, and submissiveness. They both find it acceptable to dominate, control, and harm others, to treat others as objects, to disregard the suffering of others, and to use others to satisfy one's desires. And they both hold that dominant group members are more morally worthy than are subordinate group members, that rationality makes dominant group members effective and morally worthy, while subordinate group irrationality does the opposite, and that subordinate groups are to blame for their subordination and the harms they experience.

Representations of Women and Girls in the US Media

A large body of quantitative research demonstrates that the way women and girls are portrayed in the US entertainment and news media is highly biased, with studies of television and magazine advertising, music videos, video games, television programs, and movies uncovering remarkably consistent biases that disadvantage women. For instance, sixteen articles on the US entertainment and news media that were published in special issues of the journal *Sex Roles* in 2010 and 2011 found that women are highly underrepresented in these media and that when they are represented, they tend to be "scantily dressed and relegated to stereotypical female roles" (Rebecca Collins 2011).

One of these articles, which examined magazine advertisements in *Cosmopolitan, Ladies' Home Journal, Esquire, Popular Mechanics, Reader's Digest*, and *National Geographic* between 1950 and 2000, found that women were much more likely than men to be portrayed in sexually suggestive poses, to sensually touch items in the advertisements, to be subordinate in relation to members of the opposite gender, to look and act like children, and to be psychologically removed from the situation depicted in the ad and thus to be non-agentic. Women in these advertisements were also much less likely than men to provide instruction or assistance to others and much more likely to receive instruction, suggesting that they lacked authority, knowledge, intelligence, and competence (Mager and Helgeson 2011). A study of advertising in more than fifty popular US magazines similarly found that women were treated as sex objects in more than half of the two thousand advertisements included in the study (Stankiewicz and Rosselli 2008).

Video games are also highly biased, having significantly fewer female than male characters and female characters that are regularly "cast" in stereotypical roles. In the 1980s and 1990s, for example, female characters were generally depicted as innocent and helpless princesses and damsels in distress who needed to be protected or saved by male characters. This changed in the 1990s and 2000s, when female game characters began to be cast as highly sexual objects who became more and more sexy and wore ever more physically revealing clothing as time progressed (Downs and Smith 2010; Stermer and Burkley 2012; Summers and Miller 2014).

Women are also highly sexualized in music videos, with studies finding that women in these videos are more likely than men to engage in sexual behavior, wear highly revealing clothing, and behave submissively (Conrad, Dixon, and Zhang 2009; King, Lake, and Bernard 2006). Lead female artists in these videos are also much more likely than their male counterparts to touch themselves sexually, dance in sexually suggestive ways, wear sexually provocative clothing, and display sexualized body parts (Aubrey and Frisby 2011; Wallis 2010).

Television shows and movies also exhibit a strong gender bias. Women, for instance, are highly underrepresented in movies, and female television and movie characters are less likely than their male counterparts to work in science, technology, engineering, mathematics, and computer science or to hold prestigious jobs in business, politics, health care, and academia (McDade-Montez, Wallander, and Cameron 2017; Stacy Smith et al. 2013, 2017). Female television and movie characters are also much more likely than male characters to be highly sexualized. A study of 275 prime-time television programs and 36 children's TV shows that aired in 2010 and 2011 found, for example, that female characters ages thirteen years and older were more likely than boys and men to wear sexy attire (36.2 percent versus 8.4 percent), have thin bodies (37.5 percent versus 13.6 percent) and exposed skin (34.6 percent versus 11 percent), and be referenced as attractive by other characters (11.6 percent versus 3.5 percent), with 30.8 percent of the younger female characters in these shows (ages thirteen to twenty) wearing sexy attire and 26.9 percent having exposed skin (Stacy Smith et al. 2013). Similarly, in the hundred top-grossing films of 2016, women were much more likely than men to wear sexy attire (25.9 percent versus 5.7 percent), be partially or fully nude (25.6 percent versus 9.2 percent), and be referred to as attractive by another character (10.7 percent versus 3.2 percent) (Stacy Smith et al. 2017). Finally, guests who appear on news and public affairs programs on both commercial and public television are much more likely to be male than female (Fairness and Accuracy in Reporting 2010; Dhoest, Panis, and Paulussen 2020; Hart 2014), as are the sources cited in front-page stories in the *New York Times* (Layton and Shepard 2013).

Women are thus underrepresented in a wide variety of entertainment and news media, and when they are portrayed in these media, they are much more likely than men to be thin and sexualized and much less likely to have high-powered jobs, to be sources of knowledge and expertise, and to engage in work that requires highly rational thought. Moreover, other media research shows that even when women are portrayed as being smarter than men, as being capable of thriving in high-powered, stressful, technical, or important jobs, or as otherwise falling outside traditional gender stereotypes, they are still often very thin, beautiful, and sexy and are often scripted as being quirky, unhappy, unfulfilled, or incomplete because they lack a man (Hinshaw 2009; Holtzman and Sharpe 2014). They also often end up bowing to the wishes and sexist behavior of men or otherwise conforming to or supporting stereotypical gender behavior (Walsh, Fursich, and Jefferson 2008).

Furthermore, the sexualized images of women and girls found in print and electronic media range across a broad spectrum from relatively tame to highly explicit and violent and have become increasingly ubiquitous with the rise of sophisticated electronic media delivery systems. Widespread use of these delivery systems has also helped increase the acceptance and dissemination of pornography, which completely sexualizes women, usually makes them subservient to men, and often relies on physical force, aggression, or violence against women (Dines 2009; Ezzell 2009; Jones 2018; Tolman 2013).

Women's and Girls' Body Appearance Practices

The sexualization of women and girls in print and electronic media does not simply reflect widely held cultural ideals. It also helps shape those ideals, and along with the cultural expectations of family members, employers, friends, classmates, acquaintances, and people on the street plays a key role in guiding the bodily practices of women and girls. Indeed, a wide range of qualitative and quantitative research demonstrates that the images of women and girls found in the media, in combination with the cultural expectations of others, leads women and girls as young as six years old to want to have extremely thin bodies. These images and expectations also lead women and older girls to spend considerable time, money, and psychological energy worrying about their looks and striving hard to meet cultural ideals of thinness and sexiness (Aubrey 2006; Bartky 1990; Bordo 2003; Dohnt and Tiggemann 2006; Evans and Riley 2014; R. Freedman 1986; Grabe, Ward, and Hyde

2008; Halliwell, Malson, and Tischner 2011; Hesse-Biber 2007; Jeffreys 2005; McKenney and Bigler 2016; Oppliger 2008; Perloff 2014; Rice 2014; Sinton and Birch 2006; Starr and Ferguson 2012; Tiggemann and Slater 2017; Zurbriggen and Roberts 2013).

Feminine ideals of thinness and sexiness are traditionally met through body modification practices such as dieting, exercise, hair removal, hair styling, and wearing the right clothes, jewelry, makeup, and shoes. But they are also met through body modification practices such as fat removal, surgically reducing the size of the stomach, bulimia, anorexia, and cosmetic surgery of the face, breasts, and labia (Bordo 2003; R. Freedman 1986; Hesse-Biber 2007; Jeffreys 2005). Popular culture's emphasis on sex and sexiness and the increasing mainstreaming of pornography have also contributed to the rise of related sexualized practices such as college hookup cultures, young women flashing their breasts in public, pole dancing classes for middle-class women, and women and girls wearing fashion derived from the pornography industry (Armstrong, Hamilton, and England 2010; Evans and Riley 2014; Jeffreys 2005; A. Lynch 2012).

These and other manifestations of what Ariel Levy (2005) calls raunch culture have, in turn, led to strong disagreements among feminists and gender scholars regarding the desirability of both these social practices and the increasingly sexualized portrayal of women and girls in popular culture (Evans and Riley 2014; Jeffreys 2005; A. Lynch 2012). Those supporting these sexualized practices and portrayals argue that the successes of the feminist movement in the 1970s and 1980s provided women and girls with opportunities equal to those of men and boys and thus with a broader array of choices than they had in the past. These broader choices involve not only their educations, careers, and whether and when to get married and have children but also their sexuality and how they present themselves publicly.

For these scholars and activists, then, the purported equality of opportunity that women currently experience means that women are now highly agentic and choose when and when not to have sex, what types of sexual activities they engage in, which cultural images of women they want to embody, and whether and when they want to objectify themselves based on these images. Women are, according to this argument, also knowledgeable and discerning consumers of popular images of women and of body modification practices based on these images who want to both modify their bodies and engage in forms of sexuality, sexual activity, and self-objectification that earlier waves of feminists argued supported patriarchal oppression. Moreover, the argument goes, women take great pleasure in these images, activities, and practices. When combined with the argument that women are now relatively equal in status with men, this means that these formerly oppressive images, activities, and practices now reflect women's agency and empowerment (rather than their oppression) and must not be questioned by others, in particular by radical feminists (Bay-Cheng 2012, 2015; Evans and Riley 2014; Gill 2007; Heberle 1996; Jeffreys 2005; Lamb and Peterson 2012; Lehrman 1997; A. Lynch 2012; Marcus 1992; Murnen and Smolak 2012; Roiphe 1993; Stringer 2013; Wolf 1993).

We must ask, of course, whether this is really true. Do women freely accept and choose these images, practices, and sexual activities without any serious constraints? Do these images, practices, and activities give them pleasure or pain or both? Do free choice and agency regarding bodily practices, sexuality, and self-objectification signal an end to oppression, or do these choices and this agency, regardless of whether they are experienced as pleasurable and empowering, help maintain the patriarchal order?

In my estimation, these images, practices, activities, choices, and agency do not signal women's and girls' empowerment so much as their continued oppression by patriarchal social structures. Indeed, a key mistake that proponents of the agency argument make is to conceptualize individual choice and oppression as being mutually exclusive (Gavey 2012; Gill 2012), as if oppressed people are never able to make choices, exert some form of limited agency, or experience limited agency as freedom. Proponents of the agency argument also seem to ignore the fact that given a specific set of structural constraints and incentives, people can experience as positive, pleasurable, and empowering actions that harm them in some way or go against their interests or some subset of their interests (Bartky 1988; Bordo 2003). It is also possible that women do not experience popular culture, the body modification practices they adopt, self-objectification, and increased sexual agency as positively as proponents of the agency argument claim they do.

Thus, in the following section, I present evidence that media images of women and women's body modification practices often harm women, and are thus violent. I also present evidence that women's increased sexual agency and sexualized self-objectification may not be as liberating or agentic as proponents of the agency argument make them out to be. I then demonstrate that dominant representations of women and girls in the media, women's and girls' body modification practices, and many of the sexualized practices celebrated by proponents of the agency argument support rather than undermine patriarchal social relations because they are highly consistent with the durable symbolic structure underlying patriarchal discourse.

But before proceeding, I want to clearly state that I am not arguing that women and girls lack agency. All people have agency. Nevertheless, everybody's agency is limited to some degree by the social structures and forces that surround them, with subordinate group members' agency particularly limited by these structures and forces.

In addition, we are not simply born with agency. Agency is something that is learned and that can be expanded and developed through positive experiences and reduced by negative experiences (Brooks 2018). Being sexually violated or having society portray us in ways that reduce our self-esteem, make us anxious, ashamed, or depressed, or limit our sense of autonomy and efficacy can, for instance, reduce our future agency. And this is particularly likely to be the case when the future events we experience bring the root causes of these feelings to the fore (Hopper and Lisak 2014; van der Kolk 2014).

Agency, Oppression, or Both?

A large body of quantitative research demonstrates that viewing images that portray women or girls as exceptionally thin or highly sexualized leads women and girls to objectify themselves (self-objectification), to become dissatisfied with and constantly monitor their body shape and weight (self-surveillance), and to modify their bodies and weight to meet culturally approved body ideals (Aubrey 2006; Grabe, Ward, and Hyde 2008; McKenney and Bigler 2016; Murnen and Smolak 2012; Sinton and Birch 2006). This is true even for girls between the ages of five and ten

(Dittmar, Halliwell, and Ive 2006; Dohnt and Tiggemann 2006; Harrison and Hefner 2006); and for young women, the effect appears to be particularly strong when they view images that portray women as both highly sexual and sexually agentic (Halliwell, Malson, and Tischner 2011).

Self-surveillance and self-objectification, in turn, are linked in women to sexual dysfunction and sexual dissatisfaction and in both women and adolescent girls to lower self-esteem, reduced sense of autonomy, body shame, and eating disorders. Self-surveillance and self-objectification are also positively associated with depression and anxiety and negatively associated with life satisfaction, psychological well-being, stress management, and the adoption of health-promoting behaviors. These outcomes, along with shame, eating disorders, and low self-esteem, represent potentially serious psychological health problems. They can also severely harm physical health. They can cause severe headaches, serious gastrointestinal problems, chronic sleep disorders, cardiovascular issues, and problems with the central nervous system, and can weaken the immune system and increase sensitivity to pain. They can also produce severe weight gain or loss and a range of health problems associated with weight gain and loss (Bener et al. 2012; Breines, Crocker, and Garcia 2008; de Heer et al. 2014; Holt et al. 2013; Mercurio and Landry 2008; Moradi and Yu-Ping 2008; Murnen and Smolak 2012; Pujols, Meston, and Seal 2009; Szymanski and Henning 2007; Walter et al. 2013; Western Washington Medical Group 2020).

Moreover, research suggests that women who are presented in a sexualized manner are viewed by others as being less intelligent and competent than are nonsexualized women (Glick, Larsen, and Johnson 2005; Gurung and Chrouser 2007), while preadolescent girls who are portrayed in such a manner are viewed as less intelligent, competent, capable, moral, and responsible than are nonsexualized girls (Graff, Murnen, and Smolak 2012).

More nuanced ethnographic research on adolescent girls' body practices confirms these quantitative findings but with a few important twists. For instance, three studies, one about adolescent girls who "came of age between the late 1970s and early 1990s" (Rice 2014, 5), one that investigated the lives of girls ages thirteen to sixteen in the early to mid-1990s (Bloustien 2003), and another that examined the experiences of girls ages thirteen to fourteen in the summer of 2003 (Coleman 2009), all show that adolescent girls do, in fact, adopt and discard multiple body practices and gender identities, often in enjoyable ways, as they learn what it means for them to become women. At the same time, however, the choices the girls in these studies made were all sharply constrained by the strong social pressure they felt from boys, other girls, family members, authority figures, the popular media, strangers, and acquaintances. Indeed, serious negative consequences and severe psychological pain and trauma often accompanied this social pressure, particularly in those cases where the girls chose not to conform to cultural norms or were ethnic or racial minorities and thus unable to conform to mainstream White cultural norms. These ethnographies thus make clear that teenage girls do experience agency in relation to their body modification and gender practices, but that their agency is circumscribed in ways that are often experienced as disempowering and psychologically painful and that push them to conform to broad gender norms or to be seriously punished for failing to do so.

Laina Bay-Cheng (2015) argues that this is also true for teenage girls and women in regard to their sexual agency. According to her and other scholars (Gill 2007; Jeffreys 2005; Evans and Riley 2014), the argument that for women increased choice equals increased agency and freedom is really a form of neoliberal chicanery that imposes additional rather than fewer patriarchal obligations on women. Drawing on a broad base of empirical scholarship, Bay-Cheng demonstrates that an "agency line" has now been imposed on women that intersects with a much older disciplinary line that in the past differentiated good women from bad according to whether they refrained from having sex outside marriage.

Under the new disciplinary regime, Bay-Cheng argues, it is socially acceptable for unmarried women to have sex as long as they are in control of the situation (as long as they are agentic). However, if women have sex with too many partners or if their sexual activity or lack of sexual activity is not the product of their agency but is instead the result of them being out of control or being unappealing to men, then they are socially sanctioned for their lack of sexual agency or their inability to agentically conform to cultural standards of beauty. This, of course, puts an added onus on women, who now have to manage the impressions others have not only of their sexual activity but also of their agency in relation to that activity.

The result of all this, Bay-Cheng argues, is that neoliberalism's contempt for those who make mistakes, who suffer, or who lack agency is combined with patriarchy's contempt for women who are too sexually agentic to both police and circumscribe the behavior of women and adolescent girls. Moreover, because women and adolescent girls have largely internalized neoliberalism's norms regarding agency, and because under neoliberalism lack of agency or limited agency is viewed as a mark of personal weakness rather than as resulting from unequal social relations, the new agency line leads many women to blame themselves rather than those who have abused or raped them for sexual encounters and experiences they do not want but have been forced or coerced into having. The agency line thus reinforces society's general tendency to blame women for the sexual abuse they receive: it holds that the abuse occurred either because the woman was agentic, and therefore wanted it, or because she failed to agentically stop it, and is therefore the one at fault. Blaming women for sexual harassment and unwanted sexual encounters is not, of course, a new phenomenon, but it is, according to Bay-Cheng, given added impetus by the agency line and new neoliberal standards of personal responsibility.

In addition to the foregoing, it is also unclear that women feel as sexually agentic or as consistently sexually agentic as proponents of the agency argument claim they feel. Research suggests, for example, that a sizeable proportion of young women have complied with unwanted sex, both with committed and casual partners (Bay-Cheng and Eliseo-Arras 2008; Katz and Schneider 2015). Research and anecdotal evidence further suggest that a non-trivial percentage of teenage girls engage in unwanted, porn-inspired anal sex and unwanted, porn-inspired ejaculation on their faces with their partners, due either to persuasion or coercion (Jones 2018; Marston and Lewis 2014); and Lynch (2012) demonstrates that young college women who flash their breasts in public settings often do so not because they want to but because of extreme pressure from or fear of young men and that they often regret doing so afterward.

Similarly, hookup culture is not as positive a phenomenon for young women as the agency argument suggests it should be. It is true that hookup culture is not as widespread as some of its critics claim it is, and it is also true that for some young women it provides advantages over committed relationships (Armstrong, Hamilton, and England 2010).

Nevertheless, research shows that women are often dissatisfied with hookup sex and often find the hookup experience to be "intimidating and emotionally harmful." Hookup cultures also give men more power than women and value women solely for their sex appeal, with men the ones who decide whether women are sexy enough to pass muster (Wade 2017, 243).

Adrienne Evans and Sarah Riley's (2014) ethnographic study of young women who pursue sexualized pleasure through activities such as pole-dancing, burlesque, and watching pornography also suggests that women's experiences of sexual agency and freedom are not as straightforward as proponents of the agency argument suggest they are. It is true, on the one hand, that the women in Evans and Riley's (2014, 56) study actively and enthusiastically

> engage[] in sexual consumerism to create themselves as "new sexual subjects." . . . [They also] position[] themselves as discerning, all-consuming, and constantly self-transformative. . . . [And they pursue] identities that [are] situated against historical notions of passive femininity.

But it is also true that these women have to constantly work on their bodies to attain the identities they want to attain and must regularly transform themselves because their body ideals are constantly changing. They also recognize that they can never fully attain their ideal bodies and identities, and they perceive as inferior women who are not like them. Their pursuit of what are supposed to be empowering, pleasurable, freeing, and agentic identities is thus incomplete, not fully agentic, and hierarchical, leading Evans and Riley (2014, 137) to conclude that each woman's

> dream of being a sexy, powerful, agentic woman [is] undermined by a level of constant self-surveillance, self-monitoring, and self-disciplining that feeds into forms of *insecurity, aggression, and hatred* directed at the self and at others. (emphasis added)

Finally, Nicola Gavey (2012, 722) argues that many young women are ambivalent about the current gender order and their sexual empowerment within that order:

It was notable how readily, when gently probed, many young women we interviewed expressed dissatisfaction or discomfort with various features of the gendered order of their lives and the sexism they tentatively observed. Yet they appeared to have no access to socially acceptable tools for critical engagement with it, and tended to be diffident about expressing it. With feminism not a readily accessible framework within their peer group, the only alternative seemingly was to "make the most" of their place in the order. So while we might worry about "hurting" girls by telling them they are not empowered when they think they are . . . , I wonder whether taking claims about sexual empowerment at face value is always as validating [or accurate] as it might seem.

It thus appears that in many instances, the sexualization of women and girls in popular culture, the body modification practices women and girls engage in to conform with sexualized cultural norms, the new sexual agency, and activities such as pole dancing, hookup culture, and breast flashing disempower women and girls and push them to do things they do not want to do. These practices also circumscribe women's and girls' lives and often cause them violent harm. For instance, the self-objectification, self-surveillance, self-hatred, and insecurity that both arise from and are embedded in these practices can, as explained in the preceding pages, cause severe psychological, emotional, and physical suffering and pain. These self-disciplinary and sexual-agency practices and the portrayal of women and girls in the mainstream media are, therefore, highly violent, inflicting severe harm on tens of millions of women and girls throughout the United States.

Being held in contempt for failing to meet neoliberal and patriarchal ideals regarding sexuality, agency, and beauty can also cause psychological and emotional harm (Zhou 2011), and incorrectly blaming oneself for highly traumatic sexual experiences can increase the trauma, alienation, and pain, and thus the violence, of these experiences, particularly when others do not believe that you have been harassed, coerced, or raped (Francisco 1999; K. Freedman 2014; Norman et al. 2019; Wilson, Drozdek, and Turkovic 2006).[3]

Believing in the validity of the agency line rather than the truth of one's own experiences, having others disbelieve you or accuse you of making false accusations when you have been sexually coerced and abused, lacking the tools to properly name one's personal experiences, and being portrayed as body and not mind and thus as less than fully human can also cause extreme alienation from oneself, one's experiences, and others. And alienation, in turn, can lead to drug and alcohol abuse, eating disorders, physical pain, anger, anxiety, psychological distress, and depression, all of which, in this context, are violent harms regularly experienced by women and girls as a result of the sexualized practices and portrayals described in this (and the next) chapter (Bordo 2003; Healthline 2020; Hilt, Roberto, and Nolen-Hoeksema 2013; Ifeagwazi, Chukwuorji, and Zacchaeus 2014; Ross and Mirowsky 2009; Safipour et al. 2011).

Sexualized Practices and Portrayals and Social Order

The sexualized portrayal of women and girls in popular culture and the social practices that flow from this portrayal are not just violent, however. They also support patriarchy. To demonstrate that this is true, we can first ask how women and girls might be portrayed in popular culture if we lived in a matriarchal society. One might expect, for instance, that in a matriarchal society, dominant representations of women and girls would not focus so rigidly on women's and girls' sexuality, and that when presented in popular culture, women's and girls' sexuality would be portrayed in more varied ways that align more closely with women's and girls' actual bodies and desires than with men's sexual interests and desires. One would also expect to see powerful and intelligent women and girls portrayed much more often than they currently are in the news and entertainment media and to see images and portrayals that present the full range of what it means to be a woman and girl.

But the strongest piece of evidence in favor of my claim that the practices and portrayals described in this chapter reinforce patriarchal social relations is that these practices and portrayals line up so incredibly closely with the feminine/masculine symbolic structure that has provided the foundation for patriarchy for thousands of years. This symbolic structure associates men with the mind, rational thought, science, knowledge, emotional detachment, separation from others, self-centeredness, agency, aggression, and dominance over the body and natural world. Conversely, it associates women with the body, irrationality, lack of agency, sin, sex, temptation, subordination, passivity, and uncontrolled appetite. In addition, it views women as submissive and compliant, as unable to control their bodies, minds, and passions, as the source of man's moral downfall, and as bowing to and fulfilling the wishes and desires of others.

It is thus painfully clear that our popular culture is highly patriarchal. Its sexualization of women and girls and narrow focus on their bodies, its portrayal of women and girls as wanting to fulfill men's and boys' desires and as existing for men's and boys' enjoyment, and its failure to regularly present women in scientific and other high-status and high-rationality roles all conform with the symbolic structure that has defined masculinity, femininity, and women's oppression for thousands of years.

Women's and girls' body modification practices and purported increase in sexual agency also support patriarchal oppression, not because there is anything inherently wrong or subordinating about these practices or this agency but rather because these practices and agency, like the portrayal of women and girls in the media, reinforce our culture's negative association of women with the body, sexuality, sin, temptation, and fulfillment of male desire. In other words, for women's and girls' body modification practices and sexual agency to overcome patriarchal social relations, they must be matched with revolutionary changes in the symbolic order underlying femininity, masculinity, and patriarchy. Otherwise, regardless of how positively or negatively women and girls experience them, these practices and this agency will continue to promote patriarchal oppression.

Finally, patriarchal discourse, popular culture's portrayal of women, the new sexual agency, and women's and girls' body modification practices share an important set of symbolic elements with neoliberal discourse, which, I argued earlier, supports behaving aggressively, treating others as objects, and using others to satisfy one's desires. Neoliberal discourse also views people as rational decision makers and atomized, self-centered individuals who rather than being members of hierarchically ordered social groups are solely and individually responsible for what happens to them. In addition, it blames subordinate group members and those who experience harm for their subordination and harm, considers successful people to be rational and disciplined and unsuccessful people to be irrational and undisciplined, and considers irrational people to be less than fully human and more like objects than subjects, to whom the rational can do what they want in pursuit of their goals and desires.

Patriarchal discourse thus reinforces neoliberal discourse by blaming women for their disadvantaged position in society and linking women's disadvantaged position to their supposed irrationality, passivity, inability to think clearly and scientifically, and lack of impulse control. It further reinforces neoliberal discourse by viewing its subordinate group members, women and girls, as body and, thus, as passive, mindless objects subject to the whims and desires of self-centered, rational, agentic, and aggressive men and boys.

Moreover, the key distinction that patriarchal discourse and neoliberal discourse make between the body and mind means that these discourses are both reinforced by any social practice that distances women and girls from the mind or associates them with the body, particularly when that practice is linked to a broader set of practices that reinforce each other by also doing this. As such, the sexualization of women and girls in popular culture, the body modification practices women and girls engage in to conform with sexualized cultural norms, the tremendous amount of time and energy women and girls spend modifying and worrying about their bodies, and the rise of sexualized activities such as pole dancing and breast flashing all reinforce patriarchal and neoliberal discourse, and thus overall social order, by emphasizing women's and girls' bodies and sexuality rather than their minds.

The agency line that Bay-Cheng (2015) describes also reinforces neoliberal discourse, but in this case by making women solely and individually responsible for their sexual reputations and for what happens to them sexually. As previously noted, the agency line holds that women can be sexually agentic, even sexually aggressive, but only if they rationally choose what they want, rationally control their sexual impulses so that they do not have too many sexual partners, and rationally restrain their appetites so that they conform to socially acceptable body standards, with those women who succeed or fail in these tasks held personally responsible for what happens or does not happen to them sexually. This responsibility is held by individual women, whose ability to meet their responsibilities is not viewed by the broader culture as being severely limited by the fact that they are, as a group, hierarchically subordinated to men. It is also contingent on women remaining less sexually aggressive than men.

The agency line thus accepts aggression among men and limited and highly circumscribed aggression among women. But it does so in a form that reinforces patriarchal discourse's image of women as sexually charged bodies and neoliberalism's view that people who fail are irrational and solely responsible for their failure, while those who succeed are rational and solely responsible for their successes. The agency line further supports neoliberalism by blaming subordinate group members for the harm done to them by dominant group members and by ignoring the existence of hierarchically ordered social groups, thereby reinforcing neoliberal discourse and deflecting responsibility away from the dominant group and the social structure that supports them.

It is thus clear that central to patriarchal discourse is a set of discursive elements that are also central to neoliberal discourse and as a result, that invoking either of these discourses through social practice reinforces the other, thereby promoting overall social order. It is also clear that the portrayal of women and girls in the mainstream media, female bodily and self-disciplining practices based on this portrayal, and the new agency line are all violent social practices that support overall social order by invoking discursive elements common to both patriarchy and neoliberalism. This, of course, is highly consistent with the theoretical argument I set forth in chapter 1, providing strong support for that argument and for my claim that violence is absolutely central to social life, promoting social order not just in the specific arenas in which it occurs, but throughout society as a whole.

3

Sexual Harassment and Rape

In this chapter I investigate the relationship between sexual harassment, rape, and social order, extending the argument I presented in the preceding chapter in three key ways. First, I demonstrate that as is true of the sexualized practices highlighted in the previous chapter, sexual harassment and rape reinforce dominant discourses in multiple social arenas. Second, I demonstrate that along with the sexualized practices from the preceding chapter, sexual harassment and rape (a) support the cultural, psychological, and material interests of key subordinate groups and (b) align female and male subjectivity and identity with dominant institutional practices and external social and power relations. Third, I demonstrate that the violent practices highlighted in this and the previous chapter form a coherent whole, a unified, interdependent, and violent social structure that guides the behavior, internal consciousness, subjectivity, and identity of women, men, girls, and boys, producing social order not just by reinforcing dominant discourses, meeting subordinate group interests, and "properly" aligning subjectivity and identity, but also by fundamentally forming and shaping subjectivity, identity, embodiment, and consent.

I begin with a brief discussion of sexual harassment, which, I argue later in the chapter, reinforces discursive structures that not only promote social order but also make rape more socially acceptable. I then discuss rape and society's reaction to rape, highlighting in detail the discursive and structural reasons why so few rapists end up in jail. Understanding why so few rapists are punished is important in its own right. But the main reason I discuss these discursive and structural factors is that they play a key role, as we will see, in producing overall social order.

Sexual Harassment

Sexual harassment, which can be defined as "unwelcome sexual advances, requests for sexual favors, and other verbal or physical harassment of a sexual nature" (US Equal Employment Opportunity Commission 2017), is an often unrecognized form of violence and in some cases, a prelude to rape (Burtman 2017; McMillan 2017; Rice 2014; Valenti 2016a). It is also incredibly widespread in the United States, with highly public charges of harassment levelled in recent years against a wide range of celebrities, high-level businessmen, and politicians.

But sexual harassment is not perpetrated solely by the rich and famous. In 2018, for instance, 59 percent of US women said they had experienced sexual harassment at some point in their lives, with 55 percent of women who had been harassed experiencing harassment both at work and outside work, 14 percent experiencing harassment solely at work, and 30 percent experiencing harassment solely outside work (Graf 2018). A survey of employed women ages eighteen to thirty-four conducted in 2015 similarly found that one in three women in this age group had been sexually harassed at work, with 81 percent of those who had been sexually harassed experiencing verbal harassment, 44 percent experiencing unwanted touching and sexual advances, and 25 percent receiving lewd texts or e-mails (Vagianos 2015). Moreover, other workplace surveys show that between 25 percent and 75 percent of *all* employed women (depending on the survey) have been sexually harassed at some point in their work lives, with low-wage industries and industries that traditionally have not employed women experiencing especially high rates of harassment (Feldblum and Lipnic 2016; National Women's Law Center 2016; Restaurant Opportunities Centers United Forward Together 2014; Bame 2017).

Women also experience sexual harassment in public spaces. One study found, for instance, that 65 percent of US women had experienced such harassment, with 57 percent of US women having experienced verbal harassment, 23 percent sexual touching, 20 percent following, 14 percent flashing, and 9 percent having been "forced to do something sexual" (Kearl 2014, 6).[1] In addition, most women have experienced public harassment more than once and 6 percent are harassed either often or daily (Kearl 2014).

Harassment also occurs at schools, colleges, and universities. For instance, a 2014–2015 survey of more than 150,000 students at twenty-seven US universities found that 61.9 percent of surveyed female undergraduates and 44.1 percent of surveyed female graduate and professional students had been sexually harassed at least once by someone associated with their university (Cantor et al. 2017). And during the 2010–2011 school year, a nationally representative survey of students in grades 7–12 found that

> 46% of girls had someone make unwelcome sexual comments, jokes or gestures to or about them (more than half of these girls had that happen multiple times), 16% were shown sexy or sexual pictures they did not want to see, 13% were touched in an unwelcome sexual way, and 26% were electronically sent unwelcome sexual comments, jokes or pictures or had someone post such comments, jokes or pictures of or about them. . . . [In addition,] 9% were physically intimidated in a sexual way, 7% had someone expose themselves to them, and 4% were forced to do something sexual. (Hill and Kearl 2011, 12–13; the wording in this paragraph is taken primarily from figure 2, p. 12)

In addition to being widespread, sexual harassment can cause severe psychological, emotional, and physical harm and is thus a form of violence. In Hill and Kearl's (2011) study, for example, sexual harassment at school led 37 percent of girls to feel sick to their stomachs, 34 percent to have trouble studying, and 22 percent to have trouble sleeping, with more than 10 percent having trouble sleeping for a long period of time. Among adults, women who have been sexually harassed often experience fear, anxiety, anger, shame, helplessness, self-blame, and reduced self-esteem. They sometimes also experience major depressive disorders, drug and alcohol problems, emotional exhaustion, disordered eating, and post-traumatic stress disorder. Being sexually harassed can also produce serious physical health problems, including "headaches, exhaustion, sleep problems, gastric problems, nausea, weight loss and gain, and respiratory, musculoskeletal, and cardiovascular issues." In addition, harassment in public places can lead women to objectify themselves and their bodies, which, as I have already documented, can cause severe physical and psychological harm (Feldblum and Lipnic 2016, 21; Hill and Kearl 2011; Kearl 2014, 10).

Women writing about their experiences with sexual harassment note that in addition to these consequences, the long-term effects of sexual harassment can include feelings of dehumanization, alienation, and diminishment, a reduced sense of self, a recognition that women have little social worth and occupy a subordinate position in society, an understanding that their bodies are public property and do not always belong to themselves but often to someone else, and a chronic fear that they might be harassed, raped, or physically abused at any time (Burtman 2017; Valenti 2016b; Weiner 2017). And all these consequences, in turn, can cause severe emotional and psychological harm.

Moreover, men who sexually harass women are not just behaving violently. They are also reinforcing mainstream patriarchal and neoliberal discourse, both of which (a) prize aggressive behavior by dominant group members and passive behavior by subordinate group members, (b) support treating subordinate group members as objects and using subordinate group members to satisfy the desires of dominant group members, and (c) believe that it is acceptable to harm and disregard the suffering and pain of subordinate group members. Because sexual harassment is directed at women's bodies, emotions, and psyches, it also associates women with the body and irrationality, providing additional support for neoliberal and patriarchal discourse.

Sexual harassment can thus be viewed (among other things) as a socially pervasive, regularly enacted, highly dispersed, and inherently violent social practice that promotes overall social order by reinforcing, in an emotionally and psychologically charged way, dominant discourses in multiple social arenas. As the following section makes clear, this is also true of rape, rape trial discourse, and society's reaction to rape.

Rape and Society's Reaction to Rape

In the preceding section, I treated sexual harassment as if it is independent of other forms of sexual violence. But in addition to being violent and promoting overall social order, sexual harassment exacerbates women's and girls' fear of even more extreme male violence. It can also be a prelude to rape (Burtman 2017; McMillan 2017; Valenti 2016b; Weiner 2017), which, like sexual harassment, is extremely prevalent in the United States. Data from the Centers for Disease Control and Prevention (CDCP) show, for instance, that more than 25 million women, or 21.3 percent of all women, in the United States have been raped in their lifetimes, while 43.6 percent have experienced other forms of sexual violence (Sharon Smith et al. 2018). However, these statistics are misleading because the CDCP restricts its definition of rape to *completed and attempted forced penetration* and *alcohol- and drug-facilitated penetration*, thus excluding from its rape statistics acts of *unwanted coerced penetration* (nonphysically pressured unwanted penetration), which have been experienced by just over 19.2 million US women (16 percent of US women). Unwanted coerced penetration is, of course, rape. Thus, according to the CDCP, somewhere between 21.3 percent and 37.3 percent (21.3 plus 16) of all US women have been raped.[2]

Moreover, many women who have been raped were raped or first raped as children, teenagers, or young adults:

> Completed rape (completed forced penetration and completed alcohol- or drug-facilitated penetration) . . . was first experienced by an estimated 78.7% [of completed-rape victims] before age 25 years, by an estimated 40.4% before age 18 years (*28.3% at ages 11–17 years and 12.1% at age ≤10 years*), and by an estimated 38.3% at age 18–24 years. . . . An estimated 15.2% first experienced [completed forced rape] at age 25–34 years. (Breiding et al. 2014, 11–12, emphasis added)

But despite the fact that so many women and girls in the United States have been raped, very few rape cases go to trial and only a small percentage of these trials result in a conviction. The Rape, Abuse, and Incest National Network (RAINN) estimates, for instance, that for every 1,000 rapes committed in the United States, only 310 are reported to the police, with only 57 of these leading to arrest. Of these 57 cases, only 11 are referred to prosecutors, only 7 lead to felony convictions, and only 6 result in incarceration (RAINN 2016).

There are many reasons for this stunning attrition rate. The first is that many women who are raped choose not to report their rape to the police. Some women, for example, are afraid that if they report their rape, they or their loved ones could be harmed again; some are financially or otherwise dependent on the rapist or someone they believe will take the rapist's side if the rape becomes public knowledge; and some think that reliving the trauma of the rape when questioned by police, hospital staff, prosecutors, and defense attorneys will be too difficult for them. Other women have intense feelings of shame regarding the rape;

are not sure whether they were raped, whether they were partially to blame for the rape, or whether others will blame them or say they were not raped; and some think that their family, friends, the police, or the district attorney will not believe or support them. Finally, some women do not want anyone to know what happened to them; have had bad experiences with the criminal justice system in the past; correctly believe that it is unlikely their rapist will be convicted; do not want to view themselves or be viewed by others as a victim; or are unsure whether what they have experienced is legally rape, particularly when, as is true of most women who are raped, they were raped by someone they know (Cohn et al. 2013; Corrigan 2013; Gray 2014; Peterson and Muehlenhard 2004; Wolitzky-Taylor et al. 2011).

These reactions and the specific decisions rape survivors make regarding whether to pursue criminal charges against their rapists may seem highly idiosyncratic and self-defeating to many people. However, rape survivors' reactions and decisions are very strongly conditioned by social factors that exist externally to them, in particular by the organizational routines of the criminal justice and health care systems and the social discourses that surround gender, rape, race, class, and consensual sex. Moreover, rape survivors' reactions and decisions are quite rational given these discourses and routines. Poor women who are dependent on others, for example, are not viewed kindly by our society, which tends to blame *them* for their precarious economic situation and any harm that comes to them, particularly if they are Hispanic or Black. Whites also tend to view Black men as sexually dangerous and Black women as sexually promiscuous and lacking in restraint, while Americans in general believe that poor and working-class men are more physically aggressive and violent than are middle- and upper-class men. Thus, Whites are less likely to believe Black women who say they have been raped than they are to believe White women who say they have been raped and less likely to believe Black or poor men who claim they are not rapists than they are to believe White or middle-class men who make the same claim. The race and class of the rape survivor and her attacker thus play an important role in determining whether the survivor pursues criminal charges (Cohn et al. 2013; Corrigan 2013; Wolitzky-Taylor et al. 2011).

But even White middle-class women generally have a very difficult time convincing others that they have been raped. This is true because there exists a set of very well-documented myths, or discourses, that US citizens rely on to determine whether a woman was raped or consented to having sex that predispose most Americans to believe the rapist rather than the victim (Corrigan 2013; Matoesian 2001). Thus, in the following section, I discuss these myths and their effect on the decisions rape survivors make regarding whether to report their rapes to the police. I then use this information later in the chapter to explain how rape and society's reaction to rape promote overall social order.

Rape and Consensual Sex Myths

Rape myths, which provide US citizens with a strong image of the typical rape, rapist, and rape victim, portray the typical rapist as a deranged stranger whom the rape victim does not know. This deranged stranger savagely attacks and violently penetrates the victim, marking her body with clear physical signs of violence. The typical victim, the myth holds, loudly, violently, and persistently resists the attack, immediately calls the police after the attack is over, clearly and unequivocally wants to imprison the rapist, and provides police officers, prosecutors, defense attorneys, and jurors with a clear, detailed, coherent, and consistent account of what happened to her.

Strongly linked to these rape myths is a set of myths about consensual heterosexual sex and women's and men's proper roles in managing (and manufacturing) consent to heterosexual sex. Relying on old and deeply held cultural beliefs about both proper *and* typical gender behavior, including Old Testament beliefs about Eve tempting Adam with the apple, these consensual sex myths hold that women are temptresses who intentionally or unintentionally lure men into sexual behavior that men cannot control. If women do not want to have sex, it is thus their responsibility to create clear boundaries that signal to men that they are not sexually available. When women create such boundaries, men will not have sex with them. When women do not create such boundaries, then they (a) must consciously or unconsciously want to have sex or (b) are not playing the sexual consent game properly and must therefore accept any unwanted sex they do have because they cannot expect a man who has been turned on in any way to be able to control his sexual urges.

According to these myths, then, for an alleged rape to actually be a rape, the woman, prior to the alleged rape, must not have drunk alcohol, taken drugs, or partied with others, which somehow suggest sexual availability. Nor should she have worn physically revealing clothing, flirted with the accused man or other men, or kissed or been at all physically intimate with the accused man. In addition, she should not have willingly spent time alone with the accused man or suggested in any way that she might be physically or otherwise interested in him. A woman who does not take these precautions, the myths hold, either wants to have sex or is the responsible actor in the situation and thus at fault if her behavior results in sex she does not want. And if she subsequently blames the man for what she should have prevented through proper, rational, boundary-setting behavior, she must have an ulterior motive for her accusations, such as craving attention or wanting to punish the man for some perceived slight.

These sexual consent and rape myths are widely accepted by women and men in the United States, and as has been demonstrated in numerous studies, strongly shape their views on whether a woman has been raped or has engaged in consensual sex (Aronowitz, Lambert, and Davidoff 2012; Corrigan 2013; Gray 2014; Klement, Sagarin, and Skowronski 2018; Matoesian 2001; Payne, Lonsway, and Fitzgerald 1999; Peterson and Muehlenhard 2004; Suarez and Gadalla 2010). These myths are, however, quite ludicrous. Why, for instance, should women not be able to change their minds about wanting to have sex with someone over the course of a day or evening or from one moment to the next; and according to what standard of reasonableness is having a drink, wearing revealing clothing, or kissing someone evidence that a woman wants to have sex?

It is also completely hypocritical for patriarchal discourse to elevate men above women because men are supposedly more rational and disciplined and better able to control their bodies and emotions than are women but then require women to rationally control men's sexual urges because men lack the rationality and discipline to do so themselves. Moreover, and most consequentially for my analysis, rape myths do not accurately describe the typical rape.

Indeed, only 11 percent of forcible penetration rapes and 12.4 percent of alcohol- and drug-facilitated rapes are perpetrated by strangers, with the vast majority of these *and* coerced penetration rapes carried out by acquaintances or men the victim knows well (Breiding et al. 2014). In addition, though many women do strongly resist their attacker, the psychologically normal response that most women have to the intense fear and trauma caused by rape is to physically and mentally freeze, particularly if they believe that their lives are in danger (both resisting and freezing are psychologically normal responses, but freezing is the more likely of the two). Because of this, and because many rapes occur when women have been incapacitated by drugs or alcohol, there is often either no evidence that the survivor resisted her attacker or evidence that she resisted hesitantly and feebly and then stopped resisting. For these same reasons, medical personnel and police officers often find few or no clear signs of physical violence when they examine or question rape survivors (Corrigan 2013; Hopper 2015; Hopper and Lisak 2014; Kozlowska et al. 2015; van der Kolk 2014).

Another psychologically normal response to intensely traumatic events is for people's brains to focus on and encode in memory just one or two details of the event, largely ignoring and failing to encode in memory its remaining details. People who experience traumatic events also often behave "irrationally" in comparison to how others would expect them to behave, and they often do not tell anyone about the event or wait until they have had adequate time to process it before doing so. Intensely traumatic and violent events also tend to distort people's sense of time and their ability to recall the sequence of actions leading up to, following, and occurring during the event (these reactions are normal for all people who experience traumatic events, not just rape survivors).

Rape survivors are thus very likely to remember details such as the feel of the rapist's face or beard on their skin or the smell of the rapist's aftershave but not recall more legally important details of the event that police officers, judges, juries, and lawyers want to hear. They may also be unable to recall the sequence of events leading up to and following the rape, and the details they are able to recall may change over time and be determined in part by the manner in which they are questioned by doctors, nurses, lawyers, and criminal justice officials. It is also likely that rape victims will not immediately tell their friends and family about the rape or immediately report it to the police (Brison 2002; Corrigan 2013; K. Freedman 2014; Frewen and Lanius 2015; Hopper and Lisak 2014; Kozlowska et al. 2015; van der Kolk 2014).

But though rape myths provide a very inaccurate picture of the typical rape, rapist, and rape victim, these myths, along with the organizational imperatives of the medical and criminal justice systems, strongly shape the actions and decisions made by rape survivors, their friends and families, and nurses, doctors, police officers, district attorneys, judges, and jurors. For instance, because many rape survivors accept or partially accept these myths and because most rapes do not come close to following the script laid out in these myths, many survivors feel intense shame and responsibility (or partial responsibility) for what happened to them, often wondering what they could have done, said, or worn differently to prevent the rape. Because of these myths, many rape survivors are also unsure whether what happened to them really was rape and whether failing to strongly resist their attacker, failing to immediately call the police after the attack was over, or being unable to clearly recall what happened to them will be held against them. This shame and uncertainty, along with the strong negative connotations that people living in neoliberal societies tend to associate with victimhood, make it less likely that rape survivors will want anyone to know what happened to them. And all of this, of course, makes it less likely that survivors will file or actively pursue rape complaints with the police.

But even when rape survivors recognize how absurd the cultural myths surrounding rape and consensual sex really are, they still often recognize that many people believe these myths. As a result, survivors often realize that many people will not believe them, will treat them insensitively, or will use these myths to humiliate them or make their lives difficult. They often also realize that widespread belief in these myths will make the inevitable questioning by friends, family, doctors, nurses, police officers, and lawyers more traumatic than it has to be. Moreover, these things are particularly likely to be true if the survivor is poor; a racial or ethnic minority; had been drinking, taking drugs, flirting, wearing physically revealing clothing, or showing some kind of interest in the rapist prior to the rape; or, as is often the case, there is little physical evidence to show that the survivor was raped. In these structurally constrained circumstances, and given the fact that few rapists are convicted, it is quite understandable that many rape survivors choose not to pursue a complaint with the police.

Treatment of Victims by Health Care Providers and Criminal
Justice Personnel

Women who initially want to report being raped are also often discouraged from doing so by the treatment they receive from police officers and emergency room doctors and nurses, whose medical reports play a key evidentiary role in rape trials. There are, of course, doctors, nurses, and police officers who treat rape survivors sensitively, competently, and respectfully. But many fail to believe that the women they are treating or questioning have been raped or do not view treating or helping rape victims to be a top priority. They are also often poorly trained in how to treat, question, and examine rape victims and investigate rapes (Corrigan 2013; Schwartz 2010).

As a result, rape victims are often treated extremely poorly by police officers and medical personnel. Rose Corrigan (2013) reports, for instance, that many rape victims spend five hours or more in the emergency room before being treated, with some doctors and nurses intentionally using long wait times to get rape victims to leave without care or evidence collection. Corrigan also notes that rape victims are often treated insensitively by doctors and nurses, and discusses two emergency room cases where women who had just been raped were forced to be seen in public wearing paper exam gowns.

In addition, many police officers work actively to reduce the number of rape complaints that are filed or to get victims to withdraw their complaints (Corrigan 2013), and many police officers and departments systematically alter both their records and the data they submit to the federal government to make it appear that they receive fewer rape complaints than they actually do. The result, Corey Yung (2013–2014) estimates, is that between 1995 and 2012, the 210 police jurisdictions he studied systematically erased between 796,213 and 1,145,309 complaints of forcible vaginal rape, which, of course, is just one category of rape.

Because many doctors, nurses, and police officers are either unsympathetic to rape survivors, poorly trained, or highly constrained by the organizational structures within which they work, they also often conduct medical exams or police investigations that provide weak, useless, or tainted evidence or write up flawed reports that prosecutors cannot use. This, in turn, forces district attorneys' offices to drop many rape cases that they might otherwise take to trial (Bronson 2017; Corrigan 2013).

District attorneys' offices vary, of course, in the degree to which they sympathize with rape survivors and want to pursue rape convictions. However, even those district attorneys' offices that want to aggressively prosecute rape cases are strongly constrained by rape and consensual sex myths, which force them to pursue only those cases for which they believe they can get convictions from jurors who very likely accept these myths at a conscious or unconscious level (Corrigan 2013; Datz 2017).

District attorneys' offices worry about the power of these myths because defense lawyers use them in very subtle and effective ways in the courtroom (Datz 2017; Matoesian 2001; Ponterotto 2007; Taslitz 1999). As a result, district attorneys' offices drop many cases the police investigate because they are concerned that the rape survivor and/or the rape will not be viewed as credible by the jury solely because one or both fail to meet rape and consensual sex myth criteria for what are considered a credible rape and a credible rape victim. When combined with poor police investigations, sloppy medical exams, and the structurally constrained decisions rape survivors make about whether to pursue charges against their rapists, this means that most cases that meet the legal threshold of rape never make it to court.

The widespread acceptance of rape and consensual sex myths also means that defense lawyers are usually able to use these myths to set the discursive narrative that dominates rape trial courtrooms, making it very difficult for prosecutors to win rape trial cases. To demonstrate that this is so and to show that rape trial discourse is violent and supports patriarchal and neoliberal discourse, the next section presents evidence drawn from three studies of rape trial discourse (Matoesian 2001; Ponterotto 2007; Taslitz 1999) and a more recent interview with Caryn Datz, a lawyer with extensive rape trial experience (Datz 2017).[3]

Rape Trial Discourse

The United States has a particularly adversarial courtroom culture, with extremely aggressive and often hostile cross-examination of trial witnesses. Because of this, jury decisions are often based less on the strength of the evidence than on the credibility of the witnesses as established during both direct and cross-examination (Ponterroto 2007; Taslitz 1999). To cast doubt on the veracity and credibility of the other side's witnesses, lawyers use highly specific linguistic strategies to highlight not only internal inconsistencies in witnesses' trial testimony and pretrial statements, but also inconsistencies between witnesses' testimony and cultural narratives about how the world works. Lawyers use these strategies on the one hand because of very strict courtroom rules regarding the kinds of questions witnesses can be asked and the language that can be used to ask them and on the other hand because research shows that jurors use cultural narratives to help make sense of witness testimony and to fill in crucial gaps in the evidence (Taslitz 1999).

Thus, the questions lawyers ask during cross-examination tend to highlight contrasts between what supposedly happened at a particular point in time and what jurors expect should have happened. Questions also often take on a highly repetitive form so as to reinforce points the lawyer wants to make, make the event under question seem more important than it would otherwise seem, or make it feel to jurors as if the event spread out over more time than it really did. During cross-examination, lawyers usually also force witnesses to give very short answers about very specific events or issues, often in ways that decontextualize these events or issues. This allows lawyers to control the witnesses' testimony and give a specific meaning to the evidence that might not be given to it if jurors knew the fuller context (Matoesian 2001; Ponterotto 2007; Taslitz 1999).

The adversarial system of justice that produces lawyers' linguistic strategies also "assumes that trials achieve truth through the clash of equally matched adversaries" (Taslitz 1999, 81). The problem in rape and other sexual assault trials is that the adversaries are not and cannot be equally matched because jury verdicts are determined not just by what occurs in the courtroom, where some lawyers are better than others and legal advice costs money, but also by the culturally based narratives that jurors use to evaluate courtroom evidence. And these culturally based narratives, the rape and consensual sex myths that jurors bring with them to the courtroom, give most male rapists a key legal advantage over most female victims, making it very difficult for female victims to secure justice in the courtroom (Datz 2017; Matoesian 2001; Ponterotto 2007; Taslitz 1999).[4]

Defense lawyers take advantage of rape and consensual sex myths by comparing the behavior of the rape victim before, during, and after the rape to how these myths expect she should have behaved. They ask rape victims and other witnesses about the clothing the victim wore and how revealing it was, whether the victim was drinking or doing drugs, whether she expressed interest in or flirted with the alleged rapist or other men prior to the rape, whether she was voluntarily alone with the man before the rape, and whether she kissed or was otherwise physically intimate with the man before the rape. They ask whether the victim fought back, screamed, and tried to get away from the rapist during the alleged rape and whether after the rape she immediately left the scene of the rape, immediately called the police, and immediately got a post-rape medical exam. They also ask whether she gave a clear, detailed, coherent, and consistent account of the rape to friends, family, doctors, nurses, and police officers and whether that account has changed since her initial report (Datz 2017; Matoesian 2001; Ponterotto 2007; Taslitz 1999).

The goal of these questions is to demonstrate that the victim's behavior is inconsistent with dominant cultural images of the typical rape and typical rape victim and, thus, that the alleged victim is not a victim but instead consented to the sex. Once this is established, the defense lawyer provides jurors with an emotional or irrational motive for the plaintiff's supposedly baseless rape accusations. Perhaps she hates men, is angry at the man she accused because he spurned her afterward, is a vindictive person, or wants attention. Conversely, perhaps she does not know or understand the rules governing sexual relations or is not good at following them (Datz 2017; Matoesian 2001; Ponterotto 2007; Taslitz 1999). In either case, the victim is portrayed as behaving irrationally in relation to broad social norms regarding sexual and gender relations.

In the hands of an effective defense attorney, the rape victim thus becomes the offender whose behavior is not only questioned but questionable and who is responsible for the sexual encounter because she led the man on, tempted him, played a (sexual) game whose rules she should have known, and then broke the rules and turned on the man by accusing him of rape. So, rather than being a victim or survivor, the woman becomes the active agent in the crime, a crime that has been transformed from sexual violence to false accusation and that has a male rather than a female victim (Datz 2017; Matoesian 2001; Ponterotto 2007; Stringer 2013).

Transcript excerpts from the rape trial of William Kennedy Smith (nephew to the late President John F. Kennedy) illustrate in part how defense attorneys accomplish this transformation. The Smith trial took place in 1991 after Patricia Bowman accused Smith of raping her on the beach at a Kennedy family estate in West Palm Beach, Florida. The excerpts are taken from Gregory Matoesian's (2001) book on the Smith trial, and I use excerpts from this trial rather than a more recent trial not only because rape transcripts are very difficult to obtain but also because these excerpts do a very good job of illustrating the kinds of tactics defense lawyers use at rape trials. The first excerpt is drawn from defense attorney Roy Black's opening statement, the second is from Black's cross-examination of Ann Mercer, who took Bowman home from the Kennedy estate after the rape, and the last two are from Black's cross-examination of Patricia Bowman. All the emphasized words in the excerpts come from the court transcription, which tries to mimic the voice patterns of the courtroom participants.

In the first excerpt, Black contrasts Bowman's behavior immediately after the rape with how society expects she should have behaved:

> She *goes* into the [Kennedy] house [after being raped]. She *goes* into the kitchen area according to her testimony and makes a call to her friend Ann Mercer who is an ACQUAINTANCE. That's the first [night] they have ever gone out together. . . . She doesn't call anyone in her family, the police, ANY RELATIVE, but she calls Ann Mercer and says "I've been raped, come and pick me up."

In comparing Bowman's behavior to social expectations, Black is clearly suggesting that Bowman must not have been raped. For if she had been raped, he is asking the jury, would she have gone into Smith's house afterward, would she have called someone she hardly knew instead of the police or her family, and would she have said she had been raped in such an emotionless way (Matoesian 2001)? Black obviously thinks not.[5]

The following exchange, in this case between Roy Black (DA: Defense Attorney) and Ann Mercer (AM), also asks jurors to compare behavior to social expectations. In it, Black suggests that both Ann Mercer and Patricia Bowman acted irrationally and against expectations. But he does not simply make each point once and then move on. He repeats the points he wants to make by asking repetitive questions that change only slightly each time they are asked (this line of questioning actually went on much longer than the following excerpt indicates). He also does not make the larger points he wants to make directly. Instead, he subtly suggests them to the jurors, allowing the jurors to fill in the blanks in the testimony so as to come to the conclusions he wants them to make all by themselves, a tactic that Taslitz (1999) and Datz (2017) argue is much more effective than blatantly making the point:

> DA: You say you went to the Kennedy home on the early morning hours of March 30th? Is that correct?
>
> AM: Yes.
>
> DA: Your friend says that she was *raped*? Is that right?
>
> AM: Yes.
>
> DA: But what she tells you is that she wants her *shoes*, is that correct?
>
> AM: Yes.
>
> DA: Several *times* she was worried about her shoes.
>
> AM: Yes.
>
> DA: So you went into the house, is that correct?
>
> AM: Yes.
>
> DA: Into the house, where the rapist is, right?
>
> AM: I guess you could say that, yes.
>
> DA: It's dark in there.
>
> AM: Yes.
>
> DA: You go through the kitchen, right?
>
> AM: Yes.
>
> DA: Into this little hallway.
>
> AM: Yes.
>
> DA: It's dark in this hallway, isn't it?
>
> AM: Right.
>
> DA: You meet up with this *man* who your friend says is a rapist, isn't that correct . . .
>
> AM: . . . Yes.
>
> DA: In this dark hallway, is that right?

AM: Yes . . .

DA: . . . As you go across the lawn [to find the shoes] you get to an area where there are hedges? And a concrete wall, isn't that right?

AM: Yes.

DA: And you're still with this man who's the alleged rapist, is that right?

AM: Yes.

This line of questioning, which lasted for about three and a half minutes, essentially makes the same three points over and over again: no one who has been raped is going to care about her shoes, no woman who believes that her friend has been raped will voluntarily walk alone with the rapist in multiple dark and secluded places, and no rapist will help the friend find the victim's shoes.

Finally, Black tries to establish that Patricia Bowman (PB) was both a bad mother and sexually interested in Smith. Interest in Smith would indicate to jurors that Bowman could not have been raped, and mothers who put their own interests above those of their children are generally viewed as lacking credibility, as being contemptible and of low moral worth, and as deserving the bad things that happen to them:

DA: You told us yesterday that Will invites you into the house, is that correct?

PB: Yes sir.

DA: You went to see? The house.

PB: Yes Sir.

DA: Cause you wanted to see what it *looked like* . . .

PB: . . . It's a landmark home, I, I uh—it had some interest.

DA: Even though it was *late* you wanted to see the house.

PB: I was uncomfortable about that, um—but I, I assumed there was security and Mr. Smith seemed very comfortable in, in, in showing me the house at that hour of the morning.

DA: So even though it was, *early* in the morning, you wanted to see the house . . .

PB: . . . Yes.

DA: Is that correct?

PB: Yes.

DA: Alright, even though you were concerned for example about—
uh—your *child*? you still wanted to see the house.

PB: Yes.

DA: Even though you had to get up early the next morning to take care
of her, you still wanted to see the house.

PB: I wasn't planning on spending any extended amount of time in
the home . . .

And in another line of questioning:

DA: And you thought [Will] was *interested*? in you.

PB: I don't know.

DA: As a person, right?

PB: I could understand what he was talking about, about medical
school.

DA: And you were interested in *him* as a person.

PB: He seemed like a nice *person*.

DA: Interested enough . . . to give him a ride home.

PB: I saw no *problem* with giving him a ride *home* as I stated because
it was up the street. It wasn't out of my way. He hadn't *touched* me. I
felt no *threats* from him and I assumed there would be *security* at the
home.

DA: You were interested *enough* that you were *hoping* that he would
ask for your *phone* number.

PB: That was *later*.

DA: Interested enough that when he said to come into the *house* you
went into the *house* with him.

PB: . . . It wasn't necessarily an interest with *William*, it was an interest
in the *house*.

DA: Interested enough that uh at some time during that period of time
you took off your pantyhose?

PB: I still don't *know* how my pantyhose came off.
(Matoesian 2001, 60–63)

Black's sudden mention of the pantyhose is somewhat shocking. It is
also introduced out of context of what actually happened. Black thought
that Bowman taking off her pantyhose was "proof of foreplay in the car"

(Matoesian 2001, 10) and clearly brings it up to suggest that Bowman was letting Smith know she was sexually interested in him. But the fact that before the rape Bowman and Smith walked along the beach at the Kennedy family estate suggests a very plausible nonsexual reason for why Bowman took off her pantyhose. It also highlights the important role that taking evidence out of context can play in weakening the credibility of a rape victim and transforming her from a victim to an offender who wanted to have sex and then turned against her man.

By using tactics such as these to repeatedly and negatively compare Bowman's behavior and the events at the Kennedy estate to the myths and discourses surrounding consensual sex and rape, Roy Black placed Bowman on trial, essentially charging her with the crime of falsely accusing Smith of raping her. This, as I have already noted, is quite typical of what happens to victims in rape trials. It is *not*, however, how female and male victims of other crimes are treated in the courtroom (or by the police). Andrew Taslitz (1999, 6) notes, for instance,

> In the usual robbery case . . . the victim's identification of the defendant alone results in conviction. This is so even if the lighting conditions were poor and the time for observation brief. The victim's testimony is rarely corroborated. There are usually neither fingerprints nor bruises nor eyewitnesses. Still, juries are convinced by the victim's word alone. . . . Rarely is the robbery victim portrayed as deranged or a liar.

Caryn Datz (2017) concurs. According to her, a businessman who makes himself vulnerable to being pickpocketed by getting exceedingly drunk and who fails to report the pickpocketing until the next day is never considered to be responsible for the crime or to be making it up because he had too many drinks, made himself vulnerable, delayed his report, and cannot fully recall what happened because he was inebriated. Similarly, police and jurors understand that a non-injured but rattled victim of a car accident may not behave rationally afterward, may not want to file a police report immediately, and may not be able to provide a complete, coherent, and detailed account of the accident. Moreover, none of these things will make the victim less credible or the crime less real in the eyes of the law or the deliberations of the jury. The same courtesy is not extended to rape victims, who are expected to meet an

exceedingly strict standard of rationality, recall, and coherence immediately after experiencing a highly traumatic and emotionally painful
attack that likely violated their very sense of who they are and the world
they live in.

Rape and Overall Social Order

In this and the preceding chapter I discussed four related topics: how
women are portrayed in the popular media and advertising; women's
body work practices, including women's "new sexual agency"; sexual
harassment; and rape and society's reaction to rape. My overall goal
in discussing these topics has been to demonstrate that sexual violence against women promotes overall social order by (a) reinforcing
dominant patriarchal and capitalist discourses and bodily practices, (b)
meeting the cultural, psychological, and material interests of key subordinate groups, and (c) aligning male and female subjectivity and identity
with dominant institutional practices and external social and power
relations. However, I have not yet fully achieved this key goal.

Instead, I have achieved two intermediary goals. I have demonstrated,
first, that the portrayal of women in the media and advertising, women's
body work practices, and sexual harassment are all violent, and second,
that they all reinforce dominant patriarchal and neoliberal discourses
and, thus, dominant discourses in multiple social arenas. But despite
accomplishing these tasks, I still have not demonstrated that rape and
society's reaction to rape reinforce dominant patriarchal and neoliberal
discourses and bodily practices. Nor have I explained the substantive
or theoretical importance of the fact that the four empirical phenomena I have discussed in this and the preceding chapter reinforce each
other both discursively and violently. And I have yet to show that these
violent discourses and practices promote social order by meeting the
cultural, psychological, and material interests of key subordinate groups
and aligning female and male subjectivity and identity with dominant
institutional practices and external social and power relations.

Thus, in this section, I explain how rape and society's reaction to rape
reinforce dominant patriarchal and neoliberal discourses. And in the
next section, I demonstrate that the four forms of sexualized violence
discussed in this and the preceding chapter form a tightly knit and vi-

olent social structure that reinforces discourse and bodily practice *in a particularly profound way*, thus aligning individual subjectivity and identity with dominant institutional practices and external social and power relations and meeting the cultural, psychological, and material interests of key subordinate groups. In addition, I demonstrate that rape, as both a bodily practice and discourse, reinforces less extreme patriarchal discourses and bodily practices specifically because of its extremely violent and psychologically charged nature, thereby providing additional support for my overall theoretical argument.

To demonstrate that rape and society's reaction to rape reinforce dominant patriarchal and neoliberal discourses, I need to show that they display the following neoliberal discursive elements, which I described in detail in chapter 2: it is acceptable to use others to satisfy one's desires; it is acceptable to treat others as objects; people are rational and autonomous decision makers who are solely responsible for what happens to them; people who behave irrationally deserve whatever happens to them; subordinate groups and those who experience harm are to blame for their subordination and harm; people are atomized, self-centered individuals rather than members of hierarchically ordered social groups; inequality and double standards are normal and acceptable; it is acceptable to cause pain and disregard the suffering of others (as long as the rules are being followed); aggression is acceptable.

In addition, I need to show that rape and society's reaction to rape display a set of patriarchal discursive elements that were also described in chapter 2: men are mind, women body; men are rational, women irrational and emotional; women represent deception, temptation, and sin and are the source of man's moral downfall; men have the right to dominate women's bodies; it is acceptable for men to use women to satisfy their desires; it is acceptable to treat women as objects; male aggression is acceptable, female aggression is not; women, as body, are not fully autonomous or human and are made to be controlled, used, and dominated; women are passive and submissive; men have greater moral worth than do women; men's desires are more important than women's desires; male rationality makes men effective; female irrationality and emotion make women ineffective.

At the most obvious and straightforward level, the fact that more than 21 percent (and probably well over 21 percent) of all women in the United

States have been raped and that so few rapists are punished supports most of the discursive elements listed in the previous two paragraphs. Specifically, it demonstrates widespread bodily enactment and reinforcement of discursive scripts that support objectifying others (women) and using other's (women's) bodies to satisfy male desires;[6] that view dominant group (male) aggression, male domination of women, and female passivity and submissiveness positively; that hold dominant groups to be of greater moral worth than subordinate groups; and that deem it acceptable to harm and disregard the suffering of others.

When a man or boy rapes a woman or girl, he is also treating her solely as body, symbolically stripping her of her other human characteristics and reducing her to the one aspect of her being, the body side of the mind/body dichotomy, that is at the ideological core not only of patriarchal domination, but of race and class domination too. Rape thus reinforces millennia-old symbolic structures that place men above women because of men's supposed rationality and women's supposed irrationality, emotionality, and ineffectiveness and that blame the human condition on women's irresistible sexual allure. This irresistible allure, like Eve's tempting of Adam with the apple, is tied to cultural tropes that view women as the source of man's moral downfall and separation from God. Moreover, irrationality has negative connotations not just in patriarchal discourse but in race and neoliberal discourse too, where it is used to explain failure, blame people and groups rather than the social structure for the subordination, harm, and failure they experience, and designate those who fail as less morally worthy and deserving of autonomy than those who succeed.

In addition, the fact that in the United States 12.1 percent of female victims of forced rape and alcohol- and drug-facilitated rape were first raped when they were ten years old or younger, 28.3 percent when they were between eleven and seventeen, 38.3 percent when they were between eighteen and twenty-five, 15.2 percent when they were between twenty-five and thirty-four, and 6.1 percent when they were older than thirty-four demonstrates that there are few age limits on rape as a form of male domination. It also demonstrates that a devastatingly large number of women and girls learn very early in life that the discursive rules of male domination can be imposed on them in a traumatically violent and bodily form at any time and most likely by someone they know and possibly love and trust. Patriarchal and neoliberal discursive rules are thus learned early in life by many women and girls and enacted by many men and boys in a form that is particularly emotionally and psychologically salient not only for women and girls but also for men and boys, thereby reinforcing these rules in a particularly effective way. Finally, the fact that so very few rapists are punished and that rape is so pervasively ignored and minimized by our society strongly suggests that our society supports both rape and the discursive scripts that rape simultaneously enacts and reinforces.

However, to understand the precise ways in which society's support of rape reinforces patriarchal and neoliberal discursive scripts, we must ask how specific features of this support line up with specific features of these scripts. And to do this we must compare society's rape and consensual sex myths and the courtroom strategies of rape trial defense lawyers (mechanisms of support) to society's dominant patriarchal and neoliberal discourses. In other words, while the preceding paragraphs explained how rape as a violent bodily practice displays and reinforces key patriarchal and neoliberal discursive scripts, the following paragraphs explain how the social reactions rape produces invoke and reinforce these same scripts, allowing me to trace out, in a nuanced fashion, several of the most important pathways through which rape reinforces patriarchy, capitalism, and overall social order.

As previously noted, society's rape and consensual sex myths, which play a key role in ensuring that few rapists are punished, hold that men cannot resist the female body and female sexuality. It is therefore women's and older girls' responsibility to create boundaries that convey to men and older boys that they are not sexually available. Women and girls who do not create such boundaries, the myths hold, either want to have sex or are failing to rationally and effectively play by the rules of the sexual game (think Bourdieu), thereby signaling that they are sexually available even if they are not. They are therefore responsible for whatever happens to them sexually, regardless of whether what happens is what they want. Society's rape and consensual sex myths further hold that women and girls who have been raped will violently and loudly struggle against their rapists, immediately call the police after their rape, aggressively pursue a rape conviction, and provide police officers, prosecutors, defense attorneys, and jurors with a clear, detailed, coherent, and consistent account of what happened before, during, and after the alleged rape. If they do not do these things, according to the myths, they clearly were not raped.

Our society's rape and consensual sex myths thus simultaneously associate women and girls with the body (they are highly sexual) and the mind (they can rationally and effectively create boundaries). But they do so in such a way that woman as body will nearly always win out symbolically over woman as rational mind. This is true first of all because the centerpiece of these myths, the point from which they both start, is that women are sexual temptresses who use their bodies to lure and sometimes entrap men (by falsely accusing them of rape, trying to snag a husband, and so forth). Rationally creating an effective boundary is, according to these myths, secondary to women's and girls' true natures: unlike being sexual, it may or may not occur, but even when it does occur, it does so only after they have become sexual. Moreover, most women and girls who claim to be raped are successfully accused, both inside and outside the courtroom, of failing to erect these boundaries and of intentionally making false allegations against their alleged rapists, symbolically "proving" not only that the body is primary and the rational mind secondary to women's and girls' true natures but also that women and girls really are temptresses and deceivers who work actively to demean men, undermine their moral worth, and bring them down.

As played out in the courtroom and everyday life, rape and consensual sex myths also allow men to make all sorts of irrational mistakes—such as misunderstanding or pretending to misunderstand the sexual-boundary signals women and girls convey to them, getting too drunk to accurately interpret these signals,[7] or putting themselves in a position to be either falsely or accurately accused of rape—with relatively little fear of punishment. Women and girls, on the other hand, cannot make any sexual mistakes because if a woman or girl does make such a mistake, if she breaks even one of the rules that rape and consensual sex myths hold sacred, she risks not only being raped but also becoming the responsible party, guilty in the eyes of society of enticing a man or boy to have sex with her and then falsely accusing him of rape. In addition, if she wears revealing clothing, has a beer, gets stoned, flirts, is friendly with the man before the rape, behaves like a normal human being and experiences trauma that prevents her from doing things such as struggling with her attacker, immediately phoning the police, or providing a complete and coherent account of her rape, then her behavior and decisions are declared irrational and held against her because they do not coincide with what the myths say a rational person would do.

It is therefore clear that rape and consensual sex myths reinforce dominant patriarchal and neoliberal discourse. They associate women with the body, temptation, deception, irrationality, and men's moral and social downfall and identify women as sexual objects that men cannot resist. They tell us that if women fail to play by the rules, which they are supposedly too irrational to follow, then men can do with them what they want and it will be the woman's fault if she is harmed by being forced to have sex she does not want. Thus, not only do these myths, when socially enacted, tell us that men's desires are more important than women's desires and that women are irrational sexual objects, but consistent with neoliberal discourse, they tell us that it is okay to objectify others and use them to fulfill our desires; it is okay to harm and disregard the suffering of others so long as the rules are being followed and those being harmed are irrational; and it is okay to blame those who experience harm for their suffering.

Because these myths rely on double standards and justify the domination of women by men and the unequal treatment of women and men, they also make inequality and double standards seem normal. There are several ways they do this. As enacted in social life, these myths say that unlike women, men can make mistakes and be irrational without being responsible or at fault for what happens to them. They say that women are responsible for their behavior and men's behavior but that men do not have to be responsible at all. They say that man is mind and woman body, but that only women can rationally control men's sexual urges. Finally, they say that women are passive, but when it comes to erecting sexual boundaries and preventing rape, they have to do so aggressively.

These double standards clearly support patriarchy. But all forms of inequality rely on double standards and the acceptance of unequal social relations, both in practice and in discourse. Thus, learning to accept or be oblivious to double standards and inequality in one social arena supports overall social order by making it easier to accept or be oblivious to them in other social arenas, particularly when, as is often the case, different arenas have similar double standards (this is true too for the double standards I discuss later in this section). For instance, neoliberal discourse, like patriarchal discourse, is more accepting of mistakes made by members of the dominant group than it is of mistakes made by subordinate group members, and generally holds capitalists blameless for the inequality and suffering that they and the system they dominate cause (except in those rare cases where a member of the capitalist class egregiously violates the rules of the game).[8] Thus, when rape and sexual consent myths allow men but not women to make mistakes, blame women rather than men for the harm women suffer at the hands of men, and hold accountable only the most egregious male violators of society's sexual consent myths, they reinforce overall social order by supporting neoliberal and other discourses that do the same things for and to their dominant and subordinate groups.

Rape and sexual consent myths also make order-producing sexual violence significantly less visible. This supports overall social order by making the social order seem more benign, just, equal, and moral than it really is, by making men and boys feel superior to women and better about themselves than they otherwise would, by reinforcing patriarchal discourse's claims regarding who is and is not rational and able to control their impulses, and by helping ensure that the sexual violence continues. These myths, for instance, keep many women from accusing their attackers, reduce the number of official rape complaints that make it to court, and make it less likely that juries will convict alleged rapists, thereby keeping most rapes out of the public eye. These myths also ensure that either the victim or the rapist rather than the social order is blamed for the rape, guaranteeing one of two order-producing outcomes: the rape is dismissed because people believe that it did not happen (the women made a false accusation regarding what was really consensual sex) or people view the rapist and not society as being defective in some way.

Broad acceptance of rape and sexual consent myths also makes it more difficult for non-elites to organize collectively to challenge the social order. For instance, by reinforcing discursive scripts that make patriarchal, neoliberal, and other forms of domination and violence seem natural, these myths restrict the ability of non-elites in multiple institutional arenas to see and think outside the discursive and material boundaries of their domination. And this, in turn, makes it exceedingly difficult for non-elites to name and describe their domination, imagine alternatives to it, or recognize that the harm they do to other non-elites might not benefit them nearly as much as would working with those they harm to overcome the shared and unshared oppressions they experience.

Rape and consensual sex myths thus support overall social order in several important ways, and this is true not only because they are widely believed but also, as prior research makes clear (see the preceding section), because they guide the behavior of women and men in their everyday lives and the reactions that a very wide range of people—rape survivors, friends, family, acquaintances, police officers, nurses, doctors, district attorneys, defense lawyers, judges, and jurors—have to rape and rape accusations. Rape and consensual sex myths, and the discursive scripts they support, are thus regularly and routinely brought into play in social life, including when women who have been sexually harassed or raped decide whether to publicly accuse their harasser or rapist and when friends, family, acquaintances, and others react to rape and harassment accusations. But because of their centrality to social life and individual identity and subjectivity, they are also brought into play when women and girls are portrayed in stereotypical ways in the media; when they engage in bodily practices and ways of moving and holding their bodies shaped by these portrayals; when they walk down the street, go to work, and enter other public places; when they are watched and observed by others; when they decide whether to drink, smoke, and do drugs; when they are sexually harassed and raped; and when they and men fantasize about each other and flirt, have sex, and decide whether to have sex with each other. These myths thus play a key role in supporting patriarchal and neoliberal discourse and the overall social order.

Rape trials also support patriarchal and neoliberal discourse and overall social order. They do this in large part, of course, by reinforcing rape and consensual sex myths, which defense lawyers constantly invoke by highlighting any and all discrepancies between these myths on the one hand and the victim's behavior and the alleged rape on the other. But rape trials support dominant patriarchal and neoliberal discourse in other ways as well. Two of the most important ways they do this are by presenting an individualistic rather than a social account and a decontextualized rather than a complex, contextualized account of what happened.

In particular, by using cross-examination tactics designed to destroy the credibility of the victim, defense lawyers repeatedly isolate and highlight the actions of the victim as an individual. This diverts attention away from the power differentials and patterns of relations that exist between men and women and from how these power differentials and unequal relations, along with trauma, discourse, myth, and popular portrayals of women and men, promote both aggressive male sexual behavior and female vulnerability. It also diverts attention away from how these factors push women to behave in ways that diverge from society's mythical expectations of them. Similarly, by employing repetitive questioning techniques that distort time, extract evidence from its proper context, and make certain events and actions seem more important than they really were, and by using objections to interrupt prosecuting attorneys' more contextualized questioning of victims, defense lawyers present decontextualized accounts of events to juries that highlight certain actions but not others and that strip these actions of the meanings they originally had and that jurors likely would attribute to them if they were properly contextualized (Matoesian 2001; Taslitz 1999).

Prosecuting attorneys try to overcome these tactics, which make victims' actions before, during, and after their rapes seem less coherent, rational, and consistent than they really were. But courtroom rules, the underlying assumption that "trials achieve truth through the clash of equally matched adversaries" (Taslitz 1999, 81), and the linguistic tactics these rules and assumptions force lawyers to employ make this difficult to do. Indeed, the assumption of equally matched adversaries, by denying the existence of group-based inequality, implicitly treats adversaries as individuals rather than as members of hierarchically ordered social groups. When combined with the logic and tactics of courtroom trials, this often forces even prosecuting attorneys to decontextualize and individualize evidence and behavior.

Decontextualization and individualization in rape trials support patriarchal social relations in at least two ways. First, they make it difficult for women to challenge patriarchal discourse by making it difficult or impossible for them to tell their stories. Second, individualization diverts blame away from men and patriarchal social relations by placing it on either the victim or in those cases where the rapist is prosecuted, the rapist, who is then differentiated from other men by being described in savage and animalistic terms that apply to the individual man and not the social system or men in general (rapists should, of course, be held personally accountable for their behavior, but in such a way that patriarchal social relations are held accountable too).

Decontextualization and individualization also support neoliberalism, which views people as atomized individuals rather than as members of hierarchically ordered social groups and which relies on decontextualization to prevent subordinate groups from properly describing, explaining, and developing alternatives to inequality, exploitation, and the overall social order. The simplification of complex social and psychological processes and relationships inherent in rape trial decontextualization is also inherent in modern society's quantification and bureaucratic rationalization of social life, found, for example, in statistical analyses of complex social and economic behavior and neoliberalism's goal of evaluating all human behavior and morality against a crude cost/benefit "calculus of utility, benefit, [and] satisfaction" (Brown 2003).

In these and numerous other arenas of modern life, highly unequal and highly political events and relationships are depoliticized, normalized, and justified by being turned into technocratic, variable-based phenomena in which history, culture, and social structure are ignored, atomized individuality is emphasized, and social and psychological processes are reduced to a handful of characteristics (such as the dollar value of all goods and services produced in a country or the number of times a rape victim violated norms that benefit men) that are both countable *and* valued by dominant groups. Thus, when rape trials depoliticize and dehistoricize sexuality and sexual relations by turning them into a contest between socially isolated individuals, and when they reduce female and male behavior and psychology to a handful of isolated traits valued and highlighted by patriarchal discourse, they do not only support patriarchal discourse. They also train people to accept modern society's and neoliberalism's use of decontextualization and individualization to depoliticize and simplify social, political, economic, and psychological life and normalize and justify inequality, oppression, and the overall social order.

Rape trial decontextualization and individualization also contribute to an important double standard. On the one hand, they turn the rape victim into a lone and isolated actor who in the hands of an effective defense attorney becomes the chief agent and perpetrator of the sexual act that is the subject of the trial. On the other hand, to turn the rape victim into the perpetrator, the defense attorney has to situate the victim and rapist within a set of cultural myths that differentiate between people according to their gender and that expect women and girls to behave in a certain way and men and boys to behave in another. Decontextualization and individualization are thus used to highlight female agency and to apportion responsibility to individual actors, but only by comparing the behavior of the victim and rapist to group-defined characteristics and traits. Consciously regarding people as atomized individuals while judging them according to group-based stereotypes is not, of course, confined solely to patriarchal discourse. It is a double standard found in neoliberal and racial discourse too. It is therefore supportive of both patriarchy and the overall social order. Moreover, as I argued earlier, learning to accept double standards in one social arena likely makes it easier to accept them in other social arenas, thereby further supporting the social order.

In this regard, rape trials highlight two other patriarchal double standards worth mentioning. The first is discussed by Gregory Matoesian (2001), who argues that in the courtroom, adversarial cross-examination tactics and patriarchal discursive myths highlight *in an emotionally charged way* inconsistencies between rape victims' behavior and what society expects of them. To the extent that defense lawyers rely on jurors' emotions to win rape trials, this means that they are using emotional rather than fully rational arguments to convince jurors that the alleged victim is too emotional and irrational to be trusted. It is thus acceptable, according to this double standard, for dominant groups and those in positions of authority but not for those who belong to subordinate groups to make emotional appeals to others and for those sitting in judgment but not those who are judged to be swayed by emotion. This supports overall social order not only because it normalizes the use of double standards, but also because this particular double standard is employed in other institutional arenas as well.

The final double standard I will discuss is that rape victims are not treated like victims of other crimes. As noted earlier, when male and female robbery victims claim that a crime has been done to them by a specific person, their claims are not immediately questioned, even when their recollection of events is incomplete or they engaged in behavior that made it more likely they would be robbed. Female victims are thus viewed as rational enough to accurately identify suspects, human enough to be trusted despite being traumatized or forgetting crime scene details, and honest enough to not frame alleged suspects, but only if they are victims of crimes that are not sexual in nature. When the crime is sexual in nature and committed by a man and when challenging the crime challenges male domination of women, then women are suddenly treated as though they are irrational, deceitful, untrustworthy, emotional, and dangerous.

One might argue, of course, that what happens at rape trials is not discursively consequential because most US citizens never participate in such trials. However, a quick perusal of the LexisNexis database of news coverage demonstrates that many rape trials are covered by news outlets, often with enough detail to highlight at least some of the rape and sexual consent myths employed in these trials. Moreover, coverage of celebrity rape trials, such as the one in which William Kennedy Smith was accused, is more extensive, providing much greater detail and explanation regarding the myth-based rationales used to blame rape victims and acquit rapists (see, for instance, Bowley and Pérez-Peña 2017a, 2017b; Chira 2017; Margolick 1991). US citizens are thus quite aware of the discursive arguments employed in rape trials.

More importantly, one would expect evidence to play a greater role and cultural myths a lesser role in jury trials than in everyday life, or at least to play the same relative role in these two settings. That cultural myths play such an important role in jury trials thus suggests that they play as or more important a role in everyday life, a conjecture that is supported by the fact that the behavior of a very wide variety of people is shaped by rape and sexual consent myths and the fact that defense lawyers rely on these myths because most jurors already believe them. Indeed, because jury trials force lawyers to make their arguments more explicitly than people normally do in everyday life, it is likely that rape trials provide insight into how rape and sexual consent myths operate in the broader society that would be difficult to obtain by observing everyday life.

Finally, jury trials are highly ritualized events, both in terms of the rituals that occur within the courtroom, such as everyone standing when the judge and jury enter the courtroom, and the mythological role they play in the US imagination, where they are viewed as a central pillar of US freedom, justice, and democracy and a key institution ensuring that everyone is equal before the law and that only those people who evidence shows are guilty will be sent to prison. As is true in all ritualized settings, what occurs in US courtrooms thus reinforces and increases the psychological and emotional salience of discursive practices, such as those that constitute patriarchy and neoliberalism, that are already followed in the broader society.

Put differently, rape trials, which represent the highly ritualized culmination of a series of ritualized criminal justice processes, are socially consequential because they symbolically reinforce at the level of national myth the routine and regularly repeated, and thus already *ritualized* and *psychologically salient* (J. Alexander 2004; M. Alexander 2016; Randall Collins 2004; Goffman 1959), patriarchal and neoliberal performances of everyday life (performances that include all the violent practices highlighted in this and the preceding chapter). Moreover, the highly sexual, coercive, and violent nature of rape makes rape trials, rape and sexual consent myths, and society's reaction to rape even more psychologically and emotionally salient than they otherwise would be, promoting overall social order by reinforcing the symbolic structures underlying patriarchal and neoliberal discourse in a particularly strong and emotionally profound way.

Conclusion

In this and the preceding chapter I demonstrated that how women and girls are portrayed in the media and advertising, women's and girls' bodily (and sexual agency) practices, sexual harassment, and rape and society's reaction to rape each promote overall social order by reinforcing dominant patriarchal and neoliberal discourses. I extend this argument in this section by explaining how these different social practices reinforce each other, both discursively and violently, and how this in turn strengthens their overall discursive effect on social order. Specifically, I argue that these four sets of social practices can, at least for the purposes of this chapter, be thought of as nested layers, or levels, of gender relations that not only work together to reproduce patriarchy, capitalism, and overall social order but actually depend on each other to do so. I further argue that each of these levels of social practice is even more violent than I previously stated, with (a) the number of people *directly* involved in each social practice decreasing and the form the violence takes becoming more extreme, or at least more *physically* extreme, as we move from the media and advertising to rape and (b) violence playing a key role in tying the four levels together and reinforcing their discursive effect.

We have already seen, for instance, that mainstream culture's portrayal of women is extremely violent, supporting patriarchal and neoliberal discursive structures that justify harassment and rape and leading most women and girls to constantly surveil and objectify themselves and their bodies, thereby further reinforcing these discursive structures *and* harassment and rape. We have also seen that self-surveillance and self-objectification are associated with a wide range of psychological, emotional, and physical harms, including depression, anxiety, self-loathing, reduced self-esteem, bulimia, anorexia, severe headaches, serious gastrointestinal problems, chronic sleep disorders, cardiovascular issues, central nervous system problems, increased sensitivity to pain, and severe weight gain and loss.

The "new agency line" associated with the increasingly explicit sexualization of women and girls in the mainstream media and the ever-increasing intersection of patriarchy and neoliberalism can also be extremely violent, pushing women and teenage girls to engage in unwanted sexual activity, leading them to adopt bodily practices and behaviors that produce insecurity and self-hatred, leading them to blame themselves for sexual encounters they were forced or coerced into having, and in many cases producing or exacerbating trauma, shame, alienation, anxiety, humiliation, depression, substance abuse, psychic numbing, and suicidal ideation.

The portrayal of women and girls in the media and the bodily practices resulting from this portrayal are thus extremely violent according to my definition of violence. But these sexualized portrayals and bodily practices are violent in other ways as well. In reducing women and girls to a single, often highly caricatured and inaccurately depicted dimension of what it means to be human and in treating them as if their worth depends on their ability to fulfill male desires, the commercial media and advertisers, the new agency line, and associated female bodily practices tell women and girls that they are less than fully human and, as Heather Burtman (2017) and Catharine MacKinnon (1989) argue, that their bodies are not entirely their own but instead belong to men.

Moreover, in convincing many women and girls, either consciously or unconsciously, that their worth lies primarily in one aspect of their being while simultaneously denying the importance of other aspects of their being, and in convincing many other women and girls that they do not fully own their bodies and that society does not value aspects of themselves that they value (American Psychological Association 2007), the portrayal of women and girls in the media and advertising and bodily practices associated with this portrayal alienate women and girls from themselves (from the full range of characteristics that make us human), from others (you cannot fully connect with others if you are treated as a partial being), and from a full sense of belonging in society. Of course, being told that one is less than fully human and being alienated from society, from others, and from a full and complete sense of self are inherently violent attacks upon an individual's personhood and her social, psychological, and emotional well-being. Such attacks are not taken seriously by our society, but they cause extreme and violent harm to tens of millions of women and girls in the United States and hundreds of millions of women and girls around the world.

Like the portrayal of women and girls in popular culture and many of the bodily practices generated by this culture, sexual harassment is also a violent social practice. Sexual harassment ranges in intensity from men routinely looking inappropriately at women to men making sexual comments to women, exposing themselves to women, groping them, and stalking them, with many other forms of sexual harassment located along this continuum. These various forms of harassment are all violent because they treat women as less than fully human and involve men laying proprietary claim to women's bodies. They also contribute to alienation, self-surveillance, and self-objectification and, as discussed earlier, can produce severe physical and psychological health problems. Moreover, implicit within each form of harassment is the threat and fear of more extreme harassment and of extreme physical violence. This threat and fear are real and can be experienced as real for any type of sexual harassment because of the existence of each successively more intense form of harassment and the ever-present possibility of rape.

Put differently, though fewer men inappropriately proposition women than inappropriately look at them and fewer men grope or rape women than inappropriately proposition them, it is still the case that these forms of harassment form a continuous and interdependent hierarchy of male entitlement and a continuous and interdependent hierarchy of threat, invasion, fear, and violence. As a result, less extreme forms of harassment provide a foundation of acceptability and normality that makes more extreme forms of harassment possible while more extreme forms of harassment (and rape) provide a *threat* of more intense invasion and violence that (combined in some cases with a fear of losing one's job and/or access to resources) acts as an enforcement mechanism reducing the likelihood that women will privately or publicly challenge their harassers or sexual harassment.

When left unpunished, more extreme acts of harassment likely also produce greater and more intense feelings regarding the social acceptability and unavoidability of male domination that not only reinforce the acceptability and normality of less intense forms of harassment (and of media portrayals of women and girls and female bodily practices resulting from these portrayals) but make even more intense forms of harassment (and rape) more likely. In addition, periodic public acknowledgment of more extreme cases of harassment ensures that everyone knows they occur and are a threat, has never led to broad changes in gender behavior (see my discussion at the end of the section), and likely leads many men to think, "I may engage in a less extreme form of harassment but I would never do *that* and am not like *that.*" This, in turn, likely makes many men believe that they are not part of the problem, while giving them psychological and ideological cover to continue engaging in less extreme forms of harassment and less extreme gendered behaviors (such as looking at sexualized images of women in the popular media) that support the continued perpetration of rape and more intense forms of harassment.

The other key reason why each form of sexual harassment supports the social acceptability of the other forms of harassment, and why the US media's portrayal of women and girls, female bodily practices resulting from this portrayal, women's and girls' new sexual agency, sexual harassment, rape, and society's reaction to rape all reinforce each other, is that they share a common patriarchal discursive foundation that is invoked whenever anyone engages in any of these practices. We know, for instance, that these practices all sexualize and focus attention on women's and girls' bodies, downplay or ignore women's and girls' rational minds, and treat women and girls as objects whose chief purpose and desire in life is to fulfill men's and boys' desires.[9] These practices also all symbolically say that it is okay for men and boys to behave aggressively toward women and girls, lay proprietary claim over women's and girls' bodies, and take what they want from women and girls. And though the specific details of men's and boys' proprietary claims, desires, and aggressions vary across the practices they engage in—from men and boys looking at sexualized images of women and girls to men and boys staring at them, watching them have sex, showing them their body parts, telling them what they want to do to them, raping them, and blaming them for what men and boys do to them—these are still all instances of men and boys taking what they want from women and girls and laying aggressive proprietary claim to women's and girls' sexualized and objectified bodies.

It is thus quite clear that the practices described in this and the preceding chapter all support the same core set of discursive elements and therefore cannot be treated as being independent of or symbolically different from one another. It is also quite clear that conscious or unconscious acceptance of the discursive elements of any one of these practices will foster conscious or unconscious acceptance of many and possibly all the discursive elements of the other practices (even if consciously one does not support the other practices). And these two facts, along with the rest of the evidence presented in this and the preceding chapter, confirm two important points I raised earlier: first, that the four levels of gender relations highlighted in these two chapters reinforce each other both discursively and violently; and second, that because of this, they form a coherent whole, a unified and violent social structure that guides the social behavior, internal consciousness, subjectivity, and identity of women, men, girls, and boys, and in so doing promotes overall social order by (a) reinforcing dominant discourses in multiple social arenas and (b) aligning female and male subjectivity and identity with dominant patriarchal and neoliberal institutional and discursive practices and dominant patriarchal and neoliberal social and power relations.

Violence plays a key role in reinforcing these practices, relations, and discourses and in aligning individual subjectivity and identity with them for two key reasons. First, violence affects individuals at a very deep psychological level and when linked to dominant cultural and symbolic structures can greatly increase the psychological and emotional salience of these structures and the broader discursive, material, and cultural orders these structures support, especially when combined in ritualized and non-ritualized forms with sex and sexuality (Reed and Adams 2011).

Second, for the rules of proper thought, behavior, feeling, motivation, and meaning embedded in discourse to have social force, they must be enforced in some way. People must also be regularly reminded of what these rules are. Many mechanisms exist for enforcing and reminding people of social rules, including ridicule, humor, ostracization, sanctions, and the creation, within individuals, of dispositions and generative schemes that align individual identity and subjectivity with the rules in such a way that people willingly and unthinkingly consent to them. However, one of the most important enforcement and memory mechanisms is violence. If you break the rules, society can stone you, shoot you, or throw you in jail, both to punish you and remind you and others of what is and is not acceptable. Similarly, men can sexually harass and rape women, thereby consciously or unconsciously punishing women and reminding both women and men of the social rules constituting patriarchy and neoliberalism.

But violence plays a more subtle role in rule enforcement and memory too. For instance, when society tells a woman how she should look and behave, the ridicule and negative comments she receives if she does not look or behave as she "should" and the ways in which she is treated when she does achieve society's beauty and behavioral ideals may lead her to objectify herself in ways that are violent. And this violence, by increasing the psychological and emotional salience of the discursive rules upon which society's beauty ideals and her self-objectification are based, likely increases the chances that she will internalize these rules and ideals and that these rules, ideals, and self-objectification will come to form an important part of her subjectivity and identity. Thus, violence, in its myriad physical, psychological, and emotional forms, can create consent to the overall social order by producing subjectivities and identities that are aligned with the discursive, material, and cultural order, and thus with dominant institutional practices and external social and power relations. And this is particularly likely to be the case when the different forms of violence operating in a particular social field, such as gender relations, reinforce the same sets of discursive rules and these rules operate in multiple social fields.

Discursive rules are not, of course, learned solely by subordinate group members. In the field of gender relations, for instance, violent and nonviolent discursive displays are enacted regularly both in institutional settings and in everyday life and are thus experienced and carried out widely and repeatedly by women, men, girls, and boys, shaping the subjectivities and identities of everyone in society. The specific psychological processes by which this violence and these discursive displays are internalized and come to form an important aspect of subjectivity and identity are likely to be different for women and girls than for men and boys given the different positions they hold in the social hierarchy and the fact that patriarchy advantages men and boys and disadvantages women and girls.[10] But the regular and ritualistic repetition of these displays, their violence, and the fact that regardless of where and at what level of gender relations they occur they reinforce the same discursive elements over and over again ensure that they promote overall social order.

Consistent with the argument I set forth in chapter 1, it is thus clear that the bases of social order that Foucault and Bourdieu highlighted in their theory and research do not operate independently of violence. Indeed, the evidence presented in this and the preceding chapter demonstrates quite clearly that subjectivity, identity, habitus, discourse, discipline, bodily movement, and embodied knowledge are all shaped and formed to a significant degree by violence and thus cannot be conceptualized independently of violence.

Sexual violence also helps produce Gramscian consent, in this case by meeting the material, cultural, and psychological interests of key subordinate groups. It does this in two broad ways. First, by supporting the patriarchal subordination of women, sexual violence provides men, most of whom belong to a subordinate economic class or race/ethnic group, with specific material, cultural, and psychological advantages. Gender inequality and patriarchy ensure, for example, that men earn more than women and that women do more housework and childcare than men, giving men specific material advantages and making them feel better about themselves. Sexual violence also reinforces a patriarchal symbolic structure that tells men they are better than women and that women are supposed to service their needs, thereby supporting a cultural value system that benefits men and providing men with important psychological benefits. It is also quite clear that the perpetrators of sexual violence receive direct physical and psychological benefits from the violence they perpetrate, including a sense of power and control they may not experience elsewhere in their lives.

Second, we live in a neoliberal society that blames victims for the harms inflicted on them and a patriarchal society that believes that female victims of sexual violence are not victims but rather liars who either wanted the sex they are complaining about or failed to rationally play by the rules of the sexual game. It is thus likely that some and perhaps many women and men who have not been sexually violated receive a psychological boost from sexual violence because it proves that they are better than those who have been violated or who claim to have been violated. This psychological boost and the psychological, cultural, and material benefits highlighted in the previous paragraph may pale in comparison to the psychological, cultural, and material benefits subordinated women and men could potentially receive in a less violent and less hierarchical society. But within the confines of our current social order, they are still experienced as benefits and, thus, help produce consent to the overall social order.

Sexualized violence against women is not, of course, the only form of gender or sexual violence that reinforces overall social order. Intimate partner abuse, child abuse (both sexual and nonsexual), and violence against lesbian, gay, bisexual, transgender, and queer people are highly prevalent in the United States, and it is likely that these forms of violence reinforce patriarchal and neoliberal discourse, align subjectivity and identity, and support subordinate group interests in ways both similar to and different from the sexualized violence highlighted in this and the previous chapter. Sexual violence against heterosexual, cisgender men likely also does these things, in large part because men who are sexually violated are usually described as embodying feminine traits. This and the preceding chapter, then, almost certainly underestimate the role that gender and sexual violence play in promoting overall social order.

Some might argue, however, that rather than underestimating I am likely overestimating the role gender and sexual violence play in promoting overall social order because not everyone accepts and internalizes all the discursive elements highlighted in this and the preceding chapter or accepts and internalizes them equally. I disagree with this argument. Sexualized violence and the discursive elements it reinforces do not have to be accepted by everyone or by everyone equally to be socially consequential. As long as sexualized violence reinforces discursive elements drawn from society's dominant discourses, as long as these discourses are not successfully challenged (and are thus widely accepted), and as long as a wide range of more and less violent patriarchal practices are supported by the same set of discursive elements, both the violence and the discursive elements will be consequential. Moreover, just because people consciously or publicly reject specific discursive elements or specific violent actions does not mean that they have rejected them at a deeper unconscious level or that they do not accept other discursive elements and other violent actions drawn from the same dominant discourses. People can also publicly reject things that they privately and consciously accept, and they can certainly reject specific violent actions while supporting many of the discursive elements underlying these actions.

Take, for instance, the intense challenge to workplace sexual harassment that arose in the United States in late 2017 and early 2018 in response to highly public charges of harassment leveled against many prominent politicians, businessmen, and media stars. On the one hand, this challenge resulted in widespread condemnation of sexual harassment and widespread calls for eliminating it. But it also generated, or at least did not undermine, widespread support for several of the accused men, with nearly half of Alabama voters voting for an alleged sexual harasser, many Democrats arguing that Al Franken should not have vacated his Senate seat for repeatedly harassing women, and many voters continuing to support President Trump despite the existence of multiple harassment and rape allegations against him. Moreover, even among mainstream observers who condemned both sexual harassment and the men accused of perpetrating it, there was little discussion of how harassment and rape are linked to the portrayal of women and girls in the media, to the way men and boys generally treat women and girls, or to *broad patterns* of gender inequality. There was also virtually no discussion of the need to reconfigure or radically change patriarchal discourse or broad patterns of gender relations, either because doing so would be good in and of itself or because sexual harassment and rape cannot be eradicated if this is not done.

The *New York Times*, for instance, came out strongly against workplace sexual harassment, and several major news and entertainment corporations fired male employees accused of it. But the *New York Times* and these major media companies continued to run advertisements and produce magazines, movies, and television shows that sexualized and objectified women and girls and that supported the dominant patriarchal and neoliberal discourses that underlie sexual harassment, rape, society's reaction to sexual harassment and rape, and overall social order. Men and boys also continued to objectify women and girls, who, in turn, continued to objectify themselves.

The *New York Times* also ran a front-page article on December 30, 2017, at the height of public revelations regarding workplace sexual harassment, in which it repeatedly argued that in Japan, rape is taken much less seriously and punished much less severely than it is in the United States (M. Rich 2017). Regardless of whether there is any truth to this claim, the story essentially presented rape and society's reaction to rape as much less serious problems in the United States than in Japan despite the fact that virtually every issue raised in the story—prejudice against women; police not taking rape investigations seriously; victims correctly expecting that they will not be taken seriously by the police; women not always describing nonconsensual sex as rape; women not always reporting their rape to the police; women experiencing shame because of being raped; rape cases not moving forward if there are no signs of physical violence or if the woman was drinking; people thinking that rape is not that harmful and/or that it is an extension of normal male sexual behavior; and rapists not being punished—is a serious problem in both the United States and Japan. Moreover, the article is explicitly framed as a comparison of Japan, where rape allegations are largely ignored, and the United States, where sexual misconduct allegations supposedly receive widespread media and public attention.

This type of comparative article, which is found periodically in the *New York Times* and other news sources and can be written for virtually any issue, essentially says that though we may have problems in the United States, our problems are not nearly as bad as they are in other nations. This implies, of course, that our problems and our nation are really not that bad. It further implies that though we might have to change some of our practices, we do not need to make any major or drastic changes to most of these practices or to our social, cultural, and symbolic structures, thereby leaving these structures, most of these practices, and the overall social order intact.

One can easily imagine that many men feel similarly about themselves, thinking (either consciously or unconsciously) that because there are many men who are worse than they are, they do not have to give up any of their patriarchal beliefs and behaviors, let alone most or all of them. One can also easily imagine that the extremely high prevalence of and implicit social support for rape and sexual harassment in the United States lead many women who do not consciously support harassment and rape to accept less extreme patriarchal beliefs and behaviors that nonetheless reinforce the symbolic structure underlying rape and harassment. Thus, though variation in the acceptance of patriarchal discourse and sexual violence can potentially provide space for challenging this discourse and violence, it need not do so. And this is particularly likely to be the case when even those who question the more extreme manifestations of this discourse and violence fail to recognize that the symbolic structure underlying their own discursive belief systems is essentially the same as that underlying the more extreme manifestations they feel so good about railing against, thereby ensuring that they will not question the symbolic structure that supports all patriarchal behavior, including sexual harassment and rape.

It should be quite clear, then, that variation in US citizens' conscious and unconscious acceptance of sexualized violence and the discursive scripts underlying this violence does not contradict or undermine the argument I have presented in this and the preceding chapter. Nor does it mean that sexual harassment and rape are likely to end. Indeed, so long as our society's dominant patriarchal and neoliberal discourses remain dominant, sexual harassment, rape, and other forms of sexual and gender violence are going to persist. In turn, this violence will continue to promote overall social order in the ways I have theorized it will: by reinforcing dominant discourses in multiple social arenas, meeting the material, cultural, and psychological interests of key subordinate groups, aligning individual subjectivity and identity with dominant institutional practices and external social and power relations, and producing and shaping subjectivity, identity, habitus, discourse, discipline, and embodied knowledge.

4

Police Violence against Black People

It is no longer necessary for the police to have any reason to believe that people are engaged in criminal activity or actually dangerous to stop and search them.
—Michelle Alexander (2010, 64)

Barack Obama's two terms as president allowed too many of us to think that the worst, at least, of the dark current of racism in America had run its course.
—Adam Hochschild (2018, 46)

The 2008 election of Barack Obama to the presidency of the United States led many observers to argue that racism in the United States was dead or dying. While it should have been clear to all that this was not true, it was not until 2014, when Americans witnessed not only the highly publicized police killings of Michael Brown and Eric Garner but also the national reaction to these killings, that it became clear to many that racism and racial violence in the United States are, in fact, alive and well.

The nation's reaction to these killings took multiple forms, including mass protests against police violence, a national debate over the meaning and appropriateness of police violence, the rise to national prominence of the Black Lives Matter movement, and a growing recognition among much of the public that Blacks are much more likely than Whites to be killed by the police.[1] However, these killings and the demonstrations and debates that followed also increased support among many Whites for the police and for police use of force and reinforced the belief erroneously held by many Whites that policing and police violence are not racially biased. These killings, demonstrations, and debates also helped propel Donald Trump to the presidency in 2016.

Indeed, one of the key pillars of Trump's 2016 presidential campaign was his strong and racially motivated support for law and order. To make this support clear to voters, Trump publicly endorsed police brutality and argued that we needed to restore security and safety, be vigilant against rampant crime, and "give power back to the police" (Newton 2018). He also regularly made claims such as the following (Keneally 2018; Moodley 2015; Qiu 2016):

- "The overwhelming amount of violent crime in our cities is committed by blacks and Hispanics."
- "There's killings on an hourly basis virtually in places like Baltimore and Chicago."
- "There are places in America that are among the most dangerous in the world. You go to places like Oakland. Or Ferguson. The crime numbers are worse."

And in a tweet that included an image of a "masked, dark-skinned man with a handgun, . . . [Trump] retweeted a false claim by White nationalists that 81% of White murder victims are killed by Black people" (J. Greenberg 2015).

In response to all this, many Democrats and much of the liberal news media argued that police violence against Black people and Trump's racist political rhetoric fell far outside the normal boundaries of US history and politics, or at least US history and politics since the civil rights era, and were thus un-American. Though likely securing votes for the Democratic Party and likely making liberals feel better about themselves and superior to Trump supporters, this argument was in other respects quite strange, because as those who made it should have known, rather than being un-American, violence against Black people and racist political rhetoric are as American and bipartisan as apple pie.

Indeed, the use of physical, psychological, and emotional violence against African Americans is integral to the history of the United States, being employed continuously from the colonial era to the present, including during slavery, Jim Crow, and the country's current sixty-year war on crime and drugs (M. Alexander 2010). Used as a means of social and labor control by Whites and the various governments that make up the United States, this violence has killed and injured far more African Americans, both currently and historically, than the number of Whites who have been killed and injured by Black people. Moreover, as I discuss in detail in the next chapter, over the past fifty to sixty years, leaders of both the Republican and Democratic Parties have routinely employed racist rhetoric and enacted racist policies that have greatly increased police and other state violence against African Americans.

Thus, the reactions to the killings of Michael Brown and Eric Garner recounted here are based on a series of falsehoods that need to be corrected: violence against African Americans and racist political rhetoric are *not* un-American; police violence is *more* widespread and *more* racially biased than many, perhaps most, White Americans believe; and both liberal *and* conservative politicians have employed violent and racist anti-crime rhetoric and supported increased police violence in Black neighborhoods. Put differently, the reactions recounted here reveal a set of contradictions, or tensions, between history and memory, fact and fiction, that are found not just among conservatives, working-class Whites, and the right-wing media, as many liberals and liberal media outlets claim, but also among liberals, the liberal media, and the middle and upper classes.

These tensions and the violence and political rhetoric that underlie them are the focus of this and the next chapter, promoting social order, I argue, by (a) creating divisions between subordinate groups that make it difficult for them to challenge the social order, (b) reinforcing dominant discourses in multiple social arenas, (c) aligning White subjectivity and identity with dominant institutional practices and external social and power relations, (d) promoting the psychological, cultural, and material interests of many Whites, and (e) forming and shaping subjectivity, identity, interests, and consent. Police violence and anti-Black political rhetoric also promote social order, we shall see, by creating and solidifying a distrust of mainstream institutions among many Black people, making violence against African Americans largely invisible to most Whites, making Blacks rather than Whites and the state look violent and irrational, and making the social order seem more benign, just, equal, and moral than it really is.

To demonstrate that police violence against African Americans promotes social order in these and other ways, this chapter describes the role police violence plays in the lives of Black Americans. This violence takes many forms, including killings, extreme physical violence, the constant patrolling of poor and working-class Black neighborhoods, and the disproportionate stopping, frisking, and harassing of Black people while they are walking, driving, and engaged in other routine activities. As we shall see, police violence against African Americans occurs and is threatened so regularly that it impinges directly upon the lives of most Black people, restricting their freedoms and rights on a daily basis and in many cases, helping shape their thoughts, emotions, psychology, behavior, subjectivity, and identity.

To demonstrate that Democratic and Republican politicians' violent anti-crime rhetoric promotes overall social order in the ways I claim it does, I devote the next chapter, chapter 5, to an examination of the race and crime discourses employed by US presidents, presidential candidates, politicians, and political analysts from the late 1940s to the late 1990s. As we shall see, this was a period in which the Democratic and Republican Parties both employed highly racist rhetoric that regularly and continuously linked African Americans to crime. Indeed, the history I recount in chapter 5 shows that though Democratic and Republican motivations and discourses were never perfectly identical during this period, they were often strikingly similar, and during the 1980s and 1990s nearly interchangeable. It further demonstrates that from the 1970s to the late 1990s both Democrats and Republicans strongly supported racially biased crime and drug legislation that greatly increased police violence against Black people and that they usually did so for the same reason: to win elections by swaying White voters with symbolically coded, and thus deniable, racist appeals.

One might try to justify the Democratic Party's strategy of supporting racially biased crime and drug legislation by arguing that the party had to adopt this strategy because it had proved so successful for Republicans that the Democrats could not win elections without adopting it too. One might also argue that the rhetoric Democrats used to justify their crime and drug policies was less blatantly racist than that used by Republicans. But the fact of the matter is that *both* parties adopted this strategy because they thought they could not win elections without doing so; and though Democratic politicians' rhetoric may often have been less blatantly racist than that of their Republican counterparts, their rhetoric was not always that subtle or that different from Republican rhetoric. And like Republican rhetoric, Democratic rhetoric drew directly from and strongly reinforced key symbolic structures underlying society's dominant racist discourses.

The theoretical and empirical upshot of all this, I will argue, is that racist political rhetoric, police violence against African Americans, and tensions between memory, history, and forgetfulness have helped create and reinforce deep social and political divisions that make it difficult for non-elites to work together to challenge the social order. These divisions exist not only between Blacks and Whites, as many would expect, but also between Whites who take different positions on police violence and racist political rhetoric, imbue these differences with great moral, cultural, and political significance, and fail to see that their political leaders do not differ nearly so much on race, rhetoric, and policing as they would like to think they do.

The inability of Whites to see the historical similarities in Democratic and Republican policing policies and rhetoric and their failure to recognize that subtle racist rhetoric and politicians who support racist policies without using racist rhetoric are both still racist also means that liberal Whites are able to support racist politicians and/or policies without recognizing the racism inherent in doing so. This is true too for many conservative Whites. But because liberal Whites generally recognize the racism inherent in conservative but not liberal crime policies and rhetoric, they not only tend to ignore the similarities they share with conservative Whites, they also tend to look down on and strongly condemn conservative Whites and their beliefs.

This in turn, I argue, promotes social order by increasing already existing culture war divisions between liberal and conservative Whites and supporting liberal Whites' psychological and cultural interests by making them feel superior to White conservatives. Liberal Whites' psychological and cultural interests and sense of superiority are likely also supported, as are divisions between them and African Americans, by the fact that many liberal Whites seem to have consciously or unconsciously accepted the less blatant but still racist rhetoric that prominent Democratic politicians have often employed to promote their law and order policies, thereby further promoting social order.

The racist rhetoric Democratic and Republican politicians employ to gain support for their crime and drug policies also reinforces race, gender, and class discourses that rely on the same logic and symbolic structure as does the rhetoric. This supports overall social order by reinforcing dominant discourses in multiple social arenas and aligning White subjectivity and identity, which are strongly shaped by rhetoric and discourse, with dominant institutional practices and external social and power relations. The mass arrest and imprisonment of Black people resulting from the war on crime and drugs also reinforces society's dominant racial discourses by appearing to empirically confirm the rhetorical association politicians have made between African Americans, crime, violence, criminality, and laziness, falsely proving to many Whites that the political rhetoric and racist discourses have a "factual" basis and making many Whites feel better about themselves by making them feel superior to African Americans. And these outcomes, in turn, promote overall social order by reinforcing the discursive logic underlying racism, sexism, and classism and supporting the psychological and cultural interests of many White people.

I turn now to an extended discussion of police violence against African Americans. My goals in presenting this discussion are to clearly delineate the extent to which police violence and the criminal justice system intrude into the lives of Black people; to demonstrate that this violent intrusion is based not on the behavior of African Americans but rather on the racist policies and practices of police departments and the US criminal justice system; to highlight the myriad ways in which this intrusion and violence harm Black people and Black neighborhoods; and to show how police and criminal justice violence promote overall social order in the United States.

Given my wide-ranging goals and the many ways in which police violence harms African Americans and promotes overall social order, I divide this discussion into four parts. I first examine the rules governing police stops and searches, demonstrate that these stops and searches are routine, violent, and racially biased, and describe the extensive ways in which police violence harms Black people, particularly those living in poor urban neighborhoods. I then turn my attention to the violent consequences of mass incarceration, in particular to its effects on young, poorly educated African Americans, their families, and their communities. After this, I summarize the many ways in which mass incarceration and the police and criminal justice system violently harm Black people, and I conclude the chapter by discussing how the tremendously high levels of police violence directed against Black people promote overall social order in the United States. Put differently, I spend most of this chapter demonstrating that the police and criminal justice system inflict tremendously high (and pervasive) levels of violence on Black people, in ways that are both familiar *and* unfamiliar to most White Americans and that are often (though by no means always) of relatively minor interest to those who study the police and criminal justice system. However, it is not until the end of the chapter, when I have presented evidence sufficient to test my theoretical argument, that I am able to demonstrate that police and criminal justice system violence promote overall social order in the multiple ways I theorize they do. I therefore wait until the end of the chapter to demonstrate this.

Finally, I would like to note that much, though by no means all, of the evidence I present in this chapter highlights the period between 2000 and 2014. I highlight this period for two reasons. First, mass incarceration and police stop and search practices reached their peak during these years. Second, this time period falls immediately after the Democratic Party's most intense efforts, as described in the following chapter, to throw large numbers of Black people in jail. This time period is thus extremely important for understanding the role that police and criminal justice system violence, national politics, and Democratic (and Republican) Party discourse play in promoting overall social order in the United States.

Police Violence and African Americans

Police violence against Black people takes many forms, from the constant presence of police in poor urban Black neighborhoods to the disproportionate stopping, searching, and frisking of Black people as they go about their everyday lives to their disproportionate killing at the hands of the police. Because killings represent the extreme end of the police violence continuum, I begin my discussion with this form of violence. However, the bulk of this section highlights less extreme (though still extreme) forms of police violence that occur much more regularly than police killings, that place police killings in a context that gives them their precise social force and meaning, and that play as or more important a role than do police killings in restricting and controlling Black lives, shaping Black and White subjectivity and identity, and promoting overall social order.

Research demonstrates that Black people are much more likely than White people to be killed by the police. The *Washington Post* (2022), for instance, found that between January 1, 2015, and April 1, 2022, police in the United States shot and killed 5,945 people, with Blacks two and a half times more likely than Whites, given their relative population sizes, to be killed in these shootings. Similarly, the *Guardian* found that Black men between the ages of fifteen and thirty-four "were nine times more likely than other Americans to be killed by police officers" (Swaine et al. 2015); and using Bayesian statistical methods, Cody Ross (2015) found that the probability of being Black, unarmed, and shot by the police was 3.49 times the probability of being White, unarmed, and shot by the police and equal to the probability of being White and armed and shot by the police.

Police killings are incredibly devastating to families, friends, and communities. Nevertheless, more routine exercises of police power and violence also cause extreme harm to Black people, and in their cumulative effect can likewise devastate individuals, families, and communities. Take, for example, the excessive use of police stops and frisks as a means of social control in poor urban Black neighborhoods. This widespread practice, in which the police "temporarily detain people on the street, question them, and possibly . . . search them" (Center for Constitutional Rights 2012, 3), is supported by a set of Supreme Court decisions from the past fifty years that govern the stopping, detaining, and searching of pedestrians, drivers, and others.[2]

Prior to the first of these decisions, *Terry v. Ohio* (1968), police officers could not stop and search a person without having either a warrant from a judge or probable cause. But as a result of the *Terry* decision, police officers can now stop a pedestrian or driver if the officer has nothing more than a reasonable suspicion that the person has committed, is committing, or is about to commit a crime. Based on more recent Supreme Court decisions, an officer can also stop a person if she or he commits "any objective violation of the law, no matter how minor" (Epp, Maynard-Moody, and Haider-Markel 2014, 35), including jaywalking, loitering, or having a broken taillight. Indeed, the bar is set so low that in New York City in 2012, police officers regularly stopped people for "moving furtively, wearing clothes or disguises commonly used during crimes, or being in an area with a high incidence of the offense under investigation" (Center for Constitutional Rights 2012, 4); and in Boston, in roughly three-quarters of the more than 204,000 field interrogation, observation, frisk and/or search reports filed by police officers between 2007 and 2010, the reason listed for initiating the interrogation, observation, frisk, or search was to investigate the person, which, of course, is not an explanation for the stop but the activity that needs to be explained (American Civil Liberties Union 2014).

The Supreme Court also allows police officers to use minor traffic violations as pretexts for stopping drivers who they suspect might possibly be engaged in some other illegal activity. This not only allows police officers to stop drivers based on very low levels of suspicion, but because regulations governing motor vehicles and driving are so detailed that virtually everybody violates the law every time they drive their car, it also allows officers to stop virtually any driver they want to stop. Moreover, if during the stop the officer finds evidence of some other illegal activity, that evidence is permissible in court even if the pretext the officer used is not a violation of the law but the officer says she thought it was (Armstrong 2015).

Once a pedestrian has been stopped by a police officer, the officer is allowed to pat down the pedestrian's outer clothing if the officer is reasonably suspicious that the person is armed and dangerous; and if the officer has a reasonable suspicion that the occupants of a stopped vehicle might attack him, he can pat down the occupants and search those areas of the vehicle that are within the occupants' reach. Officers can also stop and search a vehicle if "the totality of circumstances support[] reasonable suspicion of criminal activity, even if no single element of those circumstances r[i]se to the level of probable cause to justify the stop" (Epp, Maynard-Moody, and Haider-Markel 2014, 35), leading Epp and his colleagues (2014, 35) to conclude,

> It is difficult to identify what types of police stops-and-searches are not constitutionally legitimate. The line between illegal and legal is reduced to little more than whether or not the officer "articulates" a set of plausibly suspicious driver behaviors.

Finally, the Supreme Court allows police officers to search people and their property if they provide consent for the search, and this is true even if the police have no reason to suspect that a crime has, is, or will soon be committed and even when those who are searched do not realize that they can withhold their consent (police officers are not obliged to tell them this), feel that they have no choice but to give their consent, or physically comply with a request to be searched without giving their verbal consent. Most people, of course, are wary of saying no to armed police officers who want to search them, and thus agree to be searched. Moreover, drivers who refuse to be searched can be arrested for minor traffic or vehicle violations, even those that are punishable only by fines and not jail, giving the police extra leverage to extract consent from them.

The Supreme Court has thus given police officers in the United States extraordinary powers to stop, search, seize, and repress us. Indeed, in his 1968 dissent in *Terry v. Ohio*, Supreme Court Justice William Douglas noted,

> We hold today that the police have greater authority to make a "seizure" and conduct a "search" than a judge has to authorize such action. . . . To give the police greater power than a magistrate is to take a long step down the totalitarian path. (Terry v. Ohio, 392 US 1, 36, 38 [1968])

And more recently, Supreme Court Justice Sonia Sotomayor, in her 2016 dissent in *Utah v. Strieff*, stated, "This case . . . implies that you are not a citizen of a democracy but the subject of a carceral state, just waiting to be cataloged" (Utah v. Strieff, 579 US 14, 12 [2016]).

Moreover, police stops and searches can be extremely humiliating, intrusive, and traumatic. Justice Sotomayor notes, for instance, that

> the indignity of [police] stops is not limited to an officer telling you that you look like a criminal. . . . If the officer thinks you might be dangerous, he may then "frisk" you for weapons. This involves more than just a pat down. As onlookers pass by, the officer may "feel with sensitive fingers every portion of [your] body. A thorough search [may] be made of [your] arms and armpits, waistline and back, the groin and area about the testicles, and entire surface of the legs down to the feet. . . ."

[Moreover,] the officer's control over you does not end with the stop. If the officer chooses, he may handcuff you and take you to jail for doing nothing more than speeding [or] jaywalking. . . . At the jail, he can finger-print you, swab DNA from the inside of your mouth, and force you to "shower with a delousing agent" while you "lift [your] tongue, hold out [your] arms, turn around, and lift [your] genitals." (Utah v. Strieff 579, US 14, 9–12 [2016])

Of course, as Justice Sotomayor makes clear in other portions of her dissent, we are not all equally subject to police search, seizure, and de-tainment. Police officers, for example, are allowed to use race to establish reasonable suspicion as long as it is not the only or primary factor they use to do so, and they can use seemingly race-neutral factors such as wearing gang- or crime-related clothing and being in high-crime areas to justify casting suspicion on someone even though relying on these factors makes it more likely they will target African Americans and La-tinos. Urban police departments also tend to target their efforts toward high-crime areas, which tend to be located in low-income Black and Latino neighborhoods, and toward young men in these areas, who are the most likely people in these areas to commit crimes (P. Butler 2017; A. Davis 2017).

This latter point may lead some people to believe that the police are justified in focusing disproportionate attention on low-income Black and Latino neighborhoods and the young men who live in them. How-ever, most people in high-crime neighborhoods do not commit crimes (P. Butler 2017; Lurie 2019) and are thus no more deserving of experienc-ing intensive and invasive police tactics than anyone else. Young people living outside high-crime neighborhoods are also disproportionately likely to commit crimes, and there is no justifiable reason to think that young people or criminals should be subjected to more or less intense and invasive police scrutiny and treatment for activities that have noth-ing to do with the crimes they might have committed simply because of the neighborhood they live in. That is simply unjust.[3]

Research demonstrates, moreover, that Black/White disparities in violent and property crime rates disappear or nearly disappear (depend-ing on the study) when neighborhood disadvantage and other structural characteristics of cities and neighborhoods are accounted for (Chamberlain and Hipp 2015; Krivo and Peterson 2000; Krivo, Peterson, and Kuhl 2009; Light and Ulmer 2016; Sampson, Wilson, and Katz 2018; Shihadeh and Shrum 2004; Steffensmeier et al. 2010; Steinberg 2001). Research also demonstrates that the high concentration of African Americans and Latinos in extremely poor and structurally disadvantaged neighborhoods results primarily from factors such as residential and employment discrimination, poor-quality schools, and the structure of the US economy, factors over which African Americans and Latinos have no control (Massey and Denton 1993; Sampson, Wilson, and Katz 2018). As a result, Black/White differences in violent and property crime rates cannot be attributed to differences between Blacks and Whites but instead must be attributed to social-structural factors over which Whites have much greater control than Blacks.

The fact that the police focus disproportionate attention on African Americans, Latinos, and the neighborhoods they live in (A. Davis 2017) also means that African Americans and Latinos are going to have higher arrest and conviction rates and the neighborhoods they live in will have higher recorded crime rates than do other groups and neighborhoods even if African Americans and Latinos are no more likely than other groups to commit crimes. This claim is borne out in data on drug crimes, for which African Americans and Latinos are arrested and convicted at much higher rates than are Whites despite the fact that they are no more likely than Whites to use or sell drugs (M. Alexander 2010; Rothwell 2014).

Moreover, arrest and conviction disparities resulting from differential police attention are likely to be especially large if police departments devote significant time and resources to stopping and searching Black and Latino drivers and pedestrians based not on probable cause but on racially biased subjective suspicion, which is, in fact, what they do (P. Butler 2017; A. Davis 2017; Epp, Maynard-Moody, and Haider-Markel 2014). As a result, African Americans and Latinos in general and poor young African American and Latino men in particular receive much more police attention and experience much more police violence than do non-Hispanic Whites. Indeed, because the Supreme Court allows police officers to stop and frisk virtually anyone they want regardless of guilt, innocence, or even reasonable suspicion, virtually all African Americans and Latinos are subject to such scrutiny.

Numerous studies, reports, and government investigations bear this out. Several decades of research show, for example, that Black drivers are much more likely than White drivers to be pulled over by the police and to be treated poorly when they are pulled over despite engaging in relatively similar driving practices and being no more likely than White drivers to possess drugs, guns, and other contraband (Baumgartner, Epp, and Shoub 2018; Epp, Maynard-Moody, and Haider-Markel 2014; Harris 1999). In one of the most interesting of these studies, Charles Epp and colleagues (2014) found that whether Black and White drivers in Kansas City had similar or different experiences during police stops depended to a significant degree on whether they were stopped for violating more or less serious traffic laws.

Calling stops for more serious traffic violations "traffic-safety stops" and stops for less serious violations "investigatory stops," Epp, Maynard-Moody, and Haider-Markel found that African Americans were less likely than Whites to experience traffic-safety stops but more likely to experience investigatory stops. They also found that how one drives was the best predictor of traffic-safety stops, while the race of the driver best predicted investigatory stops, with Blacks "2.7 times more likely than Whites to be stopped in investigatory stops" (2014, 64). This racial disparity held for all age groups in the sample but was particularly pronounced for Black men under the age of twenty-five who, over the course of a year, had a 28 percent likelihood of experiencing an investigatory stop. Young Black men were also much more likely than any other group in the sample to experience multiple investigatory stops in a given year.

These racial differences had significant consequences. Traffic-safety stops tended to be fairly quick, to the point, and non-intrusive, with Black and White drivers treated similarly during such stops. Investigatory stops, on the other hand, were highly intrusive from the moment the police initiated the stop, with officers "ask[ing] questions, look[ing] about the car's interior, prolong[ing] the encounter while looking for anomalies and evidence of wrongdoing and, if suspicious, search[ing] the vehicle" (Epp, Maynard-Moody, and Haider-Markel 2014, 78–79). Investigatory stops thus seemed to be based more on subjectively formed suspicion than on probable cause.

In addition, during investigatory stops, Black drivers were much more likely than White drivers to be handcuffed or threatened with arrest and to have themselves or their vehicles searched. And this was so even though very few Black drivers were arrested during these stops and even though police officers were less than half as likely to find contraband when they searched Black drivers' vehicles than when they searched White drivers' vehicles. Not surprisingly, Black drivers in the study were more likely than White drivers to report feeling violated and/or traumatized by their encounters with the police, and they reported much more negative feelings about the police and their encounters with the police than did Whites.

As is true for Black drivers, Black pedestrians are also disproportionately likely to be stopped, searched, and treated poorly by the police. In Chicago, for example, 72 percent of the 250,000 people who were stopped but not arrested by the police between May 1 and August 31, 2014, were Black and 9 percent were White, despite the fact that Blacks and Whites each made up 32 percent of the city's population (American Civil Liberties Union of Illinois 2015). In Boston, moreover, 63 percent of the people listed in the more than 204,000 field interrogation, observation, frisk and/or search (FIOFS) reports that police officers filed from 2007 to 2010 were Black even though Black people made up only 24 percent of Boston's population at that time; and among those listed in these reports, Blacks were more likely than Whites to be frisked or searched and to experience repeat FIOFS encounters. These racial disparities persisted even after controlling for factors such as neighborhood crime rates and the arrest records and alleged gang involvement of those listed in these reports, and because FIOFS reports are filed for stops that do not lead to arrests, none of these encounters resulted in an arrest (American Civil Liberties Union 2014).[4]

The numbers were similarly alarming in New York City in 2011. In that year, 51 percent (350,743) of the 685,724 people who were officially stopped and frisked by the city's police department were Black and 9 percent (61,805) were White, despite the fact that Blacks and Whites made up about 23 percent and 33 percent of the city's population respectively. And of those who were stopped, force was used against 21.8 percent of Blacks and 15.8 percent of Whites, with only 12 percent of those who were stopped being arrested or given a summons and only 2 percent carrying a weapon or contraband (Center for Constitutional Rights 2011). Moreover, these racial disparities persisted even after controlling for the racial and income characteristics of the neighborhoods in which people were arrested, the strength of police patrols in these neighborhoods, and the total number of complaints reported to the police from these neighborhoods (Fagan 2012).

In addition, between 2011 and 2017 the US Department of Justice found racial bias in police stop and frisk tactics, police use of force, and/ or police vehicle stops in several medium-sized and major US cities, including Baltimore, Chicago, Ferguson (Missouri), Los Angeles, Cleveland, New Orleans, and Newark. In Baltimore, for example, it found that the police department, the BPD, often "extend[ed] stops without justification to search for evidence that would justify an arrest," often resorted to unnecessary and excessive physical force, including against juveniles, and was significantly more likely to use force against African Americans than against Whites (US Department of Justice 2016, 6).

Anyone stopped by the BPD was potentially subject to such violence. But as the Department of Justice makes clear, and as is true in virtually all cities for which research has been conducted (American Civil Liberties Union 2014; Center for Constitutional Rights 2012; P. Butler 2017; Fryer 2016), Baltimore's Black citizens were significantly more likely than its White citizens to be stopped and arrested and more likely, when stopped, to be searched and to experience excessive physical violence. As is also true in many cities, the BPD focused an inordinate amount of attention on a handful of Black neighborhoods such that these neighborhoods and the people residing in them experienced a near-constant police presence far out of proportion to that experienced by any other neighborhood or segment of the population.

The consequences of such a constant and overwhelming police presence are extremely dire. In New York City, for example, African Americans living in extremely poor and segregated neighborhoods

describe[] an environment so saturated with a hostile police presence that being stopped and harassed by police ha[s] become integrated into the fabric of daily life. . . . One [resident] said, "We expect them to jump out of a car. We expect them to just come out the staircase and scare the hell out of you . . ." [Others] describe[] the risk involved in simply being in the hallways, stairwells, or elevators of their apartment buildings, in front of their buildings, or anywhere outside including: walking on the street, on the subway, in a park, at the corner store, or while driving. . . . [One interviewee noted,] "If you show the police officers your ID that says you live [here], they tell you to go in the house or walk somewhere else; you can't be here on the block. . . . We can't be outside? . . . So what can we do? We want to go out. We don't want to be in the house." . . . [And another said,] "I can't even walk through the complex, they're always stopping you, asking you for ID. 'Do you live here?' Every single day. Do I have to go through this every single day? How many times you going to ask, do I live here? People don't even come outside anymore, because they're more fearful against the police than the folks in the neighborhood." (Center for Constitutional Rights 2012, 17, 19)

Young Black men in Boston, New York, St. Louis, and Baltimore also report being repeatedly stopped by the police, with some having been stopped thirty, forty, fifty, or more times during their teens and early twenties. Moreover, this occurs even if they have never committed a crime and almost always when they are engaged in legitimate everyday activities such as walking down the street, playing basketball, sitting on their front porches, and walking to and from school (American Civil Liberties Union 2014; Brunson 2007; Brunson and Miller 2006; Center for Constitutional Rights 2012; Dressner and Martinez 2012; Fan 2018; Gau and Brunson 2010; US Department of Justice 2016).

Young Black men also report regular police sweeps of their neighborhoods:

They'll come in like, three or four cars deep, two paddy wagons, and they'll just roll down every block that they think mainly sellin' drugs or whatever. And anybody outside, if they think you got something, they gon' check you. (Brunson and Miller 2006, 540)

These and other police stops are anything but pleasant. Young Black men report having the police yell at them, tell them they are "Fucking Mutts," threaten them with serious physical violence, grope their genitals, forcibly undress them, strip search them in public, and push and shove them. They report being thrown against walls, against police cars, and to the ground; being slapped, hit, kicked, and beaten; being choked and Tasered; and being publicly detained and humiliated for extended periods of time before being let go (M. Alexander 2010; American Civil Liberties Union 2014; Brunson 2007; P. Butler 2017; Tuttle and Schneider 2012).

The individual and neighborhood consequences of all this are profound. Those who are routinely stopped and searched describe it as humiliating, demeaning, and degrading (Center for Constitutional Rights 2012), and those who live in heavily policed neighborhoods describe feeling helpless, vulnerable, and unsafe. They talk of being constantly fearful oı the police as they walk through their neighborhoods, report feeling as though they are under constant surveillance, believe that regardless of what they do they will always be viewed as suspect and criminal, and talk about changing their behavior and altering their dress so as to avoid being stopped and mistreated by the police. As a result, they often stay away from places they want to be, such as "parks and playgrounds, basketball courts and baseball diamonds, . . . train stations and bus stops, city squares and community festivals" (American Civil Liberties Union 2014, 14). They also stay inside when they would rather be outside, report feeling trapped, tormented, and angry, experience anxiety, and take public transportation to avoid walking and driving.

Being repeatedly stopped and frisked and living in heavily policed neighborhoods also affect people's engagement with their community and their sense of status and belonging in the larger society. They feel, for instance, that they lack basic rights, are not full citizens, and do not live in a free society. There is also, as one resident notes, a

> constant fear that . . . police are going to intimidate and harass you. So stuff that you do in your community, like participate in it, like sitting on your porch or going to the store or like having fun in your community— you don't really get to do that because you have police presence in the street all the time. (Center for Constitutional Rights 2012, 18)

People living in highly policed neighborhoods also describe the police as hostile military occupiers and their neighborhoods as occupied territories that are under siege, and they often believe that the police are there not to protect them but instead to control them (Center for Constitutional Rights 2012). Indeed, Paul Butler (2017) argues that police stops and frisks are a form of sexualized social control in which police officers (a) force Black men to assume the position and physically submit to the officers' will, (b) often fondle and squeeze Black men's genitals, and (c) use this sexualized violence to enforce both individual and community submission to the police and White society. Butler also likens police stops and frisks to torture and terrorism, first, because being stopped and frisked produces psychological states—such as humiliation, submission, anxiety, fear, traumatic stress, and learned helplessness—that are similar to the psychological states produced by torture, and second, because being stopped and frisked can alter behavioral routines and produce a sense of fear and helplessness that are similar to the behavioral and psychological changes brought about by terrorism.

That stops and frisks and other negative police encounters produce lasting psychological harm has been well documented. For instance, a recent review of eleven studies finds that people who have negative interactions with the police experience nearly twice the prevalence of mental health problems—including psychological distress, depression, post-traumatic stress disorder (PTSD), anxiety, psychotic episodes, and suicidal ideation—as do others (McLeod et al. 2020). Police stops and frisks are thus not only physically violent practices, they are also psychologically and emotionally violent practices that greatly harm those subject to them.

Racially biased stops and searches also severely restrict the geographic and spatial mobility of many African Americans (see the preceding discussion), as do racially biased vehicle stops,[5] making it more difficult for African Americans to participate in the larger society and to experience economic success, personal fulfilment, and the rights associated with full citizenship. In this respect, police stop and search practices are similar to other forms of racially oriented social control, such as imprisonment, slavery, Jim Crow, and apartheid, that maintain inequality and exert control by highlighting racial divisions and violently restricting the geographic and spatial mobility of racially subordinated groups (Epp, Maynard-Moody, and Haider-Markel 2014).

Racially biased stops and searches also tell African Americans that the larger society views them as second-class citizens who are not worthy of dignity, respect, liberty, and inclusion in the larger community, but who instead must be constantly watched, monitored, and treated as enemies and objects rather than as fully human individuals (Epp,

Maynard-Moody, and Haider-Markel 2014). Racially biased stops and searches are thus not only about social control and repression deriving from restricted geographic and spatial mobility and the kinds of physical and psychological violence discussed so far. They also control and repress by sending a psychologically violent, and thus highly emotional and symbolically charged, message that society does not want to give Black people the dignity and respect all people deserve, allow Black people to participate fully and equally in society, or provide Black people with equal opportunities to experience economic success, personal fulfillment, and full and complete citizenship.

Finally, biased policing promotes racial division. It does this in large part by discriminating against African Americans, contributing to the forms of inequality and repression described in the preceding paragraph, and enforcing the geographic, social, and spatial segregation of Blacks and Whites. But just as importantly, it increases the salience of race for those African Americans who are subject to it and creates communities within the United States that have vastly different experiences with government authority. Research shows, for instance, that race is more central to the self-identity of African Americans who have experienced an investigatory traffic stop than it is for other African Americans (Epp, Maynard-Moody, and Haider-Markel 2014) and that "people who are . . . incarcerated . . . are more likely to be classified and identify as black . . . *regardless of how they were classified or identified previously*" (Penner and Saperstein 2008, 1962S, emphasis added). In addition, Black people in general and poor urban Blacks in particular are much more likely than Whites, particularly middle- and upper-class Whites, to be treated poorly, intrusively, and violently by the police. This not only helps heighten the salience of race for many Black people (P. Butler 2017; Epp, Maynard-Moody, and Haider-Markel 2014), it also means that Blacks' and Whites' experiences with government authority are so very different that their basic understandings of what their society is cannot always be reconciled with each other, increasing divisions between them and making it more difficult for them to work together to challenge the social order.

I present this latter argument in greater detail later in the chapter after I discuss mass incarceration and its pernicious effects on low-income African Americans, the subject to which I now turn.

Mass Incarceration

The racially biased stop and frisk practices highlighted in the previous section are important not just for the reasons already articulated but also because they have played a key role in this nation's half-century war on crime and drugs (recall that in this chapter, I rely primarily on data from 2000 to 2014 because this is the period when mass incarceration reached its peak). One of the key consequences of the war on crime and drugs is that it caused the US incarceration rate to skyrocket from just over 150 people per 100,000 in 1972 to nearly 800 people per 100,000 between 2006 and 2008 (this includes people in local jails and state and federal prisons). And though this rate subsequently fell, it was still 707 people per 100,000 in 2012, when 2.23 million US citizens were in prison or jail (Travis, Western, and Redburn 2014), and 537 people per 100,000 in 2021, when 1.77 million US citizens were in prison or jail (Kang-Brown, Montagnet, and Heiss 2021).

This dramatic increase in US incarceration rates hurt Black men particularly hard. Between 1960 and 2010, for instance, the incarceration rate for African Americans increased from 1,313 to 4,347 per 100,000 for men and boys and from 76 to 260 per 100,000 for women and girls. For White men and boys the rate increased from 262 to 678 per 100,000 and for White women and girls from 11 to 91 per 100,000 (Drake 2018). Thus, in 2010 Black males were 6.4 times more likely than White males, 16.7 times more likely than Black females, and 47.8 times more likely than White females to be incarcerated.

The result of all this was that in 2008 one out of every twelve Black men, one out of every nine young Black men (ages twenty to thirty-four), and one out of every three young, poorly educated Black men (without a high school diploma or GED) was incarcerated (the corresponding figures for White men were one out of eighty-seven, one out of fifty-seven, and one out of eight), with young poorly educated Black men more likely to be in prison or jail (37 percent) than employed (26 percent) (Western and Pettit 2010). Moreover, in 2019 Black men and women were still 5.7 and 1.7 times more likely, respectively, than White men and women to be incarcerated (Sentencing Project 2020); and in 2016 they were 3.5 times as likely as White adults to experience parole or probation (Horowitz and Utada 2018).

The overrepresentation of African Americans in the criminal justice system is due in part to the fact that they are more likely than Whites to commit violent crimes and property crimes. However, as noted earlier, most of the difference in Black and White violent and property crime rates can be explained by the fact that Blacks are much more likely than Whites to be poor and to live in highly disadvantaged neighborhoods, factors for which research shows that society (and not African Americans) is to blame (Massey and Denton 1993; Sampson, Wilson, and Katz 2018). Moreover, the proportion of people arrested for violent crimes who were African American declined significantly in the 1980s and 1990s at the same time as the overall violent crime rate was declining and Black/White incarceration disparities were increasing, indicating that Black violent crime rates were not the primary factor producing these increasing disparities (Travis, Western, and Redburn 2014).

African American overrepresentation in the US criminal justice system also results from the disproportionate attention that Black people and Black neighborhoods receive from the police, from the fact that African Americans are much more likely than Whites to be arrested for drug crimes even though they are equally likely to use and sell drugs, and from the fact that in the 1980s and early 1990s Blacks who were arrested for property and drug crimes, and in the 2000s Blacks who were arrested for property, drug, and violent crimes, were more likely to be imprisoned than were similar Whites who were arrested for these crimes (M. Alexander 2010; Travis, Western, and Redburn 2014). In addition, "severe sentencing laws enacted in the 1980s and 1990s [as a result of the war on crime and drugs] greatly increased the lengths of prison sentences mandated for violent crimes and drug offenses, [crimes] for which blacks are disproportionately often arrested" (Travis, Western, and Redburn 2014, 96).

Moreover, once arrested, Blacks continue to be treated worse than Whites by the criminal justice system. Because they are more likely than Whites to be poor and to require a public defender and because the caseloads public defenders manage are overwhelming, Blacks are more likely than Whites to receive subpar legal counsel (Sentencing Project 2013). Controlling for relevant factors, Blacks are also

> more likely than whites to be detained before trial, . . . increas[ing] the probability that a prison sentence will be imposed. . . . [In addition,] race

and ethnicity affect charging and plea bargaining decisions in both capital and noncapital cases, . . . [and convicted blacks], all else being equal, . . . receive somewhat longer sentences [than do convicted whites]. . . . Blacks are [also] less likely than whites to be diverted to nonincarcerative punishments . . . [and] in states that have sentencing guidelines, blacks are more likely than whites to receive sentences at the top rather than at the bottom of the guideline ranges. (Travis, Western, and Redburn 2014, 97–98)

When the evidence used against criminal defendants is similar, White jurors are also much more likely to convict Black than White defendants (Sentencing Project 2013). Additionally, Black probationers are more likely than White probationers with similar risk assessment scores, criminal histories, and probation performances to have their probation revoked and be sent to jail (Jannetta, Breaux, and Ho 2014).

Risk assessment scores, prior criminal history, and prior entanglement with the police and criminal justice system also affect jury decisions, sentencing decisions, and the decisions prosecutors make regarding whether to prosecute (Jannetta, Breaux, and Ho 2014; Kohler-Hausmann 2018; Natapoff 2018; Sentencing Project 2013). This may seem reasonable and just to many people. However, because police departments focus disproportionate attention on Black people and Black neighborhoods, because Black drug users and sellers are more likely than White drug users and sellers to be arrested, because once arrested Blacks are more likely than Whites with similar backgrounds to be imprisoned or otherwise sanctioned, and so on, Black defendants are more likely to have poor risk assessment scores, worse criminal histories, and significantly more prior contact with the police and criminal justice system than are White defendants who have behaved similarly throughout their lives. They may even have poorer scores, worse criminal histories, and more prior contact with the police than do White defendants who have engaged in higher levels of criminal activity throughout their lives (M. Alexander 2010; P. Butler 2017; Jannetta, Breaux, and Ho 2014; Kohler-Hausmann 2018; Natapoff 2018).

As a result of these and the other factors I have discussed, and in addition to the fact that arrest rates are already racially biased,

Analyses for 2004 . . . and 2008 . . . show that, relative to arrest patterns, racial disparities in imprisonment [were] much worse in the twenty-first century . . . [than in] 1979 and 1991. For 2004, 39 percent of overall disparities in imprisonment could not be explained by reference to arrests, and for 2008, 45 percent. . . . [More specifically, in] 2008, 40 percent of disparities in imprisonment for murder, 45 percent for robbery, 55 percent for aggravated assault, and 66 percent for drug offenses could not be explained by arrest patterns. (Travis, Western, and Redburn 2014, 96)[6]

It should thus be clear that the dramatic increase in incarceration brought about by the war on crime and drugs, though affecting many Americans, has had a particularly pernicious effect on African Americans. But what exactly has this effect been? In particular, how does prison affect prisoners, ex-prisoners, their families and friends, and the communities they come from and go back to? I address these questions in the following subsections, explaining at the end of each subsection why these often seemingly nonviolent effects are actually extremely violent.

The Violent Consequences of Mass Incarceration

The most obvious consequences of imprisonment are extended confinement, restricted movement, loss of decision-making authority, lack of control over one's life, inmate and guard violence, and a lack of privacy and meaningful activity. Prisoners are also wrenched away from their family, friends, and community, have the flow of their lives completely disrupted, and regularly experience uncertainty, danger, fear, and extreme physical and psychological stress.

These stressors, in turn, can produce serious physical and psychological harm. Many prisoners, for instance, experience PTSD, which occurs at much higher rates among inmates than among the general population, cannot be attributed solely to inmates' experiences prior to prison, and often results in depression, apathy, and hopelessness. Indeed, some studies report PTSD rates as high as 21 percent, 48 percent, and 65 percent among male, female, and male juvenile inmates respectively (Travis, Western, and Redburn 2014).

Many prisons are also extremely overcrowded. This makes it difficult for prison authorities to provide adequate medical care, can negatively affect prisoners' mental and physical health, and played a key role in producing extremely high rates of COVID-19 among prisoners. In addition, about 5 percent of all prisoners and 7 percent of federal prisoners are confined in some type of isolation or segregation unit that range from ones in which prisoner contact with others is fairly limited to ones in which prisoners (representing about 2 percent of the overall prison population at any given time) have virtually no contact with anyone other than prison staff.

Extreme isolation has many negative psychological consequences, including "insomnia, anxiety, panic, withdrawal, hypersensitivity, ruminations, cognitive dysfunction, hallucinations, loss of control, irritability, aggression and rage, paranoia, hopelessness, depression, a sense of impending emotional breakdown, self-mutilation, and suicidal ideation and behavior" (Haney 2003, as cited in Travis, Western, and Redburn 2014, 187–88). These psychological problems, in turn, can directly affect physical health, both in the short and the long run (Bener et al. 2012; de Heer et al. 2014; Holt et al. 2013; Travis, Western, and Redburn 2014; Walter et al. 2013; Western Washington Medical Group 2020).

Prisons are also extremely violent places, with sizeable minorities of inmates reporting that other inmates or staff have sexually assaulted them or pressured them into sexual activity and many reporting being physically injured by others (Travis, Western, and Redburn 2014, 225). Prison is also extremely boring and monotonous:

> For me, and many like me in prison . . . the major problem is monotony. It is the dull sameness of prison life, its idleness and boredom, that grinds me down. Nothing matters; everything is inconsequential other than when you will be free and how to make time pass until then. But boredom, time-slowing boredom, interrupted by occasional bursts of fear and anger, is the governing reality of life in prison. (Travis, Western, and Redburn 2014, 188)

The prison environment also changes prisoner identity and subjectivity, sometimes quite radically. Because so many decisions are made for prisoners by prison authorities and because the constant threat of victimization teaches many prisoners to be hypervigilant, distrustful, tough, and aggressive, to victimize others, and to respond to even minor insults with extreme violence, many ex-prisoners find that they are not the same people as they were when they entered prison. The psychological trauma and pain that this can cause and the trauma and pain that may have caused it in the first place are then compounded by the fact that these personality changes often make it difficult for ex-prisoners to behave in ways that conform with mainstream social norms and values. In other words, the norms, values, and behaviors that many prisoners learn in order to survive prison are often poorly adapted, and thus dysfunctional, to life outside prison, creating a subjective divide between those who have and have not been in prison and making it very difficult and painful for many ex-prisoners to reintegrate into society (Travis, Western, and Redburn 2014).

This description of how incarceration affects inmates tells only part of the story, however. A friend of mine who spent two and a half years in a maximum-security prison argues that the goal of prison authorities is to break prisoners down, treat them as if they are not human, and make them feel as if they are not human.[7] She describes forced-labor work crews where the inability to move one's body in time with other prisoners' bodies would lead one to be sent to the segregation unit, often permanently. She talks about the state in which she was imprisoned taking away inmates' rights to write each other letters, about prison authorities stopping inmates from crocheting items for each other, and about parole authorities preventing female and male parolees living in halfway houses from talking to and looking at each other.

In my friend's telling, writing to other prisoners was psychologically important to many inmates and the only opportunity that some inmates had to communicate with people outside their unit. It increased inmates' limited contact with others, allowed prisoners to learn how inmates in other units dealt with problems, and provided prisoners with the chance to open up to another person in a situation where because of violence, uncertainty, and lack of trust, one could not freely express oneself or show any sort of vulnerability to those one saw every day. When inmates lost this right, she says, their emotions, humanity, and need for human contact were denied, demoralizing and depressing everyone in the unit.

When women were denied the ability to crochet items for each other, my friend argues, yet another aspect of their humanity—their need for social relationships, respect, and self-worth—was denied them. Giving gifts they had made to other inmates had given women who had no mothers or children or who had been separated from their mothers and children the chance to be mothers or daughters, either again or for the first time. It also instilled pride and a sense of self-worth in those who had made and given the gifts. Taking this away from them was thus not simply another brutal lesson about their lack of power and control over their lives, it also denied them their innate humanity, broke them down yet again, and alienated them from themselves and others.

My friend further argues that it was very difficult for women and men denied contact with members of the opposite sex while in prison to live as parolees in halfway housing "camps" where they could not look at or talk with each other without risking imprisonment and where on those days that they were allowed to leave the camp they could not socialize with, touch, caress, or make love with each other without fear of being sent back to prison. They could, of course, socialize or have sex with other people of the opposite sex when they were away from the camp, but most people outside the camp had not been changed or trauma-tized by prison and did not understand what they had been through in prison. These former inmates were thus prevented from having human contact with members of the opposite sex who they could most easily connect with (or at least prevented from having such contact without the threat of imprisonment), denying to them one of the most basic of human needs (contact with understanding others) and alienating them from their innate humanity and, thus, from themselves.

It is therefore clear that the denial of basic human needs and the breaking of the human spirit do not necessarily end when inmates are released from prison. Indeed, there are many ways such denial and breaking occur. One of the most important of these ways is the exis-tence of thousands of government-enforced rules that deny ex-prisoners their basic humanity, alienate them from others, and make it difficult for them to survive outside prison. Referred to as hidden sentences, these legislative, administrative, and judicial rules vary greatly according to political jurisdiction, type of offense committed, type of punishment or penalty imposed, length of enforcement, and whether imposing the rule is discretionary or mandatory. Nevertheless, these sentences can haunt ex-prisoners for years, sometimes for the rest of their lives, and there are virtually no requirements that anyone "notify arrestees, criminal defendants, or convicted offenders that hidden sentences exist—much less the extent and nature of the penalties they face" (Kaiser 2016, 166). As a result, defendants deciding whether to plead guilty and prisoners being released from jail or prison are rarely informed of the full consequences of their plea deal or of the short- and long-term difficulties they will likely encounter after being released from court, jail, or prison (M. Alexander 2010; Kohler-Hausmann 2018).

The lack of information provided to people affected by hidden sentences is quite remarkable, given that

> there are, on average *about 2,100 legislative and administrative penalties [hidden sentences] per state* aimed at persons released from correctional supervision, in addition to an uncounted number imposed by judicial ruling or that accrue during and before supervision [this average includes federal penalties, which apply in every state]. (Kaiser 2016, 126, emphasis in original)

This lack of information is also remarkable given that 80 percent of hidden sentences impose permanent penalties or fail to specify a time frame by which penalties must be lifted (Kaiser 2016).

Moreover, hidden sentences, even those tied to minor misdemeanor convictions, cover a vast portion of social, political, and economic life, restricting or preventing people from obtaining things such as business and occupational licenses, government contracts, educational grants and loans, and government benefits and housing. People convicted of drug offenses, for instance, can lose social security benefits, food stamps, and access to low-income public housing, and ex-prisoners can lose access to workers' compensation, unemployment assistance, and government retirement benefits (M. Alexander 2010; Kaiser 2016). Indeed, simply being arrested can bar one from living in public housing, and misdemeanor arrests and convictions,[8] which are particularly likely for people who belong to groups or live in neighborhoods targeted by the police, can have surprisingly punitive repercussions:

> People with minor arrests and convictions . . . can lose their jobs, drivers' licenses, welfare benefits, child custody, immigration status, and housing. They may be disqualified for loans and professional licenses or sink into

debt and ruin their credit [they may even end up in debtors' prison].[9] Sometimes these things happen even when their cases are dismissed and they are never convicted at all. (Natapoff 2018, 19–20)

Depending on the offense and political jurisdiction, ex-prisoners may also lose their right to sit on juries. And in forty-eight states, prisoners convicted of felonies lose their voting rights (the exceptions are Maine and Vermont), with twelve states not returning these rights to felons after they have been released from prison (the length of time released felons are denied the vote varies across these twelve states). As a result, in 2016 there were 6.1 million people, or 2.5 percent of the voting-age population, who were not allowed to vote because they had been convicted of a felony. Moreover, in the United States as a whole, one out of every thirteen Black adults, as opposed to fewer than one out of every fifty White adults, was disenfranchised in 2016 due to a felony conviction, with one out of every five Black adults disenfranchised in Florida, Kentucky, Tennessee, and Virginia (close paraphrase of Uggen, Larson, and Shannon 2016).

Making matters worse, ex-prisoners and criminal defendants are often saddled with debts imposed by the criminal justice system that they cannot repay. For instance, they often have to pay jail book-in fees, pretrial jail per-diems, public defender application fees, bail investigation fees, pre-sentence report fees, public defender recoupment fees, work-release program fees, court fees, and probation and parole service fees. Since most ex-prisoners and many criminal defendants are poor and since ex-prisoners regularly face employment discrimination, they often have trouble paying these fees. As a result, they are often sent to jail for failure to pay their debts or are forced to pay late fees, payment plan fees, and interest on their debt (M. Alexander 2010). For others, failure to settle their debts can lead to the loss of driving privileges, making it more difficult for them to find or maintain employment. They may also lose their right to vote, as recounted in the following:

I put my life on the line for this country. To me, not voting is not right; it led to a lot of frustration, a lot of anger. My son's in Iraq. In the army just like I was. My oldest son, he fought in the first Persian Gulf conflict. He was in the Marines. This is my baby son over there right now. But I'm not able to vote. They say I owe $900 in fines. To me, that's a poll tax. You've got to pay to vote. It's "restitution," they say. I came off parole on October 13, 1999, but I'm still not allowed to vote. Last time I voted was in '88. Bush versus Dukakis. Bush won. I voted for Dukakis. If it was up to me, I'd vote his son out this time too. I know a lot of friends got the same cases like I got, not able to vote. A lot of guys doing the same things like I was doing. Just marijuana. They treat marijuana in Alabama like you committed treason or something. I was on the 1965 voting rights march from Selma. I was fifteen years old. At eighteen, I was in Vietnam fighting for my country. And now? Unemployed and they won't allow me to vote. (M. Alexander 2010, 159–60)

Ex-prisoners also often have serious trouble finding work. Not only are many ex-prisoners barred from specific categories of jobs and professions due to hidden sentencing, but in most states, employers can and regularly do discriminate against job applicants on the basis of whether applicants have prior arrests or convictions. The result is that even after controlling for other factors that affect employment and wages, ex-prisoners are more likely than the general population to be unemployed and if employed, to earn low or extremely low wages. This is particularly the case for Black men with criminal records, who, in comparison to White men with criminal records, tend both to earn less and to experience higher levels of employment discrimination (M. Alexander 2010; Decker et al. 2015; Pager 2003; Pager, Western, and Bonikowski 2009; Western and Sirois 2017). This results in a severe loss of individual, family, and community income. For instance, after controlling for relevant factors, Western and Pettit (2010, 3–4) found the following to be true:

- Serving time reduces hourly wages for men by approximately 11 percent, annual employment by 9 weeks and annual earnings by 40 percent.
- By age 48, the typical former [male] inmate will have earned $179,000 less than if he had never been incarcerated [this does not include wages lost while imprisoned].
- Incarceration depresses the total earnings of white males [as a group] by 2 percent . . . [and the total earnings] of black males [as a group] by 9 percent.

- Before being incarcerated . . . more than half [of all male inmates] were the primary source of financial support for their children.

Because former inmates are more likely than others to earn low wages or be unemployed, because government welfare and housing benefits are often unavailable to them, and because landlords and employers often discriminate against them, former inmates are also disproportionately likely to experience homelessness and destitution (M. Alexander 2010; McKernan 2017). This, combined with the discrimination they experience, their inability to provide for themselves and their families, and the fact that they cannot participate as full members of society, also means that former inmates often experience stigma, shame, depression, anger, and a sense that they are no longer members of or wanted by society. Indeed, Michelle Alexander (2010, 161–62) argues that the shame and stigma that people with criminal records regularly experience is in many ways worse than the "formal mechanisms of exclusion" they face:

> The shame and stigma . . . follow you for the rest of your life. . . . It is not just the job denial but the look that flashes across the face of a potential employer when he notices that "the box" has been checked—the way he suddenly refuses to look you in the eye. It is not simply the denial of the right to vote but the shame one feels when a co-worker innocently asks, "Who you gonna vote for on Tuesday?"

This shame and stigma, if they occur often enough and are as pervasive and emotionally traumatic as Michelle Alexander suggests they are, are clearly violent according to my definition of the term. But so is much of what I have discussed in this chapter. Indeed, whether it is being stopped, frisked, arrested, processed by the criminal justice system, or sentenced to prison, probation, or parole; whether it is being forcibly separated, or alienated, from society and oneself; whether it is being told that you do not belong, that society does not care if you suffer, and that you are less than human; and whether it is being physically and emotionally separated from children, parents, lovers, extended family, and other inmates and ex-inmates, the US criminal justice system imposes severe emotional, psychological, and physical harm on large but specific segments of the US population, primarily poor people, poorly

POLICE VIOLENCE AGAINST BLACK PEOPLE | 167

educated people, African Americans, and though I do not discuss them in this chapter, Hispanics. As described in the preceding pages, severe emotional, psychological, and physical harms are imposed, too, on those who are forced to live in physically dangerous, overcrowded, and de-humanizing prisons; those who when released from prison are denied access to jobs, benefits, and housing; those who are hungry and home-less because of hidden sentences and post-incarceration discrimination; those who experience forms of discrimination and stigmatization that are dehumanizing and that make it impossible to behave as society says they should behave; and those who are told, either in words or deeds, that they do not belong or have a place in the larger society and demo-cratic polity.

Moreover, those who are subject to these harms often experience many or most of them one after another over an extended period of time, such that the violence these harms represent is experienced by those subject to it both regularly and continuously for emotionally and temporally significant portions of their lives. And this experience is made particularly intense by the fact that most of the actions and struc-tures that produce this violence are backed by the use or threatened use of physical violence by the state. This is significant for several reasons. First, people would not consent to most or any of this if it were not backed by the actual or threatened use of violence by the state, tying all the outcomes described in this chapter to state violence. Second, because of the state's size and ability to ruin lives, people often feel particularly vulnerable in relation to state power and authority, making state vio-lence particularly unsettling and traumatic for people. Third, in a de-mocracy, the state represents the power, voice, and sentiments of society as a whole. Thus, when state violence is exercised against an individual, group, or community, and when state institutions regularly and force-fully mistreat and subordinate specific individuals, groups, and com-munities, those against whom this violence, force, and mistreatment are directed are likely to understand this violence and what it says about how others perceive them as coming not just from the state but from society too, making it particularly painful.

It is thus incumbent on those who do not experience the violence of the criminal justice system to try to imagine the psychological, emo-tional, and physical harm that long-term exposure to it would have on them. And to those who after trying to imagine this would still argue that criminals deserve to be treated this way, it is important to note once again that research clearly shows that those groups that bear the brunt of this violence do not do so because of their own behavior but because this country's social, economic, political, and criminal justice systems are so severely biased against them.

It is also important to note that those who are arrested, convicted, and imprisoned are not the only ones who suffer violently at the hands of the US criminal justice system. I have already discussed the extremely harmful individual and neighborhood consequences of police stop and frisk practices. I have also discussed the fact that the vast majority of people who are stopped and frisked and many of those who are arrested due to being stopped and frisked are innocent. Nevertheless, other victims of the US criminal justice system abound, in particular the children, families, and neighbors of those who are arrested, convicted, and imprisoned. It is to these people's experiences that I now turn.

The Effects of Mass Incarceration on Children, Families, and Communities

Approximately 2.7 million US children—one out of every nine Black children and one out of every fifty-seven White children—have a parent in prison or jail at any given time. Indeed, the situation is so bad (and racially biased) that 4 percent of White children and 25 percent of Black children have had at least one parent behind bars by the time they turn fourteen. And among seventeen-year-olds whose parents have not finished high school, 15 percent of Whites and 62 percent of Blacks have had a parent in prison at some point in their lives (Morsy and Rothstein 2016; Travis, Western, and Redburn 2014; Western and Pettit 2010).

The effect of this on children and families is severe. Families with a father in prison have incomes that on average are 22 percent lower than the year before the father was imprisoned and that remain 15 percent lower the year after the father is released from prison than they were prior to his imprisonment.[10] Not surprisingly, these families face difficulties meeting basic needs, are more likely to use public assistance, and tend to experience increased poverty, housing instability, and homelessness. Children of incarcerated fathers also experience significant increases in problematic internalizing behaviors (depression, anxiety, somatic complaints, and so forth) and externalizing behaviors (aggression, delinquency, and so forth), likely due to the emotional difficulties of being separated from their fathers and the instability, hardship, and stigma that accompany this separation (Travis, Western, and Redburn 2014; Wakefield and Wildeman 2013; Western and Pettit 2010).

These harmful consequences, in conjunction with the fact that severe behavioral problems and homelessness in youth are associated with limited economic success in adulthood, lead Sara Wakefield and Christopher Wildeman (2013, 156–57) to argue that stark racial differences in parental incarceration rates play a key role in perpetuating the intergenerational transmission of racial inequality in the United States:

> [Our] results . . . paint a bleak[] picture of the effects of mass imprisonment on the future of inequality in America. Indeed, they suggest that the long-term consequences of mass imprisonment for inequality may be even greater than the contemporaneous effects. . . . We find that mass imprisonment increased [black-white] inequalities in [overall] behavioral problems by between 5 and 10 percent. . . . [More specifically,] black-white disparities in children's internalizing behavioral problems would be between 14 percent and 26 percent smaller absent mass imprisonment . . . [,] black-white gaps in externalizing behavioral problems would be a shocking 24 percent to 46 percent smaller absent mass imprisonment, . . . [and] the black-white gap in child homelessness would [be] between 26 percent and 65 percent smaller had mass imprisonment not taken place.

These are startling findings, particularly when paired with the fact that the outcomes these findings point to are strongly linked to reduced economic success in adulthood. But as Wakefield and Wildeman note, their study likely underestimates the effect of mass incarceration on the intergenerational transmission of racial inequality because the statistical models they employed were designed to provide conservative results and because in addition to the consequences they studied, parental imprisonment harms children in other ways too. Research shows, for example, that even after controlling for relevant factors, children of incarcerated parents are more likely than other children to have speech and language problems and to drop out of school. They also tend to complete fewer years of school than do other children and tend to see their school grades decline after their parent is imprisoned. Compared to children whose parents have never been incarcerated, and controlling for relevant factors, they are 48 percent, 43 percent, 23 percent, and 22 percent more likely, respectively, to experience attention deficit hyperactivity disorder, depression, developmental delays, and learning disabilities, and they are much more likely than other children to experience migraines, asthma, high cholesterol, anxiety (51 percent more likely), and PTSD (72 percent more likely). They are also more likely than other children to be sent to prison (Morsy and Rothstein 2016).

The physical, material, and psychological harm, and thus violence, that children of incarcerated parents experience extends to other family members as well. For instance, spouses, partners, and extended family members often experience financial hardship because of the prisoner's lost income and the legal fees and prison and other expenses they must bear on behalf of the prisoner or the prisoner's dependents. Family members and friends also experience the loss of a loved one, and spouses and partners must adjust to living without their spouse or lover (Braman 2004).

In addition, the loss of a loved one and the difficulties involved in providing for and taking care of children and other family members on one's own often produce anxiety, stress, isolation, and depression among inmates' partners and spouses, which, in turn, can negatively affect children. Spouses, partners, and other family members also often experience the stigma and shame of their loved one's imprisonment very strongly, and because they live in a society that denigrates and mistreats prisoners and criminals, they are often afraid and embarrassed to tell co-workers, neighbors, community members, fellow churchgoers, and others that their loved one is in prison. Feeling as though they have to lie to protect themselves and their loved ones from the harmful opinions of others, they often become isolated and alienated not only from their co-workers, friends, and neighbors, but also from a key aspect of their humanity, how they relate to others, leading them to become self-alienated too (for instance, lying to others may violate their understanding of themselves as honest people) (Braman 2004).

This isolation and alienation and the financial and material demands that mass incarceration places on low-income families, anthropologist

Donald Braman argues, break down the social bonds that hold families, friends, and communities together. They do this in two ways. First, family members have to decide whether to risk social stigma and shame or withdraw from their friends and community. Second, extended family members have to choose between impoverishing themselves (by helping inmates' dependents) and withdrawing their social, economic, and moral support from people they care about and love. These are not appealing or reconcilable choices, particularly for people who are already poor. But as Braman argues, millions of people and families, particularly in low-income Black neighborhoods, are forced to make these choices every day, with many feeling as though they have no option but to withdraw or partially withdraw from some or many of their family and neighborhood relationships, undermining the social ties that bind friends, families, and communities together.

The material deprivation, anxiety, stress, depression, shame, stigma, isolation, alienation from self and others, and weakening of social bonds that inmates' friends, families, and communities experience are clearly forms of violence as I have defined the term: they are harms that are often severe that are caused by social structural factors, intentional policy decisions, and societal neglect (inaction). They must therefore be added to the violent consequences of mass incarceration I have already discussed if a full and proper accounting of mass incarceration is to be made.

And yet, this accounting is still incomplete. The fact that mass incarceration deepens the economic difficulties poor Black families and communities face, weakens the ties that bind poor Black families and communities together, and imprisons so many young Black men also supports dominant racial discourses that hold that a large segment of the Black population will always fail economically, turn to crime, form weak social bonds, and be inferior to Whites because they lack family and community values, are lazy, and have a weak work ethic. These discourses, in turn, are violent because they tell Black people that they are worthless, undeserving, less than fully human, unworthy of dignity and respect, and unable to maintain proper standards of thought, behavior, and responsibility, messages that can cause severe emotional and psychological harm to those against whom they are directed either because (a) the messages are internalized and at some level believed to be true or

(b) those to whom the messages are directed recognize that others think they are inferior and less than fully human. These discourses are also violent because Whites use them to support and justify a range of violent actions, policies, and outcomes, including police violence, the war on crime and drugs, mass incarceration, and racial inequality.

Mass incarceration and the war on crime and drugs thus produce outcomes that support the very stereotypes and discourses used to justify both them and Black oppression. Moreover, violence inheres in every step of the process: the discourses used to justify mass incarceration and the war on crime and drugs are violent (I discuss this in greater detail in chapter 5); mass incarceration and the war on crime and drugs are enforced violently and produce violent outcomes; and these violent outcomes provide false "empirical support" for the violent discourses and the government and individual violence that produce the violent outcomes. State and societal violence against African Americans is thus coherent, unified, and systemic, operating on multiple levels to reinforce Black oppression, White dominance, and, as we shall see in the next section, overall social order.

The fact that mainstream society generally ignores the violent consequences of mass incarceration and the war on crime and drugs also represents a form of violence.[11] One of these ignored consequences is the plight of the millions of US children who have been forcibly separated from one or both of their parents and made to live in difficult or impossible circumstances because of mass incarceration. This issue has received virtually no attention from politicians or the news media despite the fact that in 2018 the news media and the Democratic Party paid extensive attention to the plight of immigrant children separated from their families and placed in detention camps by the Trump administration.

As many Democrats correctly noted at the time, forcibly separating children from their parents and placing them in deplorable living situations simply because their parents illegally migrated to the United States is both monstrous and violent. But it is equally monstrous and violent, I would argue, to forcibly separate children from their parents and place them in difficult or impossible living situations simply to prosecute a politically motivated and racially biased war on crime and drugs (I discuss the political motivations behind this war in the following chapter). Moreover, the fact that the pain and suffering these families experience are ignored and made invisible likely makes the pain and suffering significantly worse than they otherwise would be.

This is likely to be the case for three key reasons. First, making the pain and suffering of specific non-elite groups invisible makes it less likely that other non-elite groups will ally with them to alleviate or eliminate the pain and suffering, increasing the likelihood that the violence causing these harms will continue into the future. Second, sharing one's pain and suffering with others often helps alleviate the pain and suffering. However, when society says that your pain and suffering do not exist, the public cannot and will not share it with you (as it might, for example, if your loved one died in combat). You will also have fewer people to share your pain with if, to protect yourself and your family from ill-treatment, you feel you have to lie about your pain and suffering to those you know.

Third, to be ignored and made invisible is to be silenced. It is to be told that your life, your experiences, and your situation are unimportant, that you lack worth and value, and that your pain and suffering do not matter or are not real and are, perhaps, neither violent nor what you think they are. It is to be told that you cannot be trusted to accurately describe your situation, either because you are a liar or because you are too ignorant to understand your situation, and that you are less important than and not part of the same moral community as those whose lives, experiences, and suffering are recognized and honored by the larger society (Solnit 2017).

Being ignored and made invisible are violent, therefore, not only because they increase the likelihood that violent actions, inactions, and structures that harm millions of people will persist into the future and not simply because they make it more difficult to share one's pain and suffering with others. They are also violent because they separate and alienate their victims from others and tell them that they are worthless, undeserving, less than fully human, and unworthy of dignity and respect, all of which, I previously argued, can cause severe emotional and psychological harm. Being ignored and made invisible can thus significantly worsen the pain and suffering of individuals and groups whose experiences are already violent, particularly when these experiences are central to the individual's or group's identity and subjectivity and when the denial is widespread and relatively complete. This, I argued in the last chapter, is an important and socially consequential aspect of the violence experienced by women and girls who are sexually assaulted and raped, shaping their (and others') subjectivity, identity, and behavior and helping to promote overall social order. It is likewise an important and socially consequential aspect of the violence directed against African Americans in this country.

Another important aspect of this violence is the widespread blame that Black people receive for their extremely high incarceration rates. On the one hand, unfairly blaming African Americans for the harms society does to them is to deny the true nature of their violent experiences and to suggest that these experiences are not real or violent, which, I just argued, is inherently violent. On the other hand, blaming African Americans for harms society does to them is to suggest that they are inferior to groups that do not experience these harms and perhaps less than fully human, which I have also argued are forms of violence.

But mass incarceration, the war on crime and drugs, and police violence are not just extremely violent. They also play an important role in producing overall social order, the topic to which I now turn.

Police Violence, Mass Incarceration, and Social Order

Mass incarceration, the war on crime and drugs, and police violence produce overall social order in several key ways. One way they do this is by creating a large ex-prisoner population, concentrated among specific social groups and neighborhoods, that to survive prison learned a set of norms, values, behaviors, and ways of moving and holding their bodies that are often poorly adapted, and thus dysfunctional, to life outside prison. In addition to making life more difficult for ex-prisoners, these norms, values, behaviors, and bodily dispositions create a subjective, discursive, and corporeal divide between ex-prisoners and those who have not been in prison, making it more difficult for members of these different groups to trust each other, communicate and feel comfortable with each other, and work together to challenge the social order. These difficulties are likely enhanced, moreover, by the fact that many ex-prisoners feel alienated from and have trouble trusting and forming relationships with other people (Jarrett 2018; Haney 2001).

Mass incarceration, the war on crime and drugs, and police violence also promote social order by reinforcing dominant discourses in multiple social arenas. I already noted that they reinforce dominant racial discourses that hold that a large segment of the Black population will always fail economically, turn to crime, form weak social bonds, and be inferior to Whites because they lack family and community values, are lazy, and have a weak work ethic. These discourses also hold that unlike Whites, Black people in general, and poor Blacks in particular, do not value education, are unable to control their emotions, are physically and sexually aggressive, do not plan rationally for the future, are unable to delay gratification, and are better athletes and entertainers than they are thinkers, all of which, these discourses hold, produce Black/White inequality and Black criminality.

These discourses thus associate African Americans in general, and poor Blacks in particular, with the body and Whites with the mind, in this way supporting dominant gender and class discourses that likewise associate subordinate groups with the body and dominant groups with the mind (see the preceding chapters for a detailed discussion of gender and class discourse). In other words, by providing false empirical support for dominant racial discourses, our biased criminal justice system reinforces the associations society makes between the body and subordinate group status on the one hand and the rational mind and dominant group status on the other, thereby reinforcing dominant discourses in multiple social arenas and providing strong support for the overall social order.

Mass incarceration, the war on crime and drugs, and police violence against African Americans also promote consent to the social order among many Whites by providing them with specific material and psychological benefits, related largely to work, schooling, and housing, that they would not otherwise possess. Prisoners, for instance, cannot compete for jobs in the civilian labor market,[12] and ex-prisoners, particularly Black ex-prisoners, are more likely than others to face job discrimination, be unemployed, and work in low-wage occupations. Ex-prisoners also earn significantly less than they otherwise would over the course of their post-incarceration lives, and because of hidden sentences are often unable to compete for loans, contracts, government benefits, and professional licenses, among other things. Ex-prisoners and those regularly subjected to violent police stops and searches also often experience psychological and behavioral issues that likely make it more difficult for them to succeed in school and work. In addition, routine police violence in poor Black neighborhoods restricts the geographic mobility of neighborhood residents and increases the likelihood that they will have criminal records, further limiting their ability to do well in school and compete in the labor market.

The children, partners, and spouses of prisoners and ex-prisoners are also more likely than comparable others to be poor and homeless and to experience psychological and behavioral problems that, along with ex-prisoners' reduced lifetime earnings, can interfere with their schooling and ability to succeed at work, both in the present and the future (including when the children become adults). Prisoners' extended families also often commit significant resources, relative to their means, to prisoners' immediate families, reducing the resources available to them to compete for schooling, housing, and other valued goods. It should thus be clear that prisoners, ex-prisoners, their families, and people routinely subjected to police violence are often poorly positioned to compete with others for housing, jobs, quality schooling, and other valued material goods, both in the present and the near and distant future, giving those who are not directly or indirectly caught up in the criminal justice system benefits they would be less likely to have if more people were competing for them.

Mass incarceration, the war on crime and drugs, and police violence have therefore provided important material advantages to those not caught up in the criminal justice system, advantages that like mass incarceration and police violence are distributed inequitably according to race. The result, of course, is that whether they realize it or not, many Whites benefit both materially and substantially from the violence inflicted on African Americans, making it more likely that they will support the overall social order. And though the benefits Whites receive are not tied solely to the labor market, most of them are, either directly or indirectly (labor market outcomes, for example, are strongly shaped by educational outcomes, which, in turn, are shaped by one's housing options). Thus, among other things, mass incarceration, the war on crime and drugs, and police violence are violent forms of *racial labor control* that benefit Whites by making many Blacks economic, rather than criminal, prisoners.

The economic harm mass incarceration does to poor urban Black neighborhoods, the decreased community cohesion these neighborhoods experience as a result of mass incarceration, and the contempt politicians and mainstream society generally hold for high-crime neighborhoods have also likely decreased the political power of many poor urban Black neighborhoods, benefitting Whites to the degree that this has increased their political power and ability to garner government-distributed benefits.

Whites also benefit from the fact that mass incarceration, the war on crime and drugs, and police violence reinforce dominant racial discourses that hold that Blacks (but not Whites) are violent, criminally inclined, unwilling to work, lazy, impulsive, unable to delay gratification, and so on. On the one hand, these discourses justify racial inequality, which benefits Whites. On the other hand, they make Whites feel better about themselves by telling them that they are superior to Black people and that they and they alone possess positive traits that are valued by society. The fact that reduced competition for jobs, housing, and other material resources increases the chances Whites have to succeed economically and achieve other socially valued goals also helps many Whites feel better about themselves, as does the increase in social status that accompanies successfully meeting society's valued goals. Mass incarceration, the war on crime and drugs, and police violence therefore provide many Whites with psychological, cultural, and material benefits, or wages, that make them feel better about themselves and their position in the social order, thereby increasing their support for, and thus the strength of, the social order.

The mass incarceration of young Black men also helps hide from the general public a significant portion of the racial inequality that exists in this country. Becky Pettit (2012) demonstrates, for instance, that quantitative evidence on inequality in the United States is drawn almost entirely from non-institutionalized populations. She further demonstrates that once you include the prison population in national educational, employment, and wage estimates, Black/White disparities in these areas increase so substantially that much or all of the racial progress in these areas that US government statistics suggest occurred between 1980 and 2008 is lost.

Incarcerating large segments of the poor, poorly educated, and unemployed population and failing to include them in official statistics thus make the social order appear to be more just, moral, and equal than it really is, which, in turn, likely increases overall support for the social order. Increased support for the social order is likely also provided by the fact that the violence, harm, and extreme racial inequity associated with the US criminal justice system are almost entirely hidden from the White population, making the order and Whites' position in the order seem more benign, just, moral, and equal to Whites than they really are.

Finally, the experiences African Americans have with the police are, in general, so much more negative than are the experiences Whites have with the police that African Americans and Whites talk and think about the police very differently from each other, resulting in a shared understanding among African Americans regarding their status in this country and relationship to government authority that differs fundamentally from that held by most Whites. Epp, Maynard-Moody, and Haider-Markel (2014) found, for instance, that among Kansas City drivers, African Americans were much more likely than Whites to believe that police officers discriminate by race, are untrustworthy, do not try hard to be fair, are rude to people like them, do not care about or help people like them, and are out to get people like them. Controlling for a range of factors, Epp, Maynard-Moody, and Haider-Markel also found that although traffic-safety stops have no effect on Black or White drivers' trust in the police, recently experiencing an investigatory stop decreases both groups' trust in the police, with the effect twice as large for Blacks as it is for Whites. Moreover, because White drivers experience very few investigatory stops, the number of stops a driver experiences in her or his lifetime has no effect on White drivers' trust in the police but strongly and negatively affects Black drivers' trust in the police. Thus, in Kansas City, Blacks' and Whites' experiences with police authority are clearly linked to their levels of trust in and sense of status in relation to that authority.

This conclusion is supported by a wide range of additional research that shows that positive experiences with police officers increase citizens' trust in the police (Bradford, Jackson, and Stanko 2009; Skogan 2006) while negative experiences (a) increase people's distrust of both the police and the criminal justice system and (b) decrease the likelihood that people will cooperate with the police, ask the police or other government authorities for assistance, voluntarily interact with other government agencies, and vote (Bradford, Jackson, and Stanko 2009; Gau 2010; Gibson et al. 2010; Hurwitz and Peffley 2005; Lerman and Weaver 2013, 2014; Skogan 2005, 2006; Tyler and Huo 2002; Tyler and Wakslak 2004; Weitzer and Tuch 2006). Negative experiences with the police also have a much bigger effect on levels of trust and distrust in the police (between four and fourteen times bigger) than do positive police encounters (Skogan 2006). It is therefore not at all surprising that African Americans from all demographic groups view the criminal justice system as biased and unfair, while Whites tend to believe the opposite. Moreover, people who believe that the criminal justice system is biased and unfair tend to view the overall political system as less legitimate than do others and to trust it less (Gibson et al. 2010; Hurwitz and Peffley 2005; Skogan 2006; Weitzer and Tuch 2006). Interactions with the police and criminal justice system thus affect one's relationship with, trust in, and sense of status in relation to not just these arms of government, but the US government and political system as a whole.

Of particular interest here is Amy Lerman and Vesla Weaver's (2014) study of how contact with the criminal justice system affects people's sense of citizenship and political efficacy. Relying on qualitative interview data and five publicly available quantitative datasets, Lerman and Weaver found that as contact with the criminal justice system increases from no contact to being stopped by the police to being arrested to being convicted, young people become significantly more likely to believe that government leaders do not care about people like them and significantly less likely to believe that they are full and equal citizens, that all US citizens have an equal chance to succeed, and that they can make a difference by participating in politics.[13] Young people who have experienced more serious criminal justice contacts are also much less likely to trust their federal, state, and local governments, with the percentage of respondents expressing distrust in the US government rising from 18 percent for those with no police contact to 28 percent for those who have been questioned by the police to 55 percent for those who have spent more than one year in prison (levels of distrust in state and local government were slightly lower but otherwise quite similar).

Moreover, the prisoners that Lerman and Weaver (2014, 156) interviewed believed that "government was not merely unresponsive, it was often repressive, . . . designed to control rather than serve." As a result, many of those they interviewed tried hard to avoid not only the police, but all government officials, government agencies, and politicians too. This is not an uncommon response for heavily policed people. Cathy Cohen (2010) notes, for instance, that

> many of the young black Americans who told us their stories through surveys, in-depth interviews, and focus groups have grown up with police cars patrolling their streets to make the community safe from youth like them. . . . These young black people have watched friends and schoolmates get killed routinely, and the visible presence of police and metal detectors has come to define part of their school experience. . . . These young people have seen increasing numbers of family and friends arrested, sent to prisons and jails, and "domestically deported" out of their neighborhoods and their lives. Because of such experiences, these young people have decided that their best survival strategy is to be invisible to state, community, and often family authorities. . . . These young people have chosen a politics of invisibility, disengaging from all forms of politics and trying to remain invisible to officials who possibly could provide assistance but were more likely to impose surveillance and regulations on their lives. (Cohen, quoted in Lerman and Weaver 2014, 208)

The foregoing discussion, when considered along with the rest of the evidence presented in this chapter, sheds important light on how mass incarceration, the war on crime and drugs, and police violence help produce overall social order. First, it is quite clear that these violent practices help create and solidify a distrust of mainstream institutions and a desire to remain invisible among a large segment of the poor, urban Black population that make it significantly less likely that they will want to engage in mainstream political action to change the status quo.[14] Second, it is also quite clear that mass incarceration, the war on crime and drugs, and police violence play a key role in creating and maintaining a violently enforced and racially multi-tiered society that is experienced as such by most Black people but very few White people, helping to form and maintain Black and White racial identities that are quite distinct from each other and making it very difficult for Blacks and Whites to hold a common vision of what the United States really is and should be and what it really means to live in the United States.

Most Whites, for instance, do not think of the United States as a place where they or their loved ones could be stopped, searched, or arrested every time they leave their homes or get in a car, or as a place where the government and police are often or always suspicious of them. And very few Whites live in neighborhoods where the police periodically conduct organized sweeps of the entire neighborhood, where people constantly worry that the police will attack them, or where significant numbers of people are questioned every time they walk into or out of their homes. Nor do Whites live in neighborhoods where the police regularly humiliate many of them, often in a sexualized manner, or where the police are viewed by many as an occupying army there to repress rather than help them.

The United States is therefore a nation in which (a) the shared understanding African Americans have regarding their and Whites' citizenship status and relationship to government authority differs fundamentally from that held by most Whites, (b) Blacks, but not Whites, correctly believe they live in, and routinely experience living in, a violently enforced, racially multi-tiered society, and (c) Blacks' and Whites' visions of what the United States is and should be and what it means to live in the United States differ so fundamentally as to often be unintelligible to each other, as if rather than inhabiting the same country, they live in entirely different worlds. One of the key results of all this is that it is often exceedingly difficult for Blacks and Whites to work together to challenge the social order, both in a practical, day-to-day sense and in terms of formulating coherent and consistent social movement goals.[15]

Put differently, and consistent with the language I used in earlier chapters, racially biased policing and criminal justice play a key role in promoting overall social order by forming widely divergent Black and White subjectivities and identities that greatly impede Blacks' and Whites' ability to work together to challenge elite interests and achieve radically progressive social change.[16] Racially biased policing and criminal justice, by reinforcing dominant racial discourses and treating most

Whites relatively well, also help align White subjectivities and identities with dominant institutional practices and external social and power relations, providing additional support for the overall social order. In addition, people regularly subjected to police and criminal justice violence likely alter the way they hold themselves and move their bodies. To the degree that this is true, their bodily dispositions, which can be thought of as outward manifestations of unequal, unjust, and violent social relations (Bourdieu 2001), likely become highly visible markers of "negative distinction" that divide them from other non-elites, making it even more difficult for non-elites to work together to challenge the social order.

Another, more general, way to think about all this is that the highly disparate services, treatment, and punishment that important social institutions such as the criminal justice, educational, and health care systems provide or mete out to different social groups play a key role in promoting overall social order by treating these groups so differently that each group's fundamental understanding of what its society is and what its society believes cannot be reconciled with the understandings of the other groups. In such a situation, statements and understandings that are perfectly reasonable and rational to the members of one group may seem like fantasy to the members of other groups, making dialogue and collective action difficult or impossible and increasing the likelihood that the actions and statements of each group will offend the subjectivities and identities of members of the other groups, undermining any cohesion they might otherwise attain.[17]

Of course, one key way dominant institutions create such conflicting subjectivities and identities is by treating some social groups well and others poorly. We know, for example, that though the police and criminal justice system do not always treat poor and working-class Whites well, they generally treat them and other Whites much better than they treat most African Americans. The subjectivities and identities of those Whites who are treated well by the police and criminal justice system are thus more likely than they otherwise would be and certainly more likely than the subjectivities and identities of most African Americans to be aligned in a positive and supportive way with the institutional practices of the police and criminal justice system. Those Whites who are treated well by the police and criminal justice system likely also believe (rightly or not) that these institutions serve their material interests by protecting them from criminals. And as I have argued throughout this book, partially meeting non-elites' material interests and aligning their subjectivities and identities with dominant institutional practices and external social and power relations both play key roles in promoting overall social order. It is thus likely that one way dominant institutions such as the criminal justice, educational, and health care systems promote overall social order is by treating some groups well and others poorly and violently, producing support for the overall social order among those groups they treat well and creating irreconcilable differences in subjectivity and identity among those groups they treat in greatly disparate fashion.

I recognize, of course, that the experiences Blacks and Whites have with dominant institutions vary according to their gender and class status and, thus, that the situation is more complicated than I have so far suggested. For instance, the fact that poor, urban Blacks' experiences with the police and criminal justice system are, in general, much worse than those of middle- and upper-class Blacks means that police and criminal justice violence likely unite poor, working-, middle-, and upper-class Blacks in many ways while dividing them in others. Nevertheless, my theoretical point is not only still valid, it is actually strengthened when this complexity is accounted for since it means that society has even more groups with vastly different experiences, subjectivities, identities, and conceptions of the social world that have to be reconciled if they are to work together to challenge the social order. Moreover, this task is made even more difficult by the fact that society has multiple dominant institutions, each of which treats different racial groups differently, each of which treats racial subgroups defined by different class, gender, and age combinations differently, and none of which treat any of these groups or subgroups in exactly the same way as do the other institutions.[18]

Conclusion

The evidence presented in this chapter demonstrates that we live in a country that uses extremely high levels of state-sanctioned violence to enforce Black oppression and White advantage. Though directed in particular at poor, young Black men, this violence affects all Black people in this country, who live under its constant threat. Indeed, this violence is so routinized, occurs so regularly, and plays such an important role in maintaining racial inequality, and it is based in a judicial regime that allows for such great police intrusion into citizens' lives, that it is difficult to escape the conclusion that we live in a police state, one designed to breed fear and submission not just to state authority but to White privilege too. That we live in a police state, defined as a state that rules through the exercise of police power, is a sobering conclusion. But it is one reached by many authors who have written about police violence, including not just radicals (A. Davis 2014; Kitossa 2020; Williams 2007) but as recounted earlier, also Supreme Court Justices Sonia Sotomayor (*Utah v. Strieff*, 2016) and William Douglas (*Terry v. Ohio*, 1968).

Living in a police state implies that state violence is regularly used and threatened to promote overall social order. This, of course, is consistent with my general theoretical argument. But the evidence presented in this chapter does much more theoretical work than this. In addition to providing support for several of my less central theoretical claims, such as my claim that violence promotes overall social order by making the social order seem more benign, just, equal, and moral than it really is, the evidence presented in this chapter also supports five of the six propositions that form the heart of my theoretical argument.

Specifically, the evidence demonstrates that police violence and criminal justice violence play a key role in producing overall social order in the United States by (a) creating divisions between subordinate groups that make it difficult for these groups to organize collectively to challenge the social order, (b) reinforcing dominant discourses in multiple social arenas, (c) meeting the psychological, cultural, and material interests of specific subordinate groups, (d) aligning the subjectivity and identity of many Whites with dominant institutional practices and external social and power relations, and (e) helping shape and produce subjectivity, identity, interests, and consent. Moreover, my argument that violence produces these five order-producing outcomes was also strongly supported by the evidence presented in chapters 2 and 3 on sexual violence against women, in ways that were sometimes identical to but were often very different from the ways in which the argument was supported in this chapter. Thus, my theory of violence and social order is strongly supported by evidence drawn from two very different arenas of social life, demonstrating the general utility of the theory and helping us to better understand the relationship between violence in these two arenas and social order throughout society.

As was also true in chapters 2 and 3, the violence described in this chapter forms a coherent, unified, and self-reinforcing system of order- and oppression-producing violence. Indeed, violence inheres in each of the major stages of the criminal justice process highlighted in this chapter: the discourses used to justify mass incarceration and the war on crime and drugs are violent; mass incarceration and the war on crime and drugs are enforced violently and produce violent outcomes; and these violent outcomes provide false "empirical support" for the violent discourses and government and individual violence that produce the violent outcomes. Moreover, as is the case with rape in relation to other forms of sexual violence, it is likely that police killings of Black people play an important role in enforcing Black submission to other forms of police authority and violence by providing a threat of more extreme and, in this case, lethal violence that is an ever-present possibility in all encounters that Black people have with the police. The threat of death likewise hangs over every woman who is raped, making lethal violence a key component of both racial *and* gender oppression and overall social order.

But though mass incarceration, the war on crime and drugs, police and criminal justice violence, and the discourses and ideology that un- derpin them represent a coherent, unified, and self-reinforcing system of institutional violence, they do not exist in isolation from society's other dominant institutions. Instead, these violent phenomena combine with racial violence in other institutional arenas to form a larger, but still co- herent and tightly knit, system of racial violence that operates in mul- tiple institutional arenas and social fields to produce racial oppression, White dominance, and overall social order. The different arenas, fields, and institutions making up this violent system form a coherent whole, I argue, because they reinforce each other in multiple ways: they draw upon, support, and justify the same sets of discourses and ideologies; create multiple racial divisions, often in similar ways; produce similar identities, subjectivities, and interests; and produce policies and other outcomes that form the basis for action, behavior, and thought in the other institutions, arenas, and fields.

One of the most important of the institutional arenas making up this system of racial violence is the political arena, in which policies such as the war on crime and drugs and mass incarceration are created and debated and in which racial and other violent discourses are employed in highly public and symbolic ways to win elections, reinforce important social divisions, and get favored policies passed. Other key institutional arenas include the educational, welfare, health care, and housing systems. But rather than discussing all of these violent institutions, I will turn my attention in the following chapter to the role that Democratic and Republican politicians and national electoral politics have played in (a) producing mass incarceration, the war on crime and drugs, and the policing policies described in this chapter and (b) selling them to the White public. In focusing attention on the political system, I hope to demonstrate that racial violence occurring in multiple institutional arenas can, as I just argued, form a single system of order- and inequality-producing violence. This is an important task because it is exceedingly difficult to argue that an overarching system of violence that operates in multiple institutional arenas is simply a mistake or the product of a few bad apples and not a fundamental feature of the social order.

It is to an examination of the political system that I now turn.

5

Political Violence against Black People

Well boys, no other son-of-a-bitch will ever out-nigger me again.
—George Wallace, 1958[1]

I can be nicked on a lot. But no one can say I'm soft on crime.
—Bill Clinton, 1992[2]

Over the past fifty years, two persistent political myths have held that the Democratic Party is soft on crime and the Republican Party is not and that Republicans often use racist appeals to garner votes, but Democrats do not. But though these myths accurately describe the Republican Party, the fact of the matter is that the Democratic Party has never been overly soft on crime and, like the Republican Party, has been quite willing to use racist appeals to win elections. In other words, despite cross-party differences in rhetoric and policy, the Democratic and Republican Parties are not so different from each other on the issues of crime and race as they or their supporters would like to believe, and often their policies and rhetoric are strikingly similar.

A brief discussion of the George Wallace and Bill Clinton quotes that start this chapter will help illustrate this point. George Wallace was a blatantly racist Alabama governor and US presidential candidate who after losing his first gubernatorial election in 1958 dedicated his career to defending White supremacy, championing the southern way of life, and making sure he would never be "out-n'ed" again (see the first endnote of this chapter for an explanation of the term "n'ed"). However, prior to his unsuccessful run for governor in 1958, Wallace was an economic liberal and relatively moderate on race, at least in comparison to other southern politicians, receiving the endorsement of the NAACP and losing the 1958 election "because he was considered soft on the race question at the time" (Haney López 2014, 14).

Wallace would not make this "mistake" again, winning Alabama's governorship in 1962 and gaining the support of many northern Whites by couching his newly racist politics in coded language that highlighted issues such as crime, law and order, states' rights, and local control of schools that White voters instinctively knew meant protecting them from African Americans and civil rights activists (Carter 1996; Haney López 2014).

Bill Clinton made the remark cited at the beginning of the chapter during his successful 1992 presidential campaign. Like Wallace after 1958, Clinton was pandering to White voters in response to lessons learned from earlier political failures, both his own and those of the Democratic Party. Clinton's failure was to lose the Arkansas governorship in 1981 because he had, as governor, "commuted nearly seventy [prison] sentences . . . including the life sentences of thirty-eight first-degree murderers . . . [one of whom] killed again during a robbery attempt within a year of his release" (O'Reilly 1995, 412). The Democratic Party's political failure resulted from the fact that many White voters thought that the party was soft on crime, morality, and race, leading the party to lose virtually every presidential election from 1968 to 1988 (Scammon and Wattenberg 1970; S. Greenberg 1985; Edsall and Edsall 1991a). This string of losses included Michael Dukakis's spectacular loss to George H. W. Bush, whose campaign used a pair of blatantly racist political advertisements to convince many White voters to switch their support from Dukakis to Bush. The ads, which portrayed Dukakis as unable to protect White voters from violent Black criminals, was credited as the key reason Dukakis lost the 1988 election (O'Reilly 1995).

In response to these failures, Clinton apparently decided that he could never allow White voters to view him as being soft on crime or Blacks again. Thus, upon becoming governor for a second time in 1983, he stopped commuting death sentences and "began setting execution dates" instead (O'Reilly 1995, 412). And to make sure that White voters knew where he stood during the 1992 presidential campaign, he had his photograph taken in front of a large group of mostly Black convicts at the Stone Mountain Correctional Facility in Georgia. He also refused to stop Arkansas's execution of Rickey Ray Rector, a mentally incompetent Black man convicted of killing a White police officer; and after attending Rector's execution, he made the comment cited at the beginning of the chapter that no one could say he was soft on crime. This set of more and less coded actions and words, and the anti-Black crime legislation Clinton later passed as president, told White voters that Clinton would protect them from African Americans and reinforced the linkage many White voters made between African Americans and violent crime.

It is quite clear, then, that though George Wallace was a blatantly racist segregationist and Bill Clinton was not, they both used coded racist appeals to win White votes. It is also clear that they did so not because of their racial beliefs, which did not drastically change from one election to the next, but because it became clear to them that they could not win or were unlikely to win elections without doing so. Their coded rhetoric and the racially biased and violent policies they each adopted to convince White voters of their racial bona fides were thus highly strategic. Their rhetoric and policies also greatly harmed Black people.

In certain key respects, then, it is difficult to argue that Wallace was worse than Clinton. They both relied on racist rhetoric, voter racism, racially biased policies, and state violence against African Americans to win elections. One of them used the n-word and supported the Ku Klux Klan, and the other did not. But they were both willing to harm Black people to win elections and protect Whites' perceived interests. And in some sense Clinton, like Wallace, was also saying that he would never be "out-n'ed" again. Moreover, this willingness to harm Black people to win elections was not confined to Clinton and Wallace. It was a key characteristic of both the Republican *and* Democratic Parties throughout the 1970s, 1980s, and 1990s, the period when the war on crime and drugs and police violence against African Americans increased and intensified so dramatically (see the preceding chapter).

To demonstrate that this is so, this chapter examines the race and crime rhetoric employed by US presidents, presidential candidates, politicians, and political analysts from the Truman administration in the late 1940s to the Clinton administration in the late 1990s. This history will show that throughout this period both parties employed racist rhetoric that linked African Americans to crime. It will also show that the two parties' racist anti-crime policies and rhetoric became increasingly similar over time and nearly identical in the 1980s and 1990s, with each party drawing on ideas originally formulated by the other party and with the two parties co-producing a single underlying racist crime discourse that directly and indirectly reinforced this country's dominant race, gender, and class discourses. Finally, the history will show that the reason the two parties adopted harsh anti-crime and anti-Black policies and rhetoric was that neither party believed it could win elections without doing so.

After presenting this history, I will argue that it provides strong support for my theoretical argument. To show that this is true, I will first demonstrate that the two parties' racially biased anti-crime rhetoric and policies were extremely violent. I will then demonstrate that these violent policies and rhetoric produced overall social order in five of the key ways that I argue they do. Finally, I will use the evidence presented in this chapter to demonstrate that the US political system is inherently violent, that people imprisoned because of the war on crime and drugs are really economic and political prisoners, and that White voters and politicians in both the Democratic and Republican Parties are responsible for the violent consequences of mass incarceration because so many of them supported and so few of them denounced the rhetoric and policies that made mass incarceration possible. Because the two parties' anti-crime rhetoric has helped keep racism alive in this country and because both parties have regularly relied on White voters' racism to win presidential and other elections, I also conclude that White Democrats and Republicans both bear responsibility for Donald Trump's 2016 presidential victory.

I turn now to an examination of the race and crime rhetoric employed by Democrats and Republicans from the late 1940s to the late 1990s. In tracing out the historical trajectory of this rhetoric, I pay attention to the anti-crime policies pursued by some of the presidential administrations I discuss. However, my analysis focuses more closely on political rhetoric than policy, highlighting how the two parties' rhetoric became more similar over time and how the rhetoric both parties employed justified racist anti-crime policies that for decades have severely harmed Black people and communities. It is true, as others have argued, that the war on crime and drugs and local policing practices have not been shaped solely by national-level political factors. Nevertheless, the anti-crime rhetoric and policy that Democrats and Republicans at the federal level have espoused and enacted have played a key role in legitimizing harsh anti-Black policing policies throughout the country. They have also helped keep the racism that lies behind these policies and behind mass incarceration and the war on crime and drugs alive and well, and have provided local and state politicians and the White public with many of the arguments they use to understand racial inequality, crime, and their position and status in the social order. As a result, they have played a key role in promoting overall social order in the United States.

Finally, some scholars argue that the war on crime and drugs and mass incarceration were developed primarily to enforce class rather than race oppression (see, for instance, Clegg and Usmani 2019). Though I agree that these policies have disproportionately harmed poor and working-class people, analyses such as Clegg and Usmani's do not convincingly demonstrate that the main goal of these policies was to harm the working-class and poor rather than Blacks and Latinos. Moreover, for decades these policies were sold to the White public using highly racist anti-Black rhetoric. These policies and this rhetoric have also always been extremely violent, and they have harmed poor and working-class African Americans more than any other group in the country and middle-class African Americans more than middle-class Whites. Thus, even if these policies were designed primarily to enforce class inequality (which I deny was the case), that would have no bearing on my argument, which is that these policies produced overall social order in the United States through their use of highly racist anti-crime rhetoric, the role they played in US elections, and the extremely harmful effects they have had on African Americans.

Law and Order in Post–World War II America

One of the key things to note about the development of race and crime rhetoric in US politics in the post–World War II era is that each political party's use of this rhetoric developed in reaction to the other party's use of it and each drew on a common racist discourse available to all US citizens. Thus, even when Democratic and Republican race and crime rhetorics differed in significant ways, they still held important similarities, and when the two parties' rhetorics became increasingly similar in the late 1960s and 1970s and virtually identical in the late 1980s and early 1990s, the emerging rhetorical consensus relied on ideas developed by each of the parties and their supporting intellectuals.

Naomi Murakawa (2014) traces the origins of this rhetoric back to the Truman administration's Committee on Civil Rights, which was created in 1946. This liberal-Democratic committee released its landmark civil rights report, *To Secure These Rights*, the following year. To convince readers of the importance of addressing racial inequality and civil rights, the report's authors turned to social science research that held that when minority groups are treated in highly discriminatory ways and when inequality and civil rights are left unaddressed, these groups will become violent and dangerous. The report notes, for example, that

> the cost of prejudice cannot be computed in terms of markets, produc-
> tion, and expenditures. Perhaps the most expensive results are the least
> tangible ones. . . . People who live in a state of tension and suspicion can-
> not use their energy constructively. The frustrations of their restricted
> existence are translated into aggression against the dominant group. [Es-
> teemed economist and sociologist Gunnar] Myrdal says:
>
> > Not only occasional acts of violence, but most laziness, careless-
> > ness, unreliability, petty stealing and lying are undoubtedly to be
> > explained as concealed aggression. . . . The truth is that Negroes
> > generally do not feel they have unqualified moral obligations to
> > white people. (President's Committee on Civil Rights 1947, 145–46)

Myrdal drew his arguments about Black laziness, carelessness, un-reliability, stealing, lying, violence, and concealed aggression from two sources, the novelist Richard Wright and the sociologist John Dollard (Murakawa 2014). These authors, along with Myrdal, argued that White prejudice produces in Blacks an aggression, rage, and intense anger and hatred of Whites that are normally internalized because the penalties for harming Whites are so severe. But this anger, hatred, and rage, if left unaddressed, can potentially explode, they argued, and be directed at Whites. Thus, the main character in Wright's novel *Native Son* is a Black man named Bigger Thomas whose fear of and rage at Whites leads him to kill two women, one White and one Black. And in Dollard's work, the potential that Blacks purportedly have for directing their rage and anger at Whites is viewed as being especially pronounced among the children of poor single mothers, who are supposedly unable to teach their children to control their impulses, making them especially dangerous to Whites.

Myrdal, Wright, Dollard, and the authors of the civil rights report therefore saw Black rage and aggression as a psychological effect of White prejudice (itself viewed as a purely psychological attribute) and Black family structure that took on a causal force of its own, one to be reckoned with and feared. Moreover, the authors of the report clearly linked this threat to the need to extend civil rights to Black people.

Thus, despite the fact that they wanted to protect Black people's civil rights, these authors still drew on, and presumably held, a set of beliefs that viewed Black people as lazy, impulsive, criminally inclined, aggressive, violent, and rage-filled, representing a physical, sexual, and mortal threat to Whites. These characterizations of African Americans fit well within the boundaries of this nation's dominant racist discourses, which held then, and still hold today, that African Americans are of the body and not the mind and are therefore irrational, emotional, undisciplined, physically and sexually aggressive, lazy, lacking impulse control, unable to plan for the future, lacking in proper values, criminally inclined, and dangerous. Moreover, it is difficult to believe that the authors of this report had not read the rest of the two-page section from which they drew their Myrdal quote, in which Myrdal states that middle-class Blacks also possess internalized rage, that you can walk through any urban Black neighborhood and see many real-life Bigger Thomases, or murderers of White women, walking around, and that there are Black men living in urban America ready to pick up machine guns to destroy the social order (Myrdal 1944, 763–64).

Important to keep in mind here is that this was the liberal-Democratic view of African Americans and their relationship to crime, held by a committee that wanted to protect African Americans' civil rights and that believed in government-supported racial equality. It was also the view of African Americans and crime held by the liberal-Democratic Kennedy and Johnson administrations and to a significant degree, as we shall see later, by the Clinton administration.

The Kennedy administration devoted significant attention to addressing both civil rights and Black juvenile delinquency. The administration's interest in civil rights arose in part from the pressure put on it by the civil rights movement and in part from the administration's desire to help African Americans. But it also resulted from the administration's belief that White racism and discrimination had produced a set of

Black pathologies deeply rooted in Black culture, Black family life, and Black behavior that had taken on a life and causal force of their own. These purported pathologies included frustration, resentment, poor discipline, lack of concern about education and skills development, alcoholism, drug abuse, alienation, crime, and a predisposition to social unrest. The White House further believed that if these pathologies and the inequalities underlying them remained unaddressed, they would get worse over time, leading to increased crime and, potentially, to unrest, anger, and aggression directed toward Whites and the social order. This, of course, provided the White House with additional justification for civil rights, but it also linked civil rights to Black pathology and crime (Hinton 2016).

The racist beliefs, civil rights movement pressure, and desire to help African Americans that informed the Kennedy administration's civil rights policies also shaped its approach to juvenile delinquency. This led it, on the one hand, to emphasize education and vocational training rather than punishment, but also led it to emphasize teaching African American youth behavioral and cultural traits they supposedly lacked rather than face the difficult task of promoting structural economic changes that might actually have improved Black youth's economic prospects. The administration's approach to juvenile delinquency thus highlighted what it saw as deficiencies in Black culture and behavior rather than structural deficiencies in the broader economy.

Concern about the dangers that Black youth supposedly posed to society and a belief that African Americans needed to be monitored to produce cultural and behavioral changes conducive to social order also meant that the Kennedy administration's delinquency programs gave social service personnel a "soft" surveillance role and the police a minor social service role in Black communities. And this, in turn, weakened the boundaries that existed between the social services and policing and linked welfare, the police, and African Americans closely together in the public mind.

The foregoing discussion raises two important points: first, that the Kennedy administration's understanding of African Americans and crime drew on and supported racist discourses in ways that were nearly identical to the Truman administration's understanding of African Americans and crime; and second, that the Kennedy administration tied

African Americans, crime, civil rights, violence, welfare, policing, and cultural, psychological, and behavioral pathology into a tight discursive package that shaped both the administration's internal deliberations and the messages it conveyed to the American public (Hinton 2016).

This discursive package received its fullest expression in a report that assistant secretary of labor Daniel Patrick Moynihan prepared for the Johnson administration in 1965. In this report and subsequent papers and talks, Moynihan made essentially the same argument that other liberal scholars and government officials had been making since the 1930s. However, Moynihan more clearly and forcefully argued that a breakdown in Black family structure and the large number of female-headed Black households that resulted from this were the primary causes of Black crime, poverty, delinquency, and welfare dependency. He also used welfare dependency as his primary indicator of Black "pathology," thereby closely linking African Americans to welfare dependency (A. O'Connor 2001). Finally, borrowing from social psychologist Kenneth Clark, he replaced the phrase "Black pathology" with the phrase "tangle of pathology," which sounds much more entrenched and difficult to solve, or untangle, than "Black pathology." He thus wrote,

> There is no one solution [to the Negro Problem]. Nonetheless, at the center of the tangle of pathology is the weakness of family structure. . . . [It is] the principal source of most of the aberrant, inadequate, or anti-social behavior *that did not establish, but now serves to perpetuate* the cycle of poverty and deprivation. . . . At this point, the present tangle of pathology is capable of perpetuating itself without assistance from the white world. (Moynihan 1965a, 30, 47, emphasis added)

And in an article he wrote six month later, he argued,

> From the wild Irish slums of the 19th-century . . . to the riot-torn suburbs of Los Angeles, there is one unmistakable lesson in American history: a community that allows a large number of young men to grow up in broken families, dominated by women, never acquiring any stable relationship to male authority, never acquiring any set of rational expectations about the future—that community asks for and gets chaos. Crime, violence, unrest, disorder—most particularly the furious, unrestrained

lashing out at the whole social structure—that is not only to be expected; it is very near inevitable. (Moynihan 1965b, 283)

It is thus clear that for Moynihan, neither single Black mothers nor absent Black fathers could provide their sons with the values and behavioral standards they needed to act as responsible, rational adults able to control their emotions and adhere to the discipline, persistence, and hard work necessary to maintain regular employment. The result, he clearly argued, was that most young Black men were angry, violent, and criminally inclined, ready to engage in violent unrest and disorder and to tear down the social order. Furthermore, the language he used in his various writings strongly associated Black people with concepts such as disorder, chaos, crumbling, disintegrating, aberrant, disturbed, antisocial, unstable, desperate, and deteriorating. Moynihan thus associated African Americans with the body, emotion, lack of restraint, and chaos rather than with the mind, rationality, discipline, and civilization.

Moreover, though Moynihan argued that centuries of racism and discrimination produced the Black family structure and tangle of pathology he wrote about, it is clear that he believed that this structure and pathology were now the heart of the problem. For Moynihan, then, racial inequality and crime resulted primarily from Black values and Black culture rather than from White prejudice and discrimination or a larger social structure that benefitted Whites and harmed Blacks.

Moynihan's arguments would not have mattered as much as they did if they had not found a receptive audience in the White House. But President Johnson was so enamored with Moynihan's report that Johnson had Moynihan co-author the commencement speech he gave at Howard University in June 1965. In that speech to the all-Black graduating class, Johnson argued that he was fighting racial inequality through his educational, health care, anti-poverty, and other Great Society programs. He further argued that to achieve racial equality, Blacks must receive not only the same opportunities and civil rights as Whites but extra help from the government as well. But Johnson then shifted gears and argued that though no single causal factor, all by itself, produces racial inequality and poverty, Black family breakdown was by far the most important causal factor, doing more than anything else to produce despair and deprivation in Black communities (Johnson 1965).

Johnson's speech did not describe Black family breakdown in the kinds of bleak and blatantly racist terms as did Moynihan's report, and Johnson blamed Whites for this breakdown more forcefully than did Moynihan. Johnson also supported Black civil rights and wanted to alleviate poverty for all poor Americans. Nevertheless, it is clear that the Johnson administration, like the Truman and Kennedy administrations before it, accepted the racist beliefs that lay behind the Black pathology thesis.

These racist beliefs, along with Johnson's progressive civil rights and anti-poverty values, helped inform Johnson's civil rights, crime, and anti-poverty policies and rhetoric. But Johnson's policies and rhetoric were also shaped by the more than two hundred urban riots that occurred while he was president. In response to these riots, Johnson called repeatedly and forcefully for *law and order*, arguing that neither White southerners who attacked African Americans nor Black urban rioters had the right to break the law. Indeed, in at least one speech he equated Black urban rioters, who were protesting exploitation, oppression, biased policing, and police brutality, with the Ku Klux Klan, calling both groups lawbreakers (Hinton 2016; Kirker 1964; *Los Angeles Times* 1964).

The White House, along with the liberal and conservative news media, also used the arguments laid out in Moynihan's report to help explain to the public the riots that broke out in Watts and Chicago in August 1965 (A. O'Connor 2001), helping to popularize a discourse that tied female-headed Black families to crime, delinquency, urban unrest, and violence against White people and White authority. Discussing the Watts riot, the liberal *New York Times* (1965) noted, for instance, that

> about a quarter of the Negro women of such slum areas who have been married are divorced or separated, and nearly one out of every four Negro babies born is illegitimate—the result of a breakdown of family life that . . . [along with] an unemployment rate double that for whites creates *self-perpetuating* poverty *and with it* delinquency and crime. (emphasis added)

Not to be outdone, the conservative *Wall Street Journal* (1965) published an article the next day titled "Behind the Riots: Family Life Breakdown in Negro Slums Sows the Seeds of Race Violence—Husbandless Homes Spawn Young Hoodlums." In it, the *Journal* stated,

Behind the past week's orgy of Negro rioting in Los Angeles and Chicago lies a sickness that all the new civil rights legislation is powerless to cure in the foreseeable future, the spreading disintegration of Negro family life in the big cities of the North and West.

It is thus clear that in the days following the Watts and Chicago riots, both the *New York Times* and the *Wall Street Journal* employed the same underlying racist argument to explain Black crime and Black urban unrest (other liberal and conservative news outlets used this argument too). This racist argument was developed by liberals, not conservatives, and along with other important factors shaped the various approaches that three Democratic presidents—Truman, Kennedy, and Johnson—took to addressing civil rights and crime.

In the case of the Johnson administration, which had to reconcile its progressive values and racist beliefs not just with each other but also with the values and beliefs of its White constituents and stiff pressure from conservatives, this produced somewhat contradictory anti-crime policies. On the one hand, the White House argued that Johnson's War on Poverty was both a social justice and a crime prevention program, fighting crime by addressing the root causes of it. On the other hand, because the War on Poverty would not reduce crime quickly, the White House also argued that it had to immediately strengthen the police and criminal justice system so as to punish lawbreakers and promote law and order in the short term.

Moreover, as the riots and growing dissatisfaction with the War on Poverty led urban politicians in the North to call for more law and order, as conservative attacks on the War on Poverty and Johnson's root-causes argument increased, as the Vietnam War took up ever more of Johnson's time and the nation's money, and as Johnson's concerns about law and order at home increased, his administration began emphasizing law and order more and more and the War on Poverty less and less (Hinton 2016; Murakawa 2014). This led Johnson, in his 1967 State of the Union address, to declare as one of his key objectives

an all-out effort to combat crime. . . . Our country's laws must be respected. Order must be maintained. And I will support—with all the constitutional powers the President possesses—our Nation's law enforcement officials in their attempt to control the crime and the violence that tear the fabric of our communities. . . . And so I will recommend to the 90th Congress the Safe Streets and Crime Control Act of 1967. (Johnson 1967)

As proposed, Johnson's Safe Streets Act contained many progressive elements. It also drew on the liberal goal, dating back to at least the Truman administration, of professionalizing and modernizing policing and criminal justice by recruiting better-educated personnel, improving training, making criminal sentencing more uniform, and eliminating individual discretion and procedural unfairness throughout the criminal justice system. At the same time, however, the White House wanted to provide local and state police forces with more money and better weapons and to insert police officers into various local government agencies. It also wanted to strengthen Black families, schools, and churches, which were seen as a source of crime and urban unrest because they failed to teach young African Americans proper values; and it wanted to maintain a strong and highly visible police presence in high-crime areas, in part by providing federal funding for tactical police forces in these areas (Hinton 2016; Johnson 1967; Murakawa 2014; President's Commission on Law Enforcement and Administration of Justice 1967).

This approach to crime was problematic for several reasons. First, it relied in part on the racist family-breakdown argument. Second, it assumed that crime was largely a Black problem, thereby tying Blacks to crime and criminalizing them. Third, it assumed that racial bias in policing results from the racist beliefs of individual police officers and that professionalization and modernization are necessarily progressive forces that will increase efficiency and eliminate racial bias. However, highly modernized and professional police forces can be extremely discriminatory and violent regardless of the racial beliefs of specific officers, while procedural and sentencing uniformity can produce highly biased outcomes if other aspects of policing and criminal justice remain racially biased (M. Alexander 2010).

Finally, Johnson's proposed act was problematic because Republicans and southern Democrats were able to take advantage of the ambiguities inherent in professionalization and modernization to pass a much more conservative and punitive bill than that proposed by Johnson, a bill that was more consistent with their views on race and crime than with Johnson's. But this begs the question: how exactly did conservative Republicans and southern Democrats think about race and crime and how did this differ from the liberal-Democratic view of race and crime? It is to this question that I now turn.

The Conservative Approach to Race and Crime: 1950–1964

In the 1950s and 1960s, southern Democrats and conservative Republicans, like liberal Democrats, linked African Americans with crime and African American crime with civil rights. But unlike liberal Democrats, they argued that civil rights activism represented a breakdown of law and order that caused further African American unrest and crime. Specifically, they argued that civil rights activists were criminals because they selectively chose which laws to follow and which laws to disregard. Liberal acquiescence to activist demands thus taught both activists and African Americans that criminal activity of all sorts—including, as conservatives saw it, violent crime, street crime, civil rights demonstrations, *and* urban unrest—was acceptable. This was particularly dangerous, they believed, because African Americans were (according to them) already impulsive, violent, and criminally inclined and because the integration that would result from civil rights gains would bring violent, criminally inclined African Americans into contact with innocent Whites, resulting in increased Black crime and increased physical and sexual violence against White men and women.

Racially conservative politicians argued that African American crime was also on the rise because liberals were more concerned with the disadvantages Blacks faced than with the harms African American criminals and rioters inflicted on Whites. This concern, they argued, led liberal politicians and courts to reward Black rioters, coddle Black criminals, hamper law enforcement, and harm Whites. They further argued that federal civil rights legislation and court rulings were illegal because they violated the rights of states to make and enforce their own laws and the rights of property owners to do as they wished with and on their properties, making demands for civil rights equivalent to demands to violate the law and constitution. The solution, therefore, was to vote liberals out of office, prevent and reverse civil rights gains, and give criminal justice personnel the power and tools they needed to punish lawbreakers and restore law and order.

Racially conservative politicians' views of the relationship between race, crime, and civil rights clearly differed from the views held by liberal Democrats, leading the former to emphasize much more punitive crime policies than did the latter and the latter to call for a balanced approach that relied on social services, welfare, and law and order. Yet, despite their obvious differences, liberal and conservative arguments regarding race, crime, and civil rights shared some key similarities. For instance, liberals and conservatives both associated African Americans and civil rights (either its presence or absence) with crime and violence; they both argued that African Americans are in some way deficient; and because of African Americans' purported deficiencies, neither believed that civil rights and equal opportunities would be sufficient, on their own, to overcome African American poverty, welfare dependency, violence, and crime. In addition, they both believed that African Americans are impulsive, violent, dangerous, and criminally inclined and that to improve Blacks' behavior and ensure the safety of Whites, Blacks must be monitored and controlled by the state.

Indeed, one might argue that the biggest difference between the liberal and conservative positions on race, crime, and civil rights in the 1950s and 1960s is that though they were both racist, conservatives were more honest about their racism than were liberals, both to themselves and to the general public.

This presented a problem for both parties, particularly during presidential elections. On the one hand, as the national Democratic Party became more closely associated with civil rights after 1962, it began to lose support among many Whites, especially in the South, even as it continued to rely in its crime policies on more "subtly" racist arguments that these Whites and many other Democrats likely agreed with. On the other hand, though many Whites were sympathetic to conservative racial arguments, Whites outside the South were both hesitant to support and often disgusted by racial conservatives' blatant racism and vitriolic anger against civil rights, which harmed the presidential aspirations of racially conservative politicians, whether they were from the Republican or Democratic Party (M. Alexander 2010; Haney López 2014).

The Republican Party and the racially conservative southern Democrat George Wallace were the first to figure out how to finesse this dilemma (the dilemma of how to be racist without being too openly or opaquely racist), though their initial steps in this direction did not win either of them the presidency. In short, what the Republican Party and George Wallace learned to do was to use coded racial language that allowed them to appeal to White racial resentments without sounding racist, thereby gaining the support of openly racist White voters and stealing less openly racist White voters away from liberal Democrats. But before I discuss how they did this, it is important to describe the political coalition that supported the Democratic Party from the Great Depression to the 1960s.

Prior to the Great Depression, the South was solidly Democratic and the North solidly Republican. However, in the 1930s, President Franklin Roosevelt's New Deal policies shattered this alignment, giving the Democratic Party solid support among poor and working-class Whites and Blacks in both the North and the South (though Blacks in the South could not vote). This alliance was always somewhat uneasy, with northern Democrats more liberal than southern Democrats and more inclined to support civil rights. But it was not until the early 1960s, when it became clear that the Democratic Party leadership strongly supported civil rights, that these divisions first began to threaten the coalition.

The first racial conservative to realize that he could exploit this situation and steal White votes away from liberal Democrats was George Wallace. Wallace started his political career, as I noted earlier, as an economic liberal and a relative moderate on race, at least in comparison to other southern politicians. But after losing Alabama's 1958 gubernatorial election, he moved far to the right on racial matters, winning the 1962 gubernatorial election by wooing the Ku Klux Klan and vowing to defend segregation. Indeed, he moved so far to the right that he received national condemnation for his 1963 inauguration speech, in which he declared,

> It is very appropriate . . . that from this Cradle of the Confederacy . . . we
> sound the drum for freedom as have our generations of forebears before
> us done, time and time again through history. Let us rise to the call of
> freedom . . . and send our answer to the [northern] tyranny that clanks its

chains upon the South. In the name of the greatest people that have ever trod this earth, I draw the line in the dust and . . . say, segregation today, segregation tomorrow, segregation forever. (Wallace 1963)

A half year later, Wallace stood at the entrance of the University of Alabama, facing down US deputy attorney general Nicholas Katzenbach, who was there to enforce a federal court order to integrate the university. But this time, rather than recalling the Confederacy, trumpeting White supremacy, and employing inflammatory rhetoric, Wallace focused his remarks on what he calmly described as the illegal actions of and usurpation of state power by the federal government. The nation's reaction was quite different this time, as Ian Haney López (2014, 16–17) recounts:

> More than 100,000 telegrams and letters flooded [Wallace's] office. . . . More than half of them from outside the South. Did they condemn him? Five out of every 100 did. The other 95 percent praised his brave stand in the schoolhouse doorway.
>
> The nation's reaction was an epiphany for Wallace. . . . First, Wallace realized . . . that hostility toward blacks was not confined to the South. . . . [Second, he realized] how to exploit that pervasive animosity. The key lay in seemingly non-racial language. At his inauguration, Wallace had defended segregation and extolled the proud Anglo-Saxon Southland, thereby earning national ridicule as an unrepentant redneck. Six month later, talking not about stopping integration but about states' rights and arrogant federal authority, . . . Wallace was a countrywide hero. . . . As a rejoinder to the demand for integration, [states' rights] meant the right of Southern states to continue laws mandating racial segregation. . . . Yet this was enough of a fig leaf to allow persons queasy about black equality to oppose integration without having to admit, to others and perhaps even themselves, their racial attitudes. . . .
>
> As a contemporary of Wallace marveled, "he can use all the other issues—law and order, running your own schools, protecting property rights—and never mention race. But people will know he's telling them 'a [Black person's] trying to get your job, trying to move into your neighborhood.' What Wallace is doing is talking to them in a kind of shorthand, a kind of code."

Like Wallace, the Republican Party soon realized that the national Democratic Party's support of civil rights presented it with an opportunity, in this case to win southern White votes it had traditionally lost to the Democrats. Southern Whites had voted Democratic since the end of the Civil War because of the South's defeat at the hands of Republican president Abraham Lincoln. But with African Americans overwhelmingly supporting the Democrats and the national Democratic Party supporting civil rights, conservative Republicans began to realize that southern White support for the national Democratic Party might be weakening. Thus, in a speech in Atlanta in 1961, Arizona Republican Barry Goldwater declared, "We're not going to get the Negro vote as a bloc in 1964 and 1968, so we ought to go hunting where the ducks are" (quoted in Bass and DeVries 1976, 27). To make sure everyone knew that the ducks were southern Whites, he then made an overture to these Whites by arguing that the decision to integrate schools, which was being forced upon the South by the federal government, should be made by state governments, not the US government.

Another indication that Republicans were beginning to develop a new national electoral strategy occurred in the summer of 1963 when conservative journalist Robert Novak, after attending a meeting of the Republican National Committee, noted,

> A good many, perhaps a majority of the party's leadership, envision substantial political gold to be mined in the racial crisis by becoming *in fact, though not in name*, the White Man's Party. "Remember," one astute party worker said quietly, . . . "this isn't South Africa. The white man outnumbers the Negro by 9 to 1 in this country." (Novak, quoted in Haney López 2014, 18, emphasis added)

But what did it mean to be the White man's party? What it meant first and foremost was to pander to southern Whites' racist sentiments, which the party's presidential candidate, Barry Goldwater, did in 1964. Barry Goldwater had not always been a racially conservative politician. Like many other Republicans, he voted in favor of federal civil rights legislation in 1957 and 1960. But presumably because he wanted to hunt ducks, he was one of only five non-southern senators to vote against the Civil Rights Act of 1964. Moreover, as the Republican Party's presidential candidate, he regularly employed coded racist language to signal his support of White privilege and racial discrimination. He used the phrase "states' rights," for instance, to show that he supported southern states' efforts to deny African Americans their federally guaranteed civil rights and the phrases "freedom of association" and "property rights" to indicate that he supported the rights of business owners to discriminate against African Americans and prevent them from entering their businesses. He even held a rally in which he walked among seven hundred White women dressed in white gowns and standing in a football field of white lilies to indicate that if elected, he would protect White women from the sexual advances of Black men (Haney López 2014).

And as if all this were not enough, Goldwater repeatedly linked African Americans and civil rights activists to crime and disorder, particularly in places that Whites associated with Blacks and civil rights activism. For instance, he "condemned lawlessness and disorder on American streets" (Mohr 1964, 21), argued that liberal coddling of criminals and civil rights activists led to Black crime (Murakawa 2014), claimed that the liberal Supreme Court was making it impossible for police officers to do their jobs (*New York Times* 1964), and when accepting his party's presidential nomination, called for law and order while "speaking at length of violence in the streets of our great cities" (Kenworthy 1964, 6). He also referred to crime and civil rights activism as a "growing menace in our country" and to those who engaged in crime and activism as "bullies and marauders" (Goldwater 1964).

Moreover, as the presidential campaign progressed, Goldwater increasingly used these and similar phrases to refer not only to civil rights activists and Black criminals but also to Black urban rioters. Goldwater thus tied African Americans, traditional crime, civil rights activism, rioting, liberal permissiveness, eroding law and order, and a lack of domestic safety and security into a single discursive package that he conveyed to the American public from his position as the Republican Party's presidential candidate.

Then, in a speech he gave in Minneapolis in September 1964, he added welfare to the mix, just as Daniel Moynihan did for President Johnson the following year. Reporting on this speech, Charles Mohr (1964, 21) noted that for the first time . . . [Goldwater] sought to relate [lawlessness and disorder] to liberal social welfare attitudes.

"If it is entirely proper," he said, "for government to take from some to give to others, then won't some be led to believe that they can rightfully take from anyone who has more than they?"

He [then] criticized what he called "the assumption by the state of the obligation to keep men in a style to which demagogues [liberals and radicals] encourage them."

And he declared: "This can never again be truly a nation of law and order until it is again fully a nation of individual responsible citizens."

In linking crime to welfare in this way, Goldwater was now arguing that liberal government taught African Americans—whom the public and politicians associated with welfare—that crime is okay and individual responsibility unnecessary. He was also arguing that as long as liberals ran the White House and the courts, Black lawlessness would prevail. Given this, and given that he repeatedly talked about the nation's moral decay, which he sometimes tied to rising crime rates, and that he clearly named the source of this decay, liberal permissiveness (*New York Times* 1964; Rovere 1964), it would seem that his race and crime arguments were radically different from those set forth by liberals. This was not true, however. Liberals, recall, argued that African Americans were violent, criminally inclined, and liable to social unrest because Black families, schools, and churches failed to teach Black youth proper values. Goldwater was simply shifting the blame, arguing that African Americans were violent, criminally inclined, and liable to social unrest because liberal judges and politicians were teaching Black youth the wrong values. The only difference, then, was that Goldwater blamed liberals while liberals blamed African Americans. Moreover, after Moynihan's report was released to the press the following year, both liberals and conservatives began to blame "broken" Black families for the urban unrest spreading across the nation.

Goldwater's racist message went over very well in the Deep South (Bass and DeVries 1976). But for a variety of reasons, he lost the presidential election in a landslide to Lyndon Johnson. In particular, voters did not trust Goldwater on foreign policy, and he vehemently attacked the New Deal, which most voters still supported. In addition, Goldwater was too strongly opposed to civil rights and too supportive of southern police at a time when most Whites outside the South supported civil rights and were horrified by television images of southern police viciously attacking Black activists.

Nevertheless, Goldwater's campaign provided important lessons for Richard Nixon, the Republican Party's 1968 presidential candidate. Most importantly, Goldwater taught Nixon and other Republicans that they could win in the South if they played to the region's racism, but that to win the national election, they would have to appeal to White racial resentments in a way that attracted both southern *and* northern Whites to the Republican Party as well as Whites who were more *and* less motivated by racial resentment. Nixon was able to do this, producing a seismic shift in electoral politics that is still with us today.

Richard Nixon

In private, Richard Nixon was a blatant racist (Ehrlichman 1982), and as a politician, he fine-tuned the use of coded racial language to win the 1968 and 1972 presidential elections. He also designed a racist campaign strategy—the Southern Strategy—that broke apart the Democrats' winning New Deal coalition, replacing it with an electoral coalition that won the Republican Party five of six presidential elections from 1968 to 1992. But as was true of George Wallace and Barry Goldwater, Nixon had not always used race to win elections, and when he did use race in this fashion, he did so not because of his personal beliefs but instead because it gave him an advantage over his political opponents. Indeed, early in his career, Nixon did his best to avoid racial issues, and as vice president of the United States, he was the second-most progressive civil rights advocate in the Eisenhower administration, winning "qualified praise from Martin Luther King and an honorary membership in a California NAACP chapter" (O'Reilly 1995, 278).

This all changed when he ran for president in 1968. The Republican Party viewed Nixon as a moderate candidate who would hopefully reverse the party's fortunes after Goldwater's disastrous defeat in 1964. But though Nixon was quite moderate in comparison to Goldwater, he had to contend not only with the Democratic Party's candidate, Hubert Humphrey, he also had to worry about being outflanked on the right by George Wallace, who was running for president for the American Independent Party. Nixon thus had to campaign in a more racially conservative fashion than he otherwise would have done so as to not lose too many Goldwater supporters to Wallace. At the same time, he had to avoid Goldwater's mistake of alienating both moderate Republican voters and potential Democratic Party defectors with racist rhetoric that was too openly racist (Carter 1996; Haney López 2014).

Nixon's initial strategy for meeting these goals was to rely on the most subtle of racial overtures to northern and southern Whites. He realized that many Whites who believed in the broad principle of racial equality had nevertheless become frustrated by 1968 not only with urban riots and civil rights activism but also with federal and judicial efforts to make states and localities enforce residential and educational integration (Edsall and Edsall 1991a).

For these Whites, Nixon said he supported racial equality but not federal efforts to enforce this equality, an argument that also satisfied many blatantly racist White voters who recognized that lack of enforcement meant lack of equality. In making this argument, Nixon was therefore able to (a) draw many White voters in the North and South away from the Democratic Party and (b) undermine support for the more blatantly racist candidate, George Wallace, by offering openly racist Whites a viable alternative to Wallace.

Nixon also realized that he needed to form alliances with racially conservative southern politicians (both Republican and Democratic) who would otherwise support Wallace. So early in his campaign he allied himself with several prominent southern politicians who strongly supported segregation, including Strom Thurmond, Harry Dent, Clarke Reed, James Eastland, and John Stennis, convincing them that despite his public support for racial equality, he was against efforts to integrate schools and neighborhoods through federally mandated busing and open-housing policies (Carter 1996; O'Reilly 1995).

Because these policies were very prominent public issues at the time, Nixon discussed them throughout the campaign. For instance, in response to a question about housing integration, he told southern delegates to the Republican National Convention, "I feel now that conditions are different in different parts of the country . . . [and] ought to be handled at the state level rather than the federal level" (Edsall and Edsall 1991a, 75). And in regard to the Supreme Court's efforts to integrate schools, he said,

> I want men on the Supreme Court who are strict constitutionalists, men that interpret the law and don't try to make the law. . . . I don't think there is any court in this country, any judge in this country, either local or on the Supreme Court . . . that is qualified to be a local school district and to make the decision as your local school board. (Nixon, quoted in Edsall and Edsall 1991a, 75–76)

Finally, in a television interview in North Carolina six weeks before the national election, he affirmed his support of the Supreme Court's *Brown v. Board of Education* decision, but then declared,

> On the other hand, while that decision dealt with segregation and said that we would not have segregation, when you go beyond that and say it is the responsibility of the federal government, and the federal courts, to, in effect, act as local school districts in determining how we carry that out, and then to use the power of the federal treasury to withhold funds or give funds in order to carry it out, then I think we are going too far. In my view, that kind of activity should . . . in many cases . . . be rescinded. . . . I think that to . . . force a local community to carry out what a federal administrator or bureaucrat may think is best for that local community—I think that is a doctrine that is a very dangerous one. (Nixon, quoted in Edsall and Edsall 1991a, 76)

Nixon's arguments about integration clearly echoed Wallace's arguments from a decade earlier about the illegitimacy of the federal government's efforts to dictate laws to the states. Nixon's arguments were also clearly about race since integration was so obviously a racial issue, and he employed the same coded language as George Wallace did, "where 'bloc vote' meant 'black vote,' . . . 'neighborhood schools' meant 'all-white schools,' and . . . 'hardcore unemployed, welfare cheats, laggards, muggers, rapists, . . . and street punks' meant 'black people generally'" (O'Reilly 1995, 281).

Like Wallace and Goldwater, Nixon also campaigned heavily on law and order, which had been a highly racialized issue in the United States since at least the 1950s. Indeed, during his 1968 campaign, Nixon "dedicated seventeen speeches solely to the topic" (Weaver 2007, 259), and in April of that year he released a position paper on law and order titled *Toward Freedom from Fear* (Nixon 1968a). In that paper, and in his campaign more generally, Nixon argued that crime rates had risen dramatically under President Johnson, which may not actually have been true.[3] He further argued that crime rates had risen not because people were poor, as many liberals claimed, but because the Democratic Party and liberal judges were too lenient, teaching criminals that crime pays and showing more sympathy for criminals (by whom he meant Blacks) than for their victims (by whom he meant Whites). The resulting purported increase in crime and the likelihood, as Nixon saw it, of further increases under a Democratic president were, he declared (1968a, 12936),

> a prospect America cannot accept. If we allow it to happen, then the city jungle will cease to be a metaphor. It will become a barbaric reality, and the brutal society that now flourishes in the core cities of America will annex the affluent suburbs. This nation will then be what it is fast becoming—an armed camp of two hundred million Americans living in fear.

Nixon thus presented a vision of law and order in the United States that did not mention race or use openly derogatory racial language but that pitted urban areas, where most northern Blacks lived, against suburbs, where Whites lived, and that used phrases such as "city jungle" and "brutal society" to describe those areas that Whites associated with Blacks. Nixon's vision was thus highly racialized. It also drew on and reinforced racist discourses that held Whites to be rational, civilized, nonviolent, and noncriminal and Blacks to be brutal, jungle-dwelling barbarians whose supposedly violent natures and criminal tendencies threatened the well-being and survival of White America.

Nixon also linked Blacks to primitiveness by arguing that Black violence brought to the surface Whites' most primitive fears. For instance, in a speech that ignored urban Blacks' legitimate grievances and the extreme violence the US government employed at that time against leftists around the world, Nixon painted the following portrait of Black threat—emanating from areas, such as Watts and Harlem, that Whites associated with Blacks—and White fear:

Tonight I would like to talk with you about the number one issue of 1968. . . . This is the problem of order. By order I mean peace at home and peace in the world. I mean the containing of violence, whether by armies or by mobs or by individuals. . . . There are many kinds of fear today . . . but the central fear is the most primitive—the fear of physical violence. . . . Here at home, we have been amply warned that we face the prospect of a war-in-the-making in our own society. We have seen the gathering hate, we have heard the threats to burn and bomb and destroy. In Watts and Harlem and Detroit and Newark, we have had a foretaste of what the organizers of insurrection are planning for the summers ahead. (Nixon 1968b)

African Americans were not, of course, the only people Nixon targeted. He argued, for example, that White, middle-class college protestors posed a serious threat to the social order. He also blamed college and civil rights protests, urban riots, and street crime on the same root cause: an excess of liberals, whose permissiveness, he claimed, rewarded lawbreaking and taught lawbreakers, young people, and African Americans that they could choose which rules to follow and which ones not to follow. But though Nixon targeted multiple groups, his law and order position paper, many of his speeches, and at least one of his political advertisements targeted African Americans specifically. They did this by highlighting events and policies and employing code words that clearly referred to racial issues and racial groups; by pitting Blacks and Whites against each other; and by portraying Black crime, Black activism, and Black unrest as menacing. They also did this by suggesting that African Americans threatened to destroy Whites' way of life and by indicating, in at least one speech, that the problems poor urban Blacks faced existed because they had become too dependent on government handouts and government leniency and needed to learn to be responsible for their own actions (Nixon 1968a, 1968b).

John Ehrlichman, who worked closely with Nixon for years and was one of his key presidential advisors, agrees that Nixon intentionally appealed to Whites' racial resentments:

That subliminal appeal to the antiblack voter was always in Nixon's statements and speeches on schools and housing. . . . President Nixon was

convinced that the majority of Americans did not support open housing, affirmative action, busing to achieve racial balance, Model Cities, the
Equal Opportunity Commission and the other Federal civil rights activities. . . . Throughout his public life Richard Nixon signaled to the American people where he stood on the race issue. He was never as blatant as
George Wallace or Lester Maddox, but he delivered a clear message that
was hard to miss. Nixon always couched his views in such a way that a
citizen could avoid admitting to himself that he was attracted by a racist
appeal. There were plausible reasons to be against open housing that had
nothing to do with the fact that most public-housing-project dwellers are
black. Busing is bad because it wasted education money, not because it
mixes the races. (Ehrlichman 1982, 222–23)

In the end, Nixon won a narrow victory over Hubert Humphrey
in the 1968 election. But collectively Nixon and George Wallace, who
both ran racist campaigns, won 57 percent of the vote (Edsall and Edsall
1991a). Thus, more than half of all US voters voted for a candidate who
employed highly racist rhetoric during the campaign.

Wallace's racist rhetoric was often similar to, though never identical
with, Nixon's. Wallace, for example,

portrayed the civil rights issue not as the struggle of blacks to achieve
equality—a goal increasingly difficult to challenge on a moral basis—
but as the [tyrannical] imposition on working men and women of intrusive "social" policies by an insulated, liberal, elitist cabal of lawyers,
judges, editorial writers, academics, government bureaucrats, and plan-
ners [working for or with the federal government]. (Edsall and Edsall
1991a, 77)

These social policies, which included both civil rights policies and
President Johnson's welfare policies, benefitted African Americans and
government bureaucrats, Wallace argued. But they were paid for, he
claimed, with the tax dollars of those they harmed, hardworking Whites.
Thus, in a speech he gave in Cicero, Illinois, he declared,

We don't need half a billion dollars being spent on bureaucrats in Washington of your hard-earned tax money to check every school system, ev-

ery hospital, every seniority list of a labor union [for discrimination]. And now after the election they're going to check even on the sale of your own property. (Wallace, quoted in Farber 1994, 218)

But despite the fact that a clear majority of White voters supported Wallace and Nixon, Nixon did not abandon his cautious approach to racial issues until 1970, when conservative *and* moderate political analysts began to argue that the 1968 election revealed a conservative shift in the electorate that Nixon's campaign had successfully tapped (Carter 1996). Most prominent among these analysts were Kevin Phillips (1969), Samuel Lubell (1970), and Richard Scammon and Ben Wattenberg (1970).

Though disagreeing on several key points, these analysts all argued that White working- and middle-class voters, who represented the largest group of voters in the country, were becoming increasingly disenchanted and frustrated with rising crime rates, social unrest (civil rights demonstrations, riots, and student protests), the personal costs they believed they were being forced to pay to help African Americans, and the breakdown of law and order and erosion of traditional cultural values that they believed held American society together. This frustration and disenchantment were good for the Republican Party, Scammon and Wattenberg and Phillips argued, so long as the party continued to address these concerns in the ways Nixon had done in his 1968 campaign. But they were highly problematic for the Democratic Party, which the mainstream White electorate viewed as too pro-Black, too lenient on criminals and protestors, and uncritical of those who purveyed drugs, pornography, and other activities and values these voters believed were immoral.

Phillips, for his part, did not believe that the Democrats could solve this problem, particularly if Republicans played their cards right. But Scammon and Wattenberg believed that they could. However, to do so, the Democrats would have to move to the center, where the votes were, by taking a pro–law and order approach, distancing themselves from African Americans, and separating race from the social issues that working- and middle-class Whites cared about so that Whites would no longer associate these issues with African Americans or with the Democratic Party's support for African Americans.

As Samuel Lubell pointed out, however, it was very unlikely that White voters would or could disentangle race from crime, social unrest, law and order, and the breakdown of cultural values because these issues were already so closely linked in their minds (in large part, I would argue, because both the Republican *and* Democratic Parties had so closely linked race to crime, social unrest, and family values in the 1950s and 1960s). Thus, even though Scammon and Wattenberg never tell the Democratic Party to abandon African Americans, it is difficult to read their book without believing that this was really the advice they were giving the party. More specifically, it is difficult to read their book without believing that they were telling the Democrats to behave as Nixon had done in 1968, which, of course, is the same advice they gave the Republican Party.

In any event, Nixon took Phillips's and Scammon and Wattenberg's advice quite seriously (Carter 1996; Ehrlichman 1982), which is not surprising since this advice was consistent with what Nixon had done in his 1968 campaign. Nixon began by firing or moving to ceremonial positions key executive branch civil rights supporters, by telling administration officials to slow down on desegregation, and by abandoning support for his more progressive race and welfare policies. In campaign speeches for other Republicans, he also made sure to highlight the dangers of pornography, violent demonstrations, and crime in the streets, and in his 1972 presidential campaign, he clearly stated his opposition to welfare, busing, quotas, and affirmative action and repeatedly accused the Democrats of being "out of touch with mainstream American values" (Carter 1996, 46).

Nixon's move to the right played a key role in his landslide victory over George McGovern in the 1972 presidential election, as did George Wallace's strong performance in the 1972 Democratic primaries. Indeed, until Wallace was shot and paralyzed in May of that year, he had won more votes than any other Democratic presidential candidate, causing havoc in the Democratic Party and leading many of his supporters to flee the party after he was shot. Nixon's resounding victory thus "marked a critical realignment in American politics." As described by historian Dan Carter (1996, 53–54),

> Nixon had successfully pulled a substantial number of traditionally Democratic ethnic and blue-collar workers into the Grand Old Party. And, what was most important, he had brought most of the southern Wallace voters into the Republican column.

The "gut" issues of the future would be crime, busing, drugs, welfare, inflation. All of these, said Nixon with some satisfaction, were "issues the Democrats . . . hate." [With the exception of inflation, they were also issues that the public and decades of Republican and Democratic political rhetoric associated with African Americans.]

The lessons of 1968 and 1972 were not lost on Democratic Party leaders. Today, when party leaders exhort the left wing of the party not to make the mistakes McGovern made in 1972, their argument is that being too liberal hurts the Democratic Party's electoral chances, particularly in presidential campaigns. But what they do not say, at least not openly, and what many Democratic Party leaders must have concluded in 1972, if not earlier, is that in the United States, being too liberal means not being racist enough. Scammon and Wattenberg, who were associated with the moderate wing of the Democratic Party, clearly recognized this in 1970, and by 1969 many liberal-Democratic politicians seemed to have done so as well. Vesla Weaver (2007, 261) notes, for instance, that

in the 1969 mayoral and 1970 midterm elections, there was a clear attempt [by liberal-Democratic politicians] to reposition themselves on the crime issue. . . . Seeking to suspend the charge of being soft on crime and coddling criminals, many posed in campaign photos with police and threw their support toward [highly punitive] anti-crime legislation formulated by the Nixon administration.

These liberal Democrats thus believed that they needed to support crime policies that would harm African Americans if they were going to win elections, as did Democratic senator Joe Biden in the 1970s, 1980s, and 1990s and Bill Clinton from the early 1980s until the end of his presidency in 2001. But before discussing Biden's and Clinton's anti-crime rhetoric and policies, I will discuss the racial rhetoric that Ronald Reagan and George H. W. Bush employed in their presidential campaigns in the 1980s.

Ronald Reagan and George Herbert Walker Bush

Ronald Reagan soundly defeated Jimmy Carter in the 1980 presidential election. Unlike Nixon, Wallace, and Goldwater, Reagan had always been a racial conservative. He entered politics in 1964 giving speeches in support of presidential candidate Barry Goldwater, opposed the 1964 Civil Rights and 1965 Voting Rights Acts, and as governor of California opposed anti-discriminatory housing legislation (Carter 1996; Dawson and Bobo 2004), stating, "If an individual wants to discriminate against Negroes or others in selling or renting his house, it is his right to do so" (quoted in Haney López 2014, 58).

In his electoral campaigns, and in the domestic policies he pursued as president, Reagan regularly pitted Whites against Blacks, using coded language and other symbolic actions to ensure that White voters knew he sided with them (Edsall and Edsall 1991a). For instance, after receiving the Republican nomination for president in 1980, he kicked off his campaign with a speech at a county fair outside Philadelphia, Mississippi, where three young civil rights activists had been killed by the Ku Klux Klan in 1964. The fair had been suggested to the Republican National Committee as an ideal location from which to attract "George Wallace inclined voters," and Reagan further appealed to these voters by stating in his speech that he supported states' rights (Haney López 2014, 58), by which he meant the right of states to determine for themselves whether they supported racial discrimination.

During his various campaigns and as president of the United States, Reagan also attacked affirmative action, school busing, forced school integration, welfare, and crime, all issues that Whites associated with Blacks. He talked about a Chicago "welfare queen" who, he inaccurately claimed, had eighty names, thirty addresses, and twelve social security cards, and was getting rich receiving food stamps and welfare under each of her names. He also talked about a strapping young "buck" (a very derogatory term used to describe Black men), which he later amended to young "fellow," who stood in line at the grocery story with a T-bone steak while hardworking Americans (by whom he meant Whites) stood in line with packages of hamburger meat (M. Alexander 2010; Carter 1996; Edsall and Edsall 1991a; Haney López 2014; O'Reilly 1995).

Moreover, Reagan combined his attacks on welfare, affirmative action, and integration with urgent calls for law and order. As part of this effort, he described criminals, whom he and Whites associated with Blacks, as a "new privileged class . . . [of] entitled rights holders who manipulated the 'maze of legal technicalities' to get their charges 'dropped, postponed, plea-bargained away'" (Murakawa 2014, 90–91). He also "portrayed the criminal as 'a staring face—a face that belongs to a frightening reality of our time: the face of the human predator'" (M. Alexander 2010, 49). For Reagan, African Americans thus represented both a mortal physical threat and a lazy, privileged class of people who on the one hand avoided punishments they deserved and on the other hand received social benefits that hardworking Whites paid for but did not receive.

Then, in 1982, he declared a war on drugs. The war initially gained little traction. But a few years later, the White House openly tied the war to African Americans by drawing the news media's attention to the increasing use of crack cocaine in inner-city Black communities. One important consequence of the White House's actions was the enactment of highly punitive anti-drug and anti-crime legislation both during and after Reagan's presidency. Another important consequence was an explosion of news stories from 1986 to 1989 that demonized Black people by wildly exaggerating the prevalence and harmful consequences of crack addiction in Black communities (the *Washington Post*, for instance, ran 1,565 stories on the drug scare in one year alone).

Describing crack cocaine as a plague and epidemic that threatened not just Black communities but the survival of American society as a whole, the news media repeatedly referred to Black people as crack whores, crack babies, and gangbangers (M. Alexander 2010; Reinarman and Levine 1995). Not to be outdone, politicians and government officials outside the Reagan administration also got into the act. Naomi Murakawa (2014, 122) writes, for instance, that according to some lawmakers,

> crack reduced its users to their most base selves. As a representation of black degeneration, crack cocaine made the men violent and the women lascivious, with defects transmitted genetically, as the children were born frenzied, uneducable, and menacing. This [Murakawa notes] was Moynihan's dysfunctional black family on drugs.

Indeed, Adam Walinsky, a former aide to Robert Kennedy, argued that family breakdown, not drugs, was the real problem:

Crack [is just] a scapegoat for the real problem of "disintegrating families
and neighborhoods." . . . Single black mothers [are] "prepar[ing] a disas-
ter: the steady growth in our midst of an unacculturated, unsocialized
and indigestible lump of young men." (Walinsky, quoted in Murakawa
2014, 123)

The incredibly derogatory crack-related commentary the White
House was able to generate in the news media and political arena was
highly consistent with, if sometimes more blatantly racist than, the racist rhetoric Reagan employed throughout his political career. Moreover,
Reagan's racist rhetoric was highly consistent with Nixon's, Wallace's,
and Goldwater's racist rhetoric, drawing on many of the same themes
and reinforcing many of the same negative stereotypes as had their rhetoric and placing Reagan in a long line of racial conservatives who all
made very similar racist arguments.

For instance, like his predecessors, Reagan portrayed African Americans as lazy, uncivilized, irrational, dysfunctional, irresponsible, damaged, and dangerous. He also described African Americans as taking
advantage of liberal permissiveness to threaten and harm Whites, undermine the social order, evade criminal punishment, abuse the welfare
system, avoid work, and move unwanted into White neighborhoods. In
addition, he claimed that African Americans took tax dollars and educational opportunities away from hardworking Whites who were losing
out because liberals and big government were giving in to the unjustified
demands of a group of people who, he argued, did not want to work or
accept the consequences of their bad choices.

But Reagan also employed racist rhetoric in ways his predecessors
had not done. He used affirmative action, for example, to attack middle-
class African Americans, whom he portrayed as "thriving in jobs they
had obtained, not through hard work or merit, but [solely] through
[government] action" (Haney López 2014, 70), thereby implying that
they had stolen these jobs from deserving White people.

Reagan also used the racist arguments he employed to tie the interests
of economic elites and corporations to those of working- and middle-
class Whites. These racist arguments virtually all defined government
intervention into the social and economic realms, whether in the form
of affirmative action, busing, civil rights enforcement, welfare, or tax-

ing Whites to help Blacks, as being harmful to Whites and the nation. But unlike George Wallace, who used similar arguments to support a racially based populism, Reagan used them to convince working- and middle-class Whites that all government intervention into society and the economy (except for criminal justice purposes) was bad. As a result, activities such as taxing rich people and corporations, regulating business, and using the government to intervene in the market or promote social welfare were defined as bad policy. This, of course, undermined what was left of the Democratic Party's New Deal. It also promoted the interests of corporations and economic elites, who now depended on Reagan's racism, and the violence associated with it, to secure their interests and accumulate capital (Edsall and Edsall 1991a), often in ways that were extremely violent (Downey 2015).

In using race as a wedge issue and harnessing social issues such as crime, race, and traditional values to win elections and achieve Republican goals, Reagan was, as previously noted, following in the footsteps of Richard Nixon and Barry Goldwater. Intentionally or not, he was also following the advice of political analysts such as Kevin Philips, Richard Scammon, and Ben Wattenberg. And this advice worked: Reagan won two landside presidential election victories for the Republican Party, elections in which he received a majority of southern White votes and the votes of large percentages of northern White Democrats (Edsall and Edsall 1991a).

Reagan's successor in the White House was his former vice president, George Herbert Walker Bush. Throughout most of his career, Bush had been a racial moderate who supported civil rights. Nevertheless, when he and his campaign advisors determined that he could not win the 1988 presidential election without appealing to Whites' racial fears, he did not hesitate to do so. The strategy that he and his advisors chose to pursue was to closely link the Democratic presidential candidate, Michael Dukakis, to Willie Horton, a Black Massachusetts man convicted of murder who had been released from prison on a weekend furlough program when Dukakis was governor of the state. Horton had received nine prior weekend furloughs. But after failing to return from his last furlough, Horton broke into a house in Maryland, tied up, beat, and stabbed Cliff Barnes, the young White man who lived there, and then tied up and raped Barnes's future wife, Angela Miller (Carter 1996; O'Reilly1995).

Dukakis was not governor when the prison furlough program was created, he had no role in approving Horton's furlough, and in the mid- to late 1980s, when Bush was vice president, all fifty states and the federal government had furlough programs. Moreover, two furloughed California prisoners committed murder while Ronald Reagan was governor of California (Schwartzapfel and Keller 2015). Nevertheless, Willie Horton became a central theme in Bush's campaign, with Bush and other Republicans repeatedly talking about him. Bush's campaign also released a television commercial that showed a line of convicts walking through a revolving door that lets them into and then out of prison while a voice intoned,

> As governor, Michael Dukakis vetoed mandatory sentences for drug dealers. He vetoed the death penalty. His revolving door prison policy gave furloughs to first-degree murderers not eligible for parole. While out, many committed other crimes like kidnapping and rape and many are still at large. Now Michael Dukakis says he wants to do for America what he's done for Massachusetts. America cannot afford that risk. (author's transcription of the commercial)

The commercial did not mention Willie Horton by name, and most of the actors portraying convicts in the commercial were light-skinned. But by the time the commercial aired, voters already knew who Willie Horton was, what he had done, and that he was Black, and the only convict in the commercial to glance up at the camera was dark-skinned. Moreover, two groups with close ties to the Republican Party released campaign advertisements that did explicitly link Willie Horton to Dukakis. One of these advertisements presented a picture of Willie Horton's face while declaring that "Dukakis not only opposes the death penalty, he allowed first-degree murderers to have weekend passes from prison" (author transcription). And the other advertisement features Cliff Barnes describing his and his fiancée's ordeal:

> "Mike Dukakis and Willie Horton changed our lives forever. . . . Horton broke into our home. For twelve hours, I was beaten, slashed, and terrorized. . . . My wife Angie was brutally raped." But when this "liberal experiment" failed . . . , "Dukakis simply looked away." (Carter 1996, 77)

The upshot of all this was that one of the key reasons, probably *the* key reason, that Bush defeated Dukakis in the 1988 presidential election was that Bush, who had formerly been a racial moderate, decided to use the fear of Black sexuality, Black violence, and Black crime to convince White voters that the liberal Dukakis represented an immediate, visceral, and existential threat to their safety and way of life. And as was true for Nixon and Reagan before him, Bush's use of racist rhetoric succeeded: in less than a month, "12 percent of the electorate had switched candidates" (Carter 1996, 79; O'Reilly 1995), an incredible shift that propelled Bush to victory.

The Democrats' Response to Nixon, Reagan, and Bush

Nixon, Reagan, and Bush did not just make race and crime key issues in their presidential campaigns. They also successfully spearheaded efforts to make the US criminal justice system more punitive than it had been in the mid-1960s. However, the Democratic Party was not far behind them. As previously noted, by 1969 many liberal Democrats, worried that they would be accused of being soft on crime, had taken a more conservative stance on race and criminal justice, doing things such as "posing in campaign photos with police officers" and supporting Nixon's highly punitive anti-crime legislation (Weaver 2007, 261). In addition, in the early 1970s a group of Democratic politicians argued that if the Democratic Party wanted to win elections, it had to take control of the crime issue by demonstrating that it was tougher on crime than the Republicans.

Democratic support for punitive anti-crime legislation further increased in the 1980s and 1990s as Democratic fears of being perceived as soft on both crime and drugs grew and as they increasingly realized that they could win elections by being tough on crime and drugs and, hence, on African Americans. In 1984, for instance, the Sentencing Reform Act passed the Senate on a 91–1 vote, and in 1986, 1988, and 1989 Democratic and Republican senators and congressional representatives engaged in bidding wars to see who could be tougher on drugs, with legislators' anti-drug rhetoric increasing as elections neared and fading afterward and with passage of anti-drug bills coinciding closely with the timing of elections. Thus, Democratic and Republican anti-drug rhetoric and bidding wars increased prior to the 1986 midterm elections and then faded away, with 51 of 53 Democratic senators and 222 of 251 Democratic representatives voting for that year's punitive Anti-Drug Abuse Act. The same pattern occurred in 1988, when 49 of 54 Democratic senators and 207 of 254 Democratic representatives voted for the 1988 Anti-Drug Abuse Act. Moreover, between 1988 and 1994, the Democratic and Republican Parties engaged in an increasingly intense bidding war, led by Joe Biden on the Democratic side, to see who could attach the death penalty to the largest number of crimes (Murakawa 2014; Reinarman and Levine 1995).

Of course, when Democrats began adopting punitive approaches to crime in order to win elections, they, like their Republican counterparts, were trading the lives and well-being of African Americans (and Hispanics) for their personal and their party's electoral success (M. Alexander 2010; Hinton 2016; Murakawa 2014). Nowhere was this personal and party calculus more evident than in the careers of Joe Biden and Bill Clinton.

Joe Biden

Joe Biden, a Democrat from Delaware, won his first senatorial campaign in 1972 and served in the US Senate from 1973 until 2009, when he became vice president of the United States. Biden, like many other Democrats, learned the lessons that Nixon's, Wallace's, and, later, Reagan's electoral victories had taught Republicans about the role race and crime play in US politics. In his 1972 Senate run, he thus positioned himself as a segregationist by declaring himself to be against busing, consciously distanced himself from liberalism, and talked tough on crime. He noted, for instance that he had "some friends on the far left . . . who can justify to me the murder of a white deaf mute for a nickel by five colored guys," and he called segregation a "phony issue which allows the white liberals to sit in suburbia, confident that they are not going to have to live next to a black" (Newell 2019).

Biden also played a key role from the 1970s to the 1990s in fomenting anti-crime hysteria and crafting legislation that contributed to mass incarceration. In 1973, for example, he asked arch-segregationist James Eastland for a seat on the Senate Judiciary Committee, and he worked closely with Eastland, and later with arch-segregationist Strom Thurmond, to craft highly punitive anti-crime and anti-drug legislation that greatly harmed African Americans (Murakawa 2014; Newell 2019; Reinarman and Levine 1995; Stolberg and Herndon 2019).

Indeed, Biden and Thurmond

> wrote roughly a half-dozen crime bills together, laying the groundwork for three of the most significant pieces of crime legislation of the 20th century: the Comprehensive Crime Control Act of 1984, establishing mandatory minimum sentences for drug offenses; the 1986 Anti-Drug Abuse Act, which dictated much harsher sentences for possession of crack than for powder cocaine; and the Violent Crime Control and Law Enforcement Act of 1994, a vast catchall tough-on-crime bill. (Stolberg and Herndon 2019, A19)

But Biden wanted to do more than just co-sponsor punitive anti-crime and anti-drug legislation that would dramatically increase Black incarceration rates at the federal level, legitimate harsh and racially biased criminal justice policies at the local and state levels, and provide significant resources for local and state police, prisons, and prosecutors. He also wanted the Democratic Party to claim ownership over the war on crime and drugs so as to steal the issue away from Republicans, win elections, and take back the White House. To do this, he adopted language, rhetoric, and policy positions that made him sound much like Nixon and Reagan: he described criminals as "violent thugs" and "predators on our streets," regularly argued that the opposition party and president were too soft on crime and drugs, claimed that the country needed more police officers, prosecutors, judges, and prisons, took an active role in Democratic and Republican battles over which party was tougher on crime and drugs, and made statements such as, "It doesn't matter whether or not [criminals are] the victims of society. . . . I don't want to ask, What made them do this? They must be taken off the street" (Haney López 2014; Murakawa 2014; Newell 2019; Stein 2019; Stolberg and Herndon 2019, A18). He also distanced himself from liberals by comparing himself favorably with Nixon:

> Every time Richard Nixon, when he was running in 1972, would say, "Law and order," the Democratic match or response was, "Law and order with

justice"—whatever that meant. And I would say, "Lock the S.O.B. up."
(Stolberg and Herndon 2019, A18)

Biden was not, of course, working in a vacuum. Other Democrats had
also come to believe that the key to electoral success and winning back
the White House was to employ coded racist rhetoric in exactly the same
way Nixon and Reagan had done. Biden and other Democrats were also
familiar with Kevin Phillips's (1969) and Richard Scammon and Ben
Wattenberg's (1970) analyses of the 1968 presidential election, in particular with their arguments that if Democrats did not want to become
the permanent minority party, they would have to distance themselves
from African Americans, criminals, and protestors and take a tougher
line on African Americans, crime, and immorality.

Whether Biden was following these analysts' advice or had independently drawn the same conclusions from the preceding elections as
they had, it is clear that in key ways Biden's political rhetoric and policy
prescriptions were closely aligned with those advocated by these analysts and employed by Nixon and Reagan. The same can be said of Bill
Clinton, who had access not only to Scammon and Wattenberg's and
Phillips's analyses, but also to the analyses of Thomas Edsall and Mary
Edsall (1991a, 1991b) and Stanley Greenberg (1985). Greenberg's analysis,
which was based on interviews conducted with Michigan residents who
had defected from the Democratic Party to vote for Ronald Reagan in
the 1984 presidential election, was important because Greenberg later
became senior pollster for President Clinton and advised both Bill Clinton and Al Gore during their respective presidential campaigns. One of
Greenberg's key conclusions was that

> it will be difficult to confront the problem of Democratic defection
> without facing up to the intense racial feelings of these voters. The race
> question has been deeply assimilated, as it defines attitudes toward their
> neighborhood, Detroit, the Democratic Party, Democratic themes and
> the government. These Democratic defectors believe the government has
> personally intervened to block their opportunities. Appeals to fairness,
> opportunity, etc. are now defined in racial terms and have been stripped
> of any progressive content. (Greenberg 1985, 56)

Thomas Edsall and Mary Edsall, whose book *Chain Reaction* was published as a call to the Democratic Party the year before Clinton ran for president, agreed with Greenberg that to win back the White House, the Democrats had to address the deep-seated racial resentments that drove many White voters away from the party. But their analysis also relied on many of the arguments Scammon and Wattenberg and Phillips had made in response to Nixon's 1968 election victory. In particular, the Edsalls highlighted the costs Democrats paid because mainstream White voters viewed them as too liberal, too supportive of Blacks, too soft on crime, too weak on traditional values, and too supportive of redistributive policies that forced White taxpayers to "subsidize" supposedly nonworking, non-taxpaying Blacks.

But the Edsalls did not stop there. They also relied on the kinds of racist anti-crime arguments Democrats and liberals had made in the 1940s, 1950s, and 1960s. Thus, in an article they published in the *Atlantic Monthly* in 1991, they focused readers' attention on Black violence, joblessness, drug abuse, and family disintegration:

> The emergence of predominantly black underclass neighborhoods *rife with the worst symptoms of social pathology* has proved to be one of the most disturbing developments in the United States, both for city residents and for residents of surrounding areas. . . . Racial progress has run into major roadblocks: *crime, welfare dependency, illegitimacy, drug abuse, and a generation—disproportionately black—of young men and women unwilling either to stay in school or to take on menial labor*, a group that has collided with a restructuring of the American economy and a dramatic loss of well-paid entry-level jobs. The worsening of the symptoms of *social dysfunction* over the past three decades has become a driving force in politics. (Edsall and Edsall 1991b, emphasis added)

Like Scammon and Wattenberg, the Edsalls do not openly say that the Democratic Party should abandon African Americans, get tough on crime, and abandon social welfare policies designed to help the poor. But they clearly and blatantly link African Americans to crime, welfare dependency, out-of-wedlock births (illegitimacy), family disintegration, drug abuse, joblessness, weak moral values, a nonexistent work ethic, and social pathology, and it is impossible to read their book and magazine article without concluding that abandoning African Americans and getting tough on crime, drugs, and welfare are exactly what they are recommending. Moreover, their analysis combines the key elements of liberal *and* conservative race, crime, and welfare rhetoric from the preceding forty-five years into a single discursive package in an attempt to develop a winning electoral strategy for the Democratic Party that relies on the same vision of race, crime, and welfare as that held by the Republican Party. The strategy the Edsalls propose involves a broader range of issues and tactics than those described here, but crime, welfare, and racism are central to it, and the Edsalls do not seem to care about the costs their strategy will impose on Black people and the poor or how much they and the Democratic Party will have to demonize Black people to achieve their goals.

It is thus clear that by 1992 there was strong support among key segments of the Democratic Party establishment, and reluctant support among others, for a racial politics that would attract White voters by talking and acting tough on crime, drugs, and welfare, distancing the party from African Americans and liberal permissiveness, and reinforcing a racial hierarchy that Democrats supposedly abhorred. Evidence of this support comes from many sources: the national leadership role Joe Biden took on drugs and crime in the 1970s, 1980s, and 1990s; the forceful arguments Democratic political analysts such as Scammon and Wattenberg and the Edsalls made in favor of achieving electoral success by abandoning African Americans and liberalism; the strong anti-drug and anti-crime positions taken by many Senate and House Democrats in the 1980s and early 1990s; and the fact that nearly every Democrat in the House and Senate voted in favor of punitive anti-drug and anti-crime legislation during this period, even those Democrats who thought that the legislation was racially biased and seriously flawed.

Into this situation walked Bill Clinton and the Democratic Leadership Council (DLC), whose race and crime rhetoric I examine in the following section.

Bill Clinton and the Democratic Leadership Council

The DLC, which formed in 1985 and was chaired by Bill Clinton from 1990 to 1991, was a nonprofit organization created by several prominent Democrats that crafted many of the policy ideas Clinton employed as presidential candidate and president. Its chief goal was to push the Democratic Party to the right so as to win back White voters the party had been losing to the Republicans since the late 1960s. Hiding its conservative and racist policy ideas behind a patina of seemingly race-neutral and sometimes liberal-sounding rhetoric, the DLC and its closely associated think tank, the Progressive Policy Institute (PPI), constantly argued that they wanted to find a third path, or way, that combined the best ideas that liberals and conservatives had to offer.

But a close inspection of their ideas shows that what the DLC and PPI really wanted to do was turn the Democratic Party into an alternate Republican Party by repackaging the ideas set forth by Scammon and Wattenberg, Phillips, Greenberg, and the Edsalls and by drawing heavily on the strategies and policies employed by Nixon, Wallace, and Reagan. Like the political analysts whose ideas they drew upon, the DLC and PPI argued that the Democratic Party was associated too closely with African Americans and had lost sight of a set of issues and values— related to crime, violence, welfare dependency, personal responsibility, hard work, drugs, the disintegration of traditional moral values, and family breakdown—that motivated White voters. Like these earlier analysts, and like Nixon, Reagan, and Wallace, they also argued that the Democratic Party was dominated by liberal elites who were out of touch with the lives of White voters and who failed to properly punish criminals, did not believe that rights should be linked to responsibilities, and talked about compensation for past wrongs rather than for hard work today. One PPI report noted, for example, that "for years [Democrats] have been perceived as the party that is weaker on crime and more concerned about criminals than about victims" and that unlike the Democratic Party, "the American people overwhelmingly believe that the central purpose of criminal punishment is to punish" (Galston and Kamarck 1989, 16, 19).

Liberal elites, the DLC and PPI argued, also enacted welfare policies that rewarded single parenthood, and they used Whites' tax dollars to pay for programs that benefitted Blacks, single parents, and poor people, thereby transferring wealth from middle- and working-class Whites to Black people and the poor. Moreover, like Moynihan and other 1960s Democrats, the DLC and PPI described dysfunctional families and communities as representing one of this nation's most pressing and disturbing social problems, linked in important ways to crime, drugs, welfare, a declining work ethic, eroding social values, and African Americans (Faux 1993; Galston and Kamarck 1989; Hale 1995; Marshall 1994; Marshall and Schram 1993).

Will Marshall, who founded the PPI and was the DLC's first policy director, put it like this:

> Liberals seem embarrassed by [our efforts] to bring these once and future Democrats—largely white and middle class—back into the fold. . . . [And] Faux chides [us] for focusing too much on social issues. Evidently, he sees crime, welfare dependency, illegitimacy, family dissolution, intergenerational poverty, and their concatenation in our decaying cities as chiefly economic problems. . . . Such economic reductionism . . . ignores an overwhelming consensus that our social systems cannot offer real opportunity if they fail to reward sound values: work, family, individual responsibility. . . .
>
> Readers curious about how social issues and racial polarization have dimmed liberal prospects *should refer to* Chain Reaction *by Tom and Mary Edsall* . . . [They should also] consider one especially dramatic example: . . . the decline, and perhaps the fall, of [a liberal] urban politics characterized by high taxes, poor services, *wealth transfers, and racial and ethnic entitlement.* (Marshall 1994, emphasis added)

The DLC and PPI were, of course, careful to say that they supported racial justice. Like Scammon and Wattenberg, they also argued that the social issues and values they highlighted were not related to racial issues and could thus be addressed without reducing the Democratic Party's commitment to racial justice. But in the context of US politics, this was absurd. As the DLC and PPI knew quite well, White voters linked African Americans to all the social issues and "negative" moral values highlighted in the preceding paragraphs, and it is pretty clear from the preceding quote that Marshall did as well. Addressing these social issues and values in the manner proposed by the DLC and PPI was therefore very much an attack on the Democratic Party's supposed commitment to racial justice.

Indeed, in 2010 Ed Kilgore, a senior fellow at the PPI who in 1993 wrote a chapter in the DLC and PPI manifesto, *Mandate for Change* (Marshall and Schram 1993), seemed to concur, ridiculing the idea that in American politics race can ever be separated from issues such as crime and welfare. Kilgore's 2010 piece is quite interesting because it highlights the hypocrisy of both the PPI and the Democratic Party. In the late 1980s and early 1990s, the PPI argued that the social issues it highlighted were not tied to racial issues and that the policies it proposed were therefore not racist. But in 2010 Kilgore, in a PPI blog post, condemned conservatives for making the same argument. It similarly seems that Democrats find it acceptable to accuse conservatives of playing on White racism to win elections, but when Democrats use White racism to win elections, as representatives of the DLC and PPI were doing in the 1980s and 1990s and as other Democrats were doing from the 1970s to the 1990s, it becomes something else entirely: not racism, but an honest attempt to address social issues that Whites care about. This, of course, is the argument racially conservative Republicans have been making for years, and it is not true when Republicans make it or when Democrats do.

In *Mandate for Change*, which covers a variety of policy topics, the PPI and DLC go even further. Careful to use seemingly race-neutral language, the authors of a chapter on family policy nevertheless warn of an "epidemic[] of divorce, out-of-wedlock births, and family dysfunction" and of the need to "reinforce[] the values of parental responsibility and child development" (Kamarck and Galston 1993, 153–54). They then argue that the best protection against child poverty is the two-parent family, link family breakdown to race, and argue that

> the absence of fathers as models and codisciplinarians is thought to contribute to the low self-esteem, anger, violence, and peer-bonding through gang membership of many fatherless boys. . . . Nowhere is this more evident than in the long-standing and strong relationship between crime and one-parent families. . . . The relationship is so strong that controlling for family configuration erases the relationship between race and crime and between low income and crime. (Kamarck and Galston 1993, 162)

Writing shortly after the height of the crack scare, which the news media and politicians overtly linked to African Americans and African American mothers, the authors further note that "nowhere . . . is the issue of parental responsibility more acute than with the thousands of mothers who use drugs during pregnancy, with disastrous consequences for their offspring *and society*" (Kamarck and Galston 1993, 173, emphasis added).

The chapters on crime and welfare are no better. In the crime chapter, Ed Kilgore (1993) uses terms and phrases such as "abhorrently high crime rates," "grim statistics of violent crimes," "skyrocketing crime rates," "pathology," and "barbarous" to drum up support for his arguments. He calls crime a national security issue, calls for 100,000 new police officers, and argues that Republicans have not been effective crime fighters. And though he uses almost no racial language, most of the relatively few examples of criminal settings and crime he provides are examples that highlight African Americans or situations that Whites associate with African Americans. For instance, he situates crime in public housing projects and disorderly neighborhoods and argues that "the effect of drug use on crime rates is universally accepted" immediately before discussing "pronounced" rates of drug use among African Americans (Kilgore 1993, 193).

Finally, in a chapter titled "Replacing Welfare with Work," Marshall and Kamarck (1993, 217) state, "Most alarming of all is the emergence of an angry and demoralized 'underclass' that is at once dependent on government yet isolated from society at large." They also talk about staggering rates of teen pregnancy and family breakdown, and to ensure that readers understand they are talking about African Americans, they immediately note,

> Suburban flight by a growing black middle class has left behind heavier concentrations of urban poverty and deprived many communities of role models and stabilizing institutions. Blue-collar jobs have been vanishing from our cities, so that black males without college educations face lower earnings and poorer job prospects than a decade ago. Some women's use of crack cocaine has brought new tragedies: the birth of addicted "boarder babies" and the advent of "no-parent families." (Marshall and Kamarck 1993, 217–18)

Marshall and Kamarck do not discuss White poverty or rural poverty, and they highlight the taxes that must be collected (from Whites presumably) to pay for the "police, courts, prisons, remedial education, . . . drug treatment centers, and shelters for the homeless" that they have just argued are needed because Black families and communities are supposedly dysfunctional and pathological. They argue that poor people, whom they have essentially defined as Black, do not believe in hard work, personal responsibility, or playing by the rules, and they claim that the poor (African Americans) benefit from the taxes paid by hardworking (presumably White) taxpayers that are transferred to the poor through the welfare system. In addition, they argue that poor people (African Americans) prefer instant gratification to delayed gratification and engage in self-destructive and socially destructive behaviors such as teen pregnancy, marriage avoidance, welfare dependency, criminal activity, drug abuse, and dropping out of school and work. Furthermore, they directly link family breakdown to African Americans and argue that the welfare system teaches poor people (African Americans) dysfunctional behavior, while undermining traditional American values of "work, family, individual responsibility, and self-sufficiency" (224).

What the DLC and PPI thus set forth in the late 1980s and early 1990s was a discursive political package that drew almost entirely on the racist ideas and rhetoric that the Democratic and Republican Parties had been employing to justify their policies and win elections since the mid-1960s. Some, though by no means all, of the wording they used had changed, and they combined the ideas the two parties had set forth in ways that were sometimes new. But the core racist message remained the same as that employed by so many Democrats and Republicans before them: vote for us if you are White because we will protect you, your family, and your interests from the depredations, pathologies, and dysfunctions of Black people, who are lazy, violent, and criminally inclined and would rather do drugs, collect welfare, and commit crime than go to school, work hard, and pull themselves up by their own bootstraps. Moreover, regardless of what Bill Clinton personally believed about Black people, he made the same arguments and supported the same policies as the DLC and PPI. As a result, he, like the DLC and PPI, drew heavily on the arguments, rhetoric, and strategies employed by Nixon, Reagan, Wallace, Goldwater, Scammon and Wattenberg, Phillips, the Edsalls, Biden, and so many others in the Democratic and Republican Parties who thought that using racist rhetoric and White racial resentments to win elections was perfectly acceptable.

It is not surprising then, that when running for president in 1992, Clinton presented himself as tougher on crime than the Republicans and hostile to welfare, declaring that as president he would "end welfare as we know it." Nor is it surprising that during the election campaign he golfed in front of television cameras at a Whites-only golf course, flew back to Arkansas to attend the execution of a mentally incompetent Black man convicted of killing a White police officer, and posed with Georgia senator and fellow DLC member Sam Nunn for a photograph that showed the two White politicians standing in front of Black convicts at Georgia's Stone Mountain Correctional facility (Haney López 2014; O'Reilly 1995). Stone Mountain was strongly associated, historically, with the Ku Klux Klan and White supremacy, as Clinton and the DLC had to have known. This photo, like Reagan's 1980 campaign speech in Philadelphia, Mississippi, thus made clear to White voters whose interests Clinton intended to support (Petrella 2016; N. Robinson 2016).

Stone Mountain also made clear Clinton's criminal justice intentions. Indeed, the prominent Black politician and civil rights activist Jesse Jackson compared the photo to George Bush's use of Willie Horton in the previous election, while Clinton's Democratic primary rival, Jerry Brown, asked, "Two white men and forty black prisoners, what's he saying? He's saying we got 'em under control, folks, don't worry" (cited in O'Reilly 1995, 410).

But whatever one might think of Clinton's tactics, they worked. Convincing White voters that he would be tough on crime, welfare, and African Americans, and benefitting from Ross Perot's third-party candidacy and the economic difficulties the country was facing, Clinton split the White vote with George Bush and won the election.[4] Moreover, as president, he continued to employ the kind of "subtly" racist rhetoric the DLC used, making public statements such as the following:

- We believe in preventing crime and punishing criminals, not explaining away their behavior. The purpose of social welfare is to bring the poor into the economic mainstream, not to maintain them in dependence. Government should respect individual liberty and stay out of our private lives and personal decisions. We believe in the moral and cultural values most Americans share, individual responsibility, tolerance, work, faith, and family. We believe American citizenship entails responsibilities as well as rights. (Clinton 1994)

- The country is still coming apart at the seams in many places because of family breakdown and crime, and because Government is still too much of a burden on a lot of people. (Clinton 1994)

- And I have to tell you . . . I've talked to a lot of young people who were and some who are in gangs. I once had someone go down to the penitentiary and interview every teenager who was there doing a life sentence for murder. Long before I ever thought of running for President I went to south central Los Angeles—which later became famous when it burned down. . . . And as nearly as I can determine, what has happened is a combination of the following: Number one, too many of these kids are growing up without family supports, without the structure and value and support they need. . . . Number two, too many of those kids also have no substitute for the family that's positive. . . . I mean, 30 years ago, even when kids didn't grow up in intact families in poor neighborhoods, they still lived in places where on every block there was a role model. . . . The third thing that's happened is, weekend drunks have been substituted by permanent drug addicts and drug salesmen, . . . by a drug culture that makes some people money destroying other people's lives. . . . Now, there are lots of other problems. But I'm convinced . . . [these are the] biggest ones: the breakdown of the family, the breakdown of other community supports, the rise of drugs . . . and the absence of work. (Clinton 1993)

- If we could start with some of the problems that are disintegrating forces in our society, I would like to focus on some that we don't often focus on, and those are the economic ones. We all know we have too much crime and violence and drugs and family breakdown. And I don't mean to minimize those things; they are profoundly important. But we are aware and sensitive to those things. (Clinton 1995)

In these various statements, Clinton does not directly mention race. But given White voters' deep familiarity with subtly racist political language, they consciously or unconsciously knew that he was talking about African Americans. And this was especially the case when he linked drugs, crime, violence, and family breakdown together in a single sentence or phrase, as he did in many of the remarks he made during his first term as president, or when he tied drugs, crime, violence, and family breakdown to "disintegrating forces," as he did on more than one occasion. It was also the case when he linked crime and welfare to individual responsibility and "the moral and cultural values most [but not all] Americans share," as he did in the first quote listed above. Indeed, this first quote makes no sense at all if one does not have a deep cultural familiarity with the racist arguments that underpin it, a familiarity Clinton clearly assumes White voters had when he made these remarks, particularly the last one, where he says, "*We all know* we have too much crime and violence and drugs and family breakdown." Finally, White voters knew that Clinton and the Democratic Party were targeting African Americans when they passed Clinton and Biden's 1994 Violent Crime Control and Law Enforcement Act and Clinton's 1996 Welfare Act (the Personal Responsibility and Work Opportunity Reconciliation Act), both of which were highly punitive (M. Alexander 2010; Haney López 2014).

Thus, by the mid-1990s the Democratic Party had staked its electoral fortunes on two things: (a) adopting harsh crime and welfare policies initially advocated by the Republican Party and (b) merging into a single discursive package the diverse strands of racist discourse employed by Democrats and Republicans from the late 1940s to the mid-1990s. White voters understood, even if they did not admit it to themselves, that Democratic and Republican politicians who employed these kinds of discourses and advocated these kinds of policies supported White interests at the expense of Black interests, and Clinton, Biden, and other Democrats hoped that by taking control of these issues and discourses, they could win back those White voters they had lost to the Republican Party. They and the rest of the leadership wing of the Democratic Party did not seem to care that the policies they advocated and the rhetoric they employed would severely harm poor people and Black people, and given the way the US electoral system is set up, they knew that African Americans and the truly liberal wing of the party had little choice but to support them since the only electoral alternative was to vote for the Republicans. The leadership wing thus thought the choice was obvious: continue losing elections or abandon Black people and the poor by adopting violent policies and rhetoric that would severely harm them. They, like the Republican Party, chose to abandon Black people and the poor.

Conclusion

In this and the preceding chapter, I examined the rules governing police stops and searches, demonstrated that these stops and searches are routine, violent, and racially biased, described the many ways in which police violence, mass incarceration, and the war on crime and drugs have physically, emotionally, and psychologically harmed African Americans, and demonstrated that between the late 1940s and the mid-1990s the Democratic and Republican Parties both employed highly racist rhetoric to describe African Americans, crime, and welfare and to justify mass incarceration and the war on crime and drugs. I further demonstrated that the two parties' racist rhetoric became more similar over time and virtually identical in the late l980s and early 1990s and that the two parties employed this rhetoric for the same exact reason: to win elections.

The evidence I presented on these issues is quite disturbing, most importantly because of the extreme violence that mass incarceration, the war on crime and drugs, racially biased policing, and racist political rhetoric have inflicted on Black people, but also because of what the evidence says about the United States and those who have supported the two parties' efforts to be tough on Black people. The evidence also provides strong support for my theoretical argument. I have already demonstrated that this is so for the evidence presented in the last chapter, so I will devote my attention now to demonstrating that the Democratic and Republican Parties' anti-crime rhetoric and policies were extremely violent and that they helped produce overall social order in the ways I theorized they would.

There are three key ways in which the two parties' policies and rhetoric were violent: they constantly reminded African Americans that the government and dominant White society viewed them as dangerous, inferior, and uncivilized outsiders; they reinforced dominant racial discourses that did (and do) the same; and they promoted, justified, and legitimized policing and other criminal justice practices, such as mass incarceration and the war on crime and drugs, that, as I demonstrated in the preceding chapter, have been and continue to be incredibly violent.

I have said much in previous chapters about why being described, treated, and discursively defined as dangerous, inferior, and less than human can produce severe emotional, psychological, and physical harm, and so will say no more about this topic here. But I still need to defend my claim that the two parties' rhetoric and policies are linked to mass incarceration and violent policing practices. In particular, I need to respond to the argument that some scholars have made that federal anti-crime policies and rhetoric have played little role in shaping mass incarceration and local policing practices because (a) most prisoners in this country are housed in state and local prisons and jails (rather than in federal prisons) and (b) state and local criminal justice policies are not derived directly from federal policy (Mauer 2016; Pfaff 2017).

Scholars who make this argument are correct in stating that most prisoners in the United States are not housed in federal prisons and that state and local criminal justice policies are not always directly derived from federal policy. But this does not mean that federal crime policy and discourse have contributed in only minor ways to mass incarceration and local policing and criminal justice practices (Mauer 2006, 2016). Indeed, federal policy and presidential and congressional discourse have strongly shaped state and local anti-crime discourse and policy by both extending *and* placing important limits on what is politically palatable and possible throughout much of the country and by providing local and state politicians with important signals regarding what policies and discourses are publicly acceptable *and* politically effective. Democratic and Republican Party discourse has also played a key role in legitimizing both the continued use of racism in American politics and the violent treatment of African Americans by the police and criminal justice system, which it has done by (a) demonizing African Americans and (b) portraying them as extremely dangerous, as the enemy of Whites, and as a grave threat to the social and moral order. As Michelle Alexander notes about the war on drugs, but is also true of the broader war on crime,

> Some people get so caught up in the prison data . . . that they lose sight
> of the fact that the drug war was a game-changer culturally and politi-
> cally. . . . The declaration and escalation of the War on Drugs marked a

moment in our history when a group of people defined by race and class was defined as the "enemy." A literal war was declared on them, leading to a wave of punitiveness that affected every aspect of our criminal justice system. . . . Counting heads in prisons and jails often obscures that social and political history. It also fails to grasp the significance of the drug war in mobilizing public opinion in support of harsh legislation and policies for all crimes . . . [and in] transforming local police into domestic militaries. (cited in Hager and Keller 2017, 2)

That Democratic and Republican Party discourse and policy shape how US citizens think about crime is further demonstrated by research that shows that citizen support for harsh crime policies in the 1960s and 1970s and harsh drug policies in the 1980s and early 1990s was not tied to actual rates of crime or drug use but instead resulted from (rather than preceded) federal politicians' attention to these issues (Beckett 1997).[5] In other words, US citizens and voters worried about crime and drugs not when crime and drug use increased but instead when federal politicians from both parties told them they should worry about these issues.

It is thus quite clear that presidential and congressional race and crime discourse and policy played a key role in harming African Americans throughout the period examined in this chapter by constantly reminding them that the government and dominant White society viewed them as dangerous, inferior, and uncivilized outsiders, by reinforcing dominant racial discourses that did the same, *and* by playing a key role in fostering mass incarceration, the war on crime and drugs, and racially biased policing and criminal justice. The Democratic and Republican Parties and the politicians and political analysts highlighted in this chapter—Joe Biden, Bill Clinton, Ronald Reagan, Richard Nixon, Barry Goldwater, George Wallace, Ben Wattenberg, Richard Scammon, Kevin Phillips, the analysts who wrote for the Progressive Policy Institute, and Thomas Edsall and Mary Edsall—are therefore pivotally responsible for the extreme political, police, and criminal justice violence inflicted on this country's Black people over the past fifty years.

Consistent with my theoretical argument, the two parties' anti-crime discourse has also played a key role in producing overall social order in the United States for the past fifty years. It has done this, most obviously, by promoting, justifying, and legitimizing the extremely high levels of anti-Black police and criminal justice violence that exist in this country, violence that, as I demonstrated in the previous chapter, produces social order in a myriad of ways predicted by my theory. It has also done this by reinforcing dominant discourses in multiple social arenas. Specifically, it has promoted the idea, central to all dominant discourses, that dominant groups are of the mind and subordinate groups of the body such that the former are rational, civilized, and able to work hard, plan for the future, and postpone pleasure while the latter are not.

Moreover, the two parties' anti-crime discourse has done this in a highly consistent way, both over time and across the two parties, since the 1940s when President Truman's Committee on Civil Rights described Blacks as lazy, careless, unreliable, criminally inclined, aggressive, violent, rage-filled, and a potential physical and mortal threat to Whites, a message that both parties supported throughout the time period under investigation. It is certainly the case that the two parties' rhetoric and discourse were never perfectly identical and that they changed to some degree over time. Nevertheless, the two parties relied on similar and consistent understandings of African Americans from the late 1940s to the late 1990s, with each party borrowing ideas about race and crime from the other and with the two parties co-producing a single underlying race, crime, and welfare discourse that they both used to win the presidency and seats in the House and Senate.

As a result, the Democratic and Republican Parties preached essentially the same racist message to the American public from the end of World War II to the late 1990s, making the parties' reinforcement of dominant race, gender, and class discourses particularly consistent and effective. It is true that the two parties' anti-crime rhetoric and policies were, in part, a response to the high levels of racism that already existed in this country in both the North and the South. But party leaders could have made different choices in response to this racism. They could, for example, have refused to play into it, particularly those leaders—such as Clinton, Bush, Nixon, Goldwater, and Wallace—who did not run racist campaigns until they thought they could not win elections without doing so. Indeed, it is easy to imagine that this country would be very different today if the two parties had chosen differently, with less racial animosity and inequality, less police and criminal justice violence, and fewer families and communities disrupted and devastated by this violence.

But the two parties did not choose differently, resulting in a fifty-plus-year war on crime and drugs and a fifty-plus-year war against African Americans that along with the parties' violent anti-crime rhetoric helped reinforce the racism and dominant race, class, and gender discourses that already existed in this country. Moreover, the parties' violent anti-crime rhetoric also produced and maintained important divisions in society that (a) made it difficult for subordinate groups to work together to challenge the social order and (b) supported the psychological, political, and cultural interests of many Whites. It did this in two key ways: by creating strong divisions between Blacks and Whites and by creating strong divisions between liberal and conservative Whites.

I will start with the divisions this rhetoric created between Blacks and Whites. From the 1940s to the present, Democratic and Republican politicians have employed anti-crime rhetoric that either makes Whites feel superior to Blacks or reinforces Whites' sense of superiority over Blacks, thus dividing these two groups from each other. At the same time, tens of millions of White voters in both parties have voted for White politicians who have employed racist crime (and welfare) rhetoric and supported racist crime (and welfare) policies, indicating to tens of millions of African Americans that many White voters, many White politicians, the two major parties, and the US political system do not care about them or consider them and Whites to belong to the same human, moral, and political community. This, of course, makes it difficult for Blacks and Whites to work together to challenge the social order, both because many Whites feel superior to Black people and because many Black people recognize that Whites feel this way. Moreover, this argument and conclusion hold regardless of whether White voters consciously supported these racist discourses and policies, were ignorant of these discourses' and policies' racist intent and effect, felt that they had to support their party's racist candidates so as to defeat the other party's candidates, or did not support but also did not care that these policies and discourses were racist.

For instance, those White voters who consciously supported racist anti-crime discourses, policies, and politicians or knew but did not care that these discourses, policies, and politicians were racist were clearly behaving in a racist fashion in which they saw themselves as being superior to and different from African Americans. Conversely, those White voters who felt that they had to support their party's racist candidates to defeat the other party's candidates either did not care that they were behaving in a racist fashion, and were thus being racist, or felt that the political system forced them to go against their racial beliefs by offering them no choice but to vote in a racially discriminatory manner, in which case it was the political system that was being racist. This latter dilemma, which many Whites and all Blacks have experienced, arises not because these voters are racist, but because the two parties and the political system usually only provide them with two highly racist choices, leading them to vote for what they see as the lesser of two evils.

Finally, those who say that they are ignorant of, and therefore not motivated by, the racism inherent in the two parties' discourses and policies cannot necessarily be taken at their word. First, it is quite rare for US citizens to admit that they are being racist even when they are behaving in blatantly racist ways. Second, some people consciously or unconsciously wish to remain ignorant of their racial motivations and thus intentionally or unintentionally ignore evidence that would strip them of their ignorance, making their ignorance manufactured rather than real. Third, since the late 1960s, politicians' racist anti-crime rhetoric has generally become more subtle, highlighting issues and themes that direct voters' attention to racial divisions and resentments in society while being "couched," as Nixon's longtime advisor John Ehrlichman (1982, 223) said about Nixon's rhetoric, "in such a way that a [White] citizen could avoid admitting to himself that he was attracted by a racist appeal." As a result, many liberal and conservative Whites who at a conscious level are ignorant of the racism inherent in their favored politicians' anti-crime rhetoric are likely still swayed by that rhetoric's racist appeal, indicating (to the degree that this is true) that they consciously or unconsciously believe that they are superior to African Americans and that they do not belong to the same human, moral, and political community as African Americans.

Evidence that many Whites are swayed by politicians' racist anti-crime rhetoric and that they do not see themselves as belonging to the same human, moral, and political community as African Americans can be found in the fact that so few Whites have ever challenged their own party's racist rhetoric. It can also be found in the fact that politicians from both parties have won elections using this rhetoric and have seen their electoral fortunes improve significantly and decisively after they began to employ it.

And let's be honest here. The verbal and visual rhetoric and discourse that politicians such as Clinton, Bush, Reagan, Biden, Goldwater, and Nixon have used is really not all that subtle. It is certainly more subtle than blatantly racist discourse, and has been subtle enough to allow White politicians and voters to deny that they are being racist. But only people who want to be fooled, who do not want to know what is happening right in front of their faces, can truly misunderstand what is going on. Moreover, if similarly "subtle" anti-White rhetoric was employed by Black politicians, those Whites who are currently fooled would most likely howl in fury. It is difficult to argue, therefore, that Whites who profess ignorance of the racism shaping politicians' anti-crime rhetoric are not swayed by that racism and rhetoric.

Evidence that many Whites are swayed by politicians' racist rhetoric and that they see themselves as being superior to Black people can also be found in a large body of psychological research that demonstrates that Whites often hold strong, implicit, anti-Black biases of which they likely are not consciously aware. This research also finds that many Whites associate Blacks with crime and violence, view Black boys as more culpable for their actions and less innocent than are White boys, and become more concerned about crime and more supportive of punitive carceral punishment when they think that penal institutions are more rather than less populated by Blacks (Eberhardt et al. 2004; Goff et al. 2008, 2014; Hetey and Eberhardt 2014; Hoffman et al. 2005; Jost et al. 2009; Rattan and Eberhardt 2010; Rattan et al. 2012).

A large majority of Whites also hold explicit racial biases. In the mid-2000s, for example, a national survey found that 64.4 percent, 77 percent, 40.2 percent, and 34.6 percent of Whites believed that a little, some, or a great deal of the difference in Black and White standardized test scores resulted, respectively, from African Americans lacking the motivation or willpower to perform well, failing to teach their children the values and skills required to be successful in school, possessing lower levels of intelligence than Whites, or possessing a fundamentally different genetic makeup than Whites. And even higher percentages of Whites (76.3 percent, 80.6 percent, 46 percent, and 37.6 percent respectively) believed that these factors played a little, a big, or some role in explaining why African Americans have lower incomes and worse housing than Whites (Huddy and Feldman 2009). Not surprisingly, explicit biases such as these were held by even greater percentages of Whites in the 1970s and 1980s and by similar or greater percentages of Whites in the 1990s (depending on the specific bias and the year of the study) despite the fact that Whites are often hesitant to openly admit their racial biases (Bobo et al. 2012).

These data also show that the two explanations for racial inequality most favored by Whites in these surveys were that *Blacks lacked motivation and willpower* and that *Blacks failed to teach their children proper values and skills*, both of which were pushed heavily by the Democratic and Republican Parties in these decades as key parts of their explanation for Black crime and Black poverty. And unless the survey respondents were overwhelmingly Republican, which is extremely unlikely, many of those who supported these two explanations had to be Democrats, a conclusion supported by the fact that General Social Survey data show that from the Reagan era to the Trump era (1985–2018), large percentages of self-identified liberals and Democrats supported the motivation and willpower explanation for Black/White differences in jobs, income, and housing (author tabulations of GSS data).

Finally, surveys and experimental research show that implicit and explicit racial biases have political consequences. Research demonstrates, for instance, that such biases "powerfully predict opinions on a wide variety of partisan and policy topics" and that subtle racist appeals such as those employed by Democratic and Republican politicians can activate White test subjects' racial resentments, make their "racial considerations more accessible in memory," and "by priming underlying antiblack predispositions," shape their policy and candidate preferences (Hutchings and Jardina 2009, 399–400; Mendelberg 2001; Payne et al. 2010; Valentino, Hutchings, and White 2002; Valentino et al. 2013, 4).

Thus, the divisions that arise between Blacks and Whites due to Whites' voting patterns and politicians' anti-crime rhetoric and policies do not arise because Blacks are oversensitive or because they inaccurately interpret White behavior. Rather, White voters and politicians create these divisions by behaving in a racist manner: they employ, support, or fail to condemn racist discourses and policies that benefit Whites and severely harm Blacks and vote for politicians who rely on racism to win elections. Whether White voters consciously or unconsciously support these racist discourses and policies or support them out of ignorance or a failure to condemn is irrelevant. The fact that they do support or fail to condemn them and that Democratic and Republican politicians use racism to win elections helps create and maintain discursive, material, and experiential divisions between Blacks and Whites that make it very difficult for these two groups to work together to challenge the social order, thereby promoting a social order that benefits not just Whites, but elites too. Moreover, failure to understand that their favored politicians' discourses and policies are racist or to admit that supporting or failing to condemn these politicians, discourses, and policies is racist further strengthens the divide between Blacks and Whites and, thus, overall social order and elite dominance.

The fact that so many White voters consciously or unconsciously support racist discourses and policies and thus see themselves as being superior to African Americans and as not belonging to the same human, moral, and political community as African Americans also provides these Whites with important psychological and cultural benefits. These benefits, which derive directly from the sense of superiority and difference these discourses and policies promote, strengthen overall social order by helping create, shape, and meet these Whites' perceived interests, thereby (a) building their consent to the social order and (b) aligning their subjectivity and identity with dominant institutional practices and external social and power relations.

Whites also receive important psychological and cultural benefits from divisions that anti-crime discourse and policy create between White liberals and White conservatives. These benefits and divisions promote overall social order in two key ways: by making it extremely difficult for these groups to work together to challenge elite interests and by making liberal and conservative Whites feel better about themselves, thus building their consent to the social order and aligning their subjectivity and identity with those segments of the elite and those dominant institutional practices they most closely identify with.

Anti-crime discourse and policy strongly reinforce divisions between liberal and conservative Whites because these groups fail to perceive four key things: first, that Democratic and Republican anti-crime policies and rhetoric have historically been quite similar; second, that the two parties' anti-crime policies and rhetoric draw on and reinforce a single, underlying, racist discourse; third, that the Democratic and Republican Parties both regularly use racism to win elections; and fourth, that voting for politicians of either party who use subtle racist rhetoric or who support racist policies without employing such rhetoric is still a racist thing to do. These perceptual failures, in turn, allow liberal Whites to support racist politicians and policies without recognizing that they are doing so, making them feel morally superior to and qualitatively different from conservative Whites and allowing them to strongly condemn conservative Whites for their supposedly unique racist behavior. These perceptual failures also allow conservative Whites to look down on and condemn liberal Whites by reinforcing conservatives' beliefs that liberals are too soft on African Americans, crime, and welfare and too hard on working- and middle-class Whites. Moreover, these perceptions and divisions are very emotionally charged, as anyone who pays attention to current events or social media knows, making them particularly psychologically salient and, hence, very socially consequential.

The irony, of course, is that the Democratic Party has not been soft on African Americans, crime, or welfare, while the Republican Party has been tougher on working- and middle-class Whites and, in key respects, is no more racist than the Democratic Party. Thus, these perceived differences are important not because they are real but because to a significant degree they are illusory, dividing liberal and conservative Whites from each other when they are in key respects quite similar and making them each feel superior to the other.

This sense of division and superiority is strengthened, moreover, by the fact that in the 1960s and 1970s anti-crime rhetoric was developed as part of a larger "culture war" discourse, first espoused by George Wallace, that said not only that liberals are soft on African Americans, crime, and welfare but also that they are unpatriotic, have drastically undermined American cultural values, want to force the government down everybody's throats, and do not believe in hard work, discipline, and punishment (Edsall and Edsall 1991a). Thus, when liberal and conservative Whites deride each other for their supposedly different views on crime and race, they are highlighting and strengthening not only the divisions highlighted in this chapter but broader culture war divisions that have existed between these groups since at least the 1960s, thereby further strengthening the social order.

That liberal and conservative Whites each believe they are fundamentally different from and inherently superior to the other is not an especially controversial or difficult to prove point. All one has to do is briefly examine the reporting and commentary found in the liberal and conservative news media, which since Trump's 2016 presidential election has focused ad nauseam on the stupidity, inferiority, and anti-Americanness of the opposing camp (this has continued, though to a lesser degree, into the Biden presidency). What the news media rarely, if ever, note, however, is how often liberal and conservative Whites deride each other when they are thinking and behaving similarly (whether they are politicians, citizens, or members of the news media) and how this *hypocritical and ritualistic discursive practice* allows them to push for similar actions and policies while simultaneously creating unbridgeable, morally laden divisions between them that become the focus of much media, political, and everyday attention. Nor do the mainstream news media note that these discursive practices benefit elites, including those elites who own and run the news media, by (a) reinforcing divisions among key subordinate groups, (b) providing these groups with important psychological and cultural wages, (c) aligning the subjectivity and identity of these groups' members with dominant institutional practices and external social and power relations, and (d) getting liberal and conservative members of the public to support different variants of what are essentially the same violent, order-producing policies, behaviors, and discourses (such as the war on crime and drugs, mass incarceration, racially biased policing, and racist anti-crime discourse).

This hypocritical and ritualistic discursive practice also benefits elites by manipulating non-elites into believing that the political system offers them real alternatives and by diverting energy and attention away from issues that rather than dividing subordinate groups might unite them against elites. For instance, rather than highlighting how similar a whole range of Democratic and Republican policies really are or how similar Donald Trump was to many previous presidents, the public is treated to never-ending liberal and conservative news media diatribes about how different the two parties are and how unique Donald Trump is (and was).

As a result, the public does not know that Trump's use of anti-crime and anti-Black rhetoric is not, in broad terms, any different from that of many other presidents and politicians over the past half century or that Trump is nowhere close to being the first president to cozy up to dictators, to eviscerate environmental regulations, or to use racism to win elections. Nor do the news media make it clear to the public that Trump was not the first president or politician of either party to violently separate large numbers of minority children from their parents, to champion the rights of corporations and the wealthy over those of non-elites, to fight for policies that harm poor people, immigrants, and the middle class, or to take actions that harm the climate and degrade the physical and educational infrastructures upon which Americans depend. Similarly, Barack Obama is rarely, if ever, compared to Trump for having deported more immigrants than any previous president, for helping Wall Street much more than non-elites after the 2008 financial crisis, for tightening the federal budget in ways that degrade national infrastructure, or for playing a key role in making the United States the world's biggest oil producer, thereby contributing significantly to climate change.[6]

The public is thus treated to news that leads them to question and hate their fellow citizens rather than find common cause with them, to form attachments to specific leaders and a specific political party rather than to each other, to love their political party and hate the other, and to think that if only their party were back in the White House everything would be okay when, in fact, much that is important and much that they hate would remain the same. Moreover, the inter-party acrimony that the news media promote takes up much of the available airtime on news and public affairs programming and a significant chunk of people's cognitive and emotional attention, crowding out all sorts of news and information that would be highly useful to the public and that might unite them against elites. It also builds consent to the social order by creating a belief among citizens that we live in a democracy in which voters have a real choice between the parties, and thus real democratic influence over politics and policy, when in fact much of the apparent difference between the parties is illusory.

The evidence presented in this *and* the preceding chapter thus provides strong support for my theoretical argument by demonstrating that mass incarceration, the war on crime and drugs, racially biased policing practices, and anti-crime politics and discourse promote overall so-cial order in several key ways: they (a) reinforce dominant discourses in multiple social arenas, (b) align the subjectivity and identity of key subordinate groups with dominant institutional practices and exter-nal social and power relations, (c) promote the psychological, cultural, and material interests of key subordinate groups, (d) create divisions between subordinate groups that make it difficult for them to organize collectively to challenge the social order, (e) shape and produce subjec-tivity, identity, interests, and consent, (f) create and solidify a distrust of mainstream institutions among some subordinate groups but not oth-ers, (g) divert attention away from issues that might unite subordinate groups against elites, (h) make the social order seem more benign, just, equal, and moral than it really is, (i) create a false belief among citizens that we live in a democracy in which voters have a real choice between the parties, and (j) increase citizen support for the United States' two dominant political parties, each of which is heavily funded by and each of which works diligently to meet the interests of economic elites.

But the evidence does more than this too. When one considers that the levels of police violence directed against African Americans in the United States are so incredibly high, that this violence is shaped so strongly by the electoral strategies of the Republican and Democratic Parties, and that so many presidents, presidential candidates, and politicians since the late 1960s have staked their political fortunes on inflicting both police and discursive violence on African Americans, one cannot but conclude that US political elites rely on this violence to maintain their position and power and thus, that the US political system is inherently violent. One cannot also help but conclude that political and police violence intrude so deeply, directly, and inseparably into the lives of Black people that in key respects, the United States is a police state. Moreover, because the war on crime and drugs and mass incarceration support the political interests of so many elected officials and the economic interests of so many Whites (who as a result of the war do not have to compete with as many Blacks for jobs, housing, wages, schooling, and other valued resources), because they likely reduce the political power of many urban Black neighbor-hoods, and because they pull millions of African Americans out of or significantly reduce their options in the labor market, it is also impos-sible to avoid the conclusion that the millions of people who have been imprisoned because of them are really economic and political prisoners and that both the war and mass incarceration are forms of *violent labor control* that increase overall social order by partially meeting Whites' economic, residential, and educational interests.

Finally, the evidence presented in this and the last chapter demonstrates that violence in multiple institutional arenas—in this case the political and criminal justice arenas—can combine to form a single, coherent, tightly knit system of violence that operates on multiple interacting levels to produce not only racial order but overall social order too. It further demonstrates that the various arenas, fields, policies, and institutions that make up this violent system form a coherent whole because they reinforce each other in multiple ways (for instance, see the last section of chapter 4). Moreover, these things are true for systems of sexual violence (see chapters 2 and 3) *and* for racial violence in welfare, health care, and housing, which in conjunction with racial violence in the political and criminal justice arenas forms an even larger, tightly knit system of violence than that highlighted here. These things are likely also true for other systems of institutionalized violence. It is thus critically important that when studying inequality, social order, and elite privilege we consider not only specific forms of violence or violence occurring in single institutional arenas but also large, coherent, tightly knit systems of violence that operate across multiple institutional arenas and that interact with other factors and systems to produce the outcomes and structures we want to understand, explain, and transform.

Critics of the arguments I have presented in this chapter might state that one cannot lump liberal and conservative approaches to crime together as easily as I have done. They might also claim that it is incorrect to argue that there are essential similarities between the liberal and conservative approaches to crime or to suggest that all liberals are racist and have responded to crime in the same way. My response to such charges is, first, that I have not argued that liberals and conservatives have taken the exact same approach to crime at all times or that liberals are all racist or have all responded to crime identically. Of course there are differences between and within these groups and of course not all on the left or right are racist. Nevertheless, too many scholars and laypeople want to highlight particularities rather than commonalities, as if any differences that exist between people, groups, events, ideas, and concepts means that there can be nothing important in common between them. In addition, too many people are too quick to dismiss the widespread causal power of racism and violence.

The fact of the matter is that from the late 1960s to the mid-1990s liberals and conservatives took increasingly similar positions on race and crime, with the racist discourses, policies, and anti-crime hysteria of the Democratic and Republican Parties converging almost completely in the 1980s and 1990s and with these discourses, policies, and hysteria drawing on and reinforcing the same underlying dominant racist discourse. Those who argue that the two parties' policies and discourses were never perfectly identical are of course correct. But the similarities between the parties' policies and discourses have been both large and striking, have been more important than their differences, and have played an incredibly important role in fostering mass incarceration and anti-Black violence.

At the same time, overt racism and more subtle, but still virulent, anti-Black racial attitudes still persist at dramatically high levels in this country (see my earlier discussion). It is thus irrelevant that not all liberals supported the Democratic Party's racist policies and discourse. Enough did, either consciously or unconsciously, and so few protested against them that liberals and Democrats have been complicit, along with conservatives and Republicans, in the violent devastation caused by rampant police violence and mass incarceration. By employing, supporting, or failing to condemn racist policies and discourses, they have also been complicit in the perpetuation of racism throughout this period, including the racism that fueled Donald Trump's presidential election victory and that continues to fuel his popularity and his positions on crime and immigration.

For when all is said and done, both parties have been spewing racist rhetoric for a long time, reflecting the racism that exists in this country but also keeping this racism alive and giving it specific form. The fact that in the mid-2000s at least two-thirds of Whites believed that lack of motivation and willpower and parents not teaching their children proper values and skills played at least some role in producing Black/White inequality cannot, for example, be divorced from the fact that when talking about crime and welfare, the Democratic and Republican Parties have for decades been telling voters that African Americans lack motivation and willpower and that Black families and parents are dysfunctional. Nor can White liberals deny that they are being racist when they support politicians such as Bill Clinton and Joe Biden. And they certainly cannot expect that their denials will not simultaneously make it easier for Trump supporters to deny their racism when they support Trump.

Thus, in supporting harsh crime and welfare policies, employing racist crime and welfare discourses, voting for racist politicians, and failing to take strong, principled stands against racism except in its most overt forms, White Democrats and liberals have played an important role, along with Republicans and conservatives, in both unleashing police violence against African Americans and paving the way for Donald Trump and the resurgence of the virulent White racism that propelled Trump to the White House.

It is therefore incumbent on Democrats and liberals to admit to the role they have played in supporting and promoting mass incarceration, the war on crime and drugs, police and criminal justice violence against Black people, and virulent White racism. Indeed, if they do not admit to this, it is extremely unlikely that widespread protests against police murders of Black people will ever significantly improve Black lives or alter police and criminal justice practices.

Unfortunately, Democrats and liberals do not seem to be willing to take this step, as evidenced by the Democratic Party's nomination and election of Joe Biden to the presidency of the United States, Biden's popularity among liberals, who just wanted to see Trump defeated, and Biden's and the party's obvious unwillingness to admit to the key role they played in perpetuating this country's long history of police and political violence against Black people. The fact that the identity of the party and the identity and subjectivity of so many of its supporters lie so strongly in the idea that conservatives and Republicans are racist and inhumane and that liberals and Democrats are not also strongly suggests that Democrats and liberals will never admit to the role they have played in fostering mass incarceration and police violence against African Americans, since doing so would be tantamount to attacking their own identity, subjectivity, and perceived interests. Police and political violence against African Americans will therefore continue in the future as they have in the past, producing severe harm, trauma, and misery for Black people and undergirding a social order that benefits Whites in the short term and elites in the long.

Conclusion

The Continuing Significance of Violence

Sociologists have long been interested in explaining social order, and until the mid-twentieth century saw violence, particularly state violence, as one of the key sources of such order. Since then, however, other sources of order have risen in intellectual prominence, due largely to historical circumstance and the critically important work of Antonio Gramsci, Michel Foucault, and Pierre Bourdieu. This shift in attention away from the violent sources of social order has provided us with many critically important insights into how society operates. But for several reasons, four of which I will discuss here, this shift has also been extremely problematic. First, state violence continues to play a key role in producing social order, as my discussion of police and political violence against African Americans makes clear. Second, violence is not just a centralized phenomenon controlled by elites and the state, as Gramsci and Foucault seemed to argue. Like power, violence is also highly dispersed, exercised both routinely and with great order-producing consequence in a multitude of everyday interactions. Third, violence is not just a negative, coercive power, as Foucault, Gramsci, and many other scholars have suggested. It is also a positive, productive power that in both its centralized *and* dispersed forms shapes and produces the very factors— discourses, bodily practices, subjectivities, identities, individual and group interests, generative schemes, dispositions, habitus, embodiment, consent, and so on—that Bourdieu, Foucault, and Gramsci so effectively demonstrated produce social order. Fourth, violence not only helps produce and shape, but also works both independently and interactively with the kinds of factors Bourdieu, Foucault, and Gramsci highlighted in their research to produce social order.

Given all this and given the incredibly high levels of violence that exist in the United States and around the world, I argued that to better understand society and social order, sociologists need to develop and test theoretical arguments that link violence, broadly conceived, to social order. To that end I developed a theoretical model that holds that violent and nonviolent factors work both independently *and* interactively to produce overall social order by (a) reinforcing dominant discourses in multiple social arenas, (b) creating divisions between subordinate groups that make it difficult for them to organize collectively to challenge the social order, (c) aligning the subjectivity and identity of key subordinate groups with dominant institutional practices and external social and power relations, (d) promoting the psychological, cultural, and material interests of at least some subordinate groups, and (e) shaping, creating, and maintaining social, political, economic, and institutional arrangements within and among nations that generate stable profits and secure investment opportunities.

Using evidence regarding sexual violence against women and police and political violence against African Americans, I then demonstrated that violence produces social order in the first four of the five ways that I hypothesized it would (points *a–d* in the previous paragraph), with evidence from the two chapters on sexual violence strongly supporting three of these four key hypotheses (hypotheses *a*, *c*, and *d*) and the police and political violence chapters each providing strong empirical support for all four of these hypotheses. The evidence I presented in these chapters also provided strong empirical support for many of the theoretical arguments I developed to explain why violence produces the intermediate outcomes (outcomes *a–e*) listed in the preceding paragraph (why it creates divisions between subordinate groups, promotes subordinate group interests, and so forth). These chapters also strongly supported my claim that violence is both a negative, coercive power and a positive, productive power that plays a key role in forming and shaping discourses, bodily practices, subjectivities, identities, generative schemes, dispositions, habitus, embodiment, consent, and other order-producing phenomena.

The evidence presented in these chapters and the many examples of violence provided in the theory chapter (chapter 1) thus demonstrate that violence is absolutely central to social life, strongly shaping the kinds of factors that Gramsci, Foucault, and Bourdieu highlighted in their investigations and working both independently and interactively with these factors to promote social order throughout society. Moreover, because the social order that violence promotes is highly unequal, alienating, and oppressive, violence also plays an important role in shaping and maintaining inequality, alienation, and oppression, which it does not just indirectly (through social order) but as I have amply demonstrated, directly too. Violence is therefore an integral component of stratification and must be conceptualized and theorized as such.

What all this means, of course, is that the evidence presented in this book strongly supports my overall theoretical argument as well as the more specific theoretical claims I made when presenting this argument. This book thus contributes greatly to our understanding of violence and social order, to our understanding of stratification, alienation, and oppression, and to what we know about discourse, bodily practices, subjectivity, identity, habitus, embodiment, and consent.

But as is true of all studies, there remain several important issues related to my theoretical argument that I have not explored or fully explored. For instance, as noted in the introduction, I was unable to test my claim that violence shapes and maintains social, political, economic, and institutional arrangements within and among nations that generate stable profits and secure investment opportunities. I will therefore test this claim (as well as my other theoretical claims) in a future book. In addition, though I spent considerable time explaining how the different forms of violence I highlight in this book work together, both discursively and theoretically, to produce social order, I spent less time describing other ways that they intersect. I did, of course, demonstrate that in the United States, violent anti-Black political rhetoric both justifies and is justified by violent criminal justice practices, and thus that the racial violence that occurs in the political arena and the racial violence that occurs in the criminal justice arena intersect with each other to produce social order. I also briefly noted that the violent racist rhetoric President Reagan employed to win presidential elections in the 1980s played a key role in building up White support for neoliberal economic policies that violently harmed hundreds of millions of people around the world, including working- and middle-class Whites in the United States.

But violence occurring in different social arenas intersects in other ways as well. Widespread economic violence in the United States, for example, creates a large low-income population that is more easily re-cruited into the military. And this, in turn, increases support for the military and for military violence abroad among those low-income peo-ple who now depend, either directly or indirectly, on the military for their livelihoods. Violence against African Americans and women also promotes psychological acceptance of aggressive and violent behavior that likely increases support for US military adventures abroad, while US military adventures abroad severely harm the global environment, have violently harmed and killed tens of millions of people around the world (Downey 2015), and are justified using racist and patriarchal dis-courses that, as we have seen, severely harm US citizens. Finally, the mass incarceration of African Americans, US military violence abroad, and neoliberal trade policies that severely harm the working and middle classes likely create a fear, distrust, and resentment of people of color and foreigners that translates into strong citizen support for policies and behaviors that severely harm undocumented immigrants.

I could, of course, provide additional examples of how different forms of violence intersect. But the foregoing examples, in combination with my extensive discussion throughout the book of how different forms of sexual violence reinforce each other, how different forms of anti-Black violence intersect across institutional arenas, and how race, gender, and class violence reinforce each other discursively, make it quite clear that the different forms of violence that exist in the world intersect constantly and in highly complex ways across multiple social arenas to severely harm individuals and social groups and produce inequality, alienation, oppression, and social order.

And this, in turn, raises the question of how we might go about chal-lenging a social order that is founded so strongly on such highly varied and complexly intersecting violences, particularly when these intersect-ing violences form highly stable, overarching, and coherent social struc-tures that fundamentally shape our psyches, bodies, and cultures and when the forms these violences take are so much more varied than what I was able to investigate in this book.

For in addition to the forms of violence investigated here, our lives and society are also shaped and ordered by intimate partner violence, child abuse, violence directed against immigrants, and anti-Black vio-lence occurring in institutional arenas not highlighted in this book. They are also strongly shaped and conditioned by the high levels of police, political, and other violence directed against Native Americans, Latinos, Asian Americans, and Muslims and by the widespread violence directed at lesbian, gay, bisexual, transgender, and queer people. In addition, the global economic system upon which we rely depends on physical violence against workers and immigrants, low wages, workplace health and safety violations, and environmental pollution and disruption, which collectively harm hundreds of millions of people around the world, while our national economic and health care systems work together to disproportionately harm poor people and racial and ethnic minorities, ensuring that people from these groups are more likely than others to have severe health problems, including those related to COVID-19. Over the past several decades, government violence has also been regularly unleashed against protestors and activists engaged in a wide range of political struggles within the United States, including struggles over globalization, free trade, Native American rights, water rights, and police violence. Moreover, the United States regularly perpetrates military violence abroad, operates hundreds of military bases within the United States and globally, which greatly harm people and the environment around the world, and spends more money on its military and exports more weaponry than any other country in the world.

Efforts to challenge this violence and the social order this violence supports must therefore account for (a) the infiltration of this violence into every aspect of social, political, economic, discursive, ideological, cultural, and community life, (b) the fact that this violence is highly durable, complex, structured, and global, (c) the ways in which this violence reaches into our bodies, subjectivities, identities, and conscious and unconscious thought, and (d) the fact that we must overcome multiple forms of violence and multiple, violent discursive structures simultaneously since these discursive structures and this violence reinforce each other so strongly. Efforts to challenge our violent social order must also overcome our society's and the world's ubiquitous social divisions and hierarchies that, by making us believe ourselves to be different from and morally superior to others, allow us to both accept widespread violence and inflict it on others. In addition, these efforts must account for the fact that the discursive structures and violence highlighted in this book do not only shape the way members of dominant groups think and behave. They also shape the way members of subordinate groups think and behave.

People of color can, for instance, be racist, sexist, and homophobic; gay and lesbian people can be racist, nativist, and transphobic; and police and political violence directed against Black people can promote anti-Black sentiments and increase support for anti-Black policing among non-Black people of color. Indeed, much has been written on how efforts to achieve racial and gender justice are weakened by divisions and prejudices such as these that exist within and between subordinate groups (for instance, see Crenshaw 1991; Taylor 2017; and Vargas 2008).

Addressing the issues highlighted in the preceding paragraphs will, of course, be extremely difficult and will require social movements and activists to overcome their many differences in order to achieve a broad-based goal of eradicating all violence, hierarchy, and social division (see Pellow 2014 for an extended discussion of this). It will also require that every one of us radically change the way we think and behave and the way we perceive the world and each other. And this, in turn, will require us to radically rebuild the discursive, ideological, cultural, *and* material structures that shape our thought and behavior, our subjectivities and identities, how we relate to each other, and how we move through the world. It will also require us to rethink our relationship to the natural world, in part because this relationship produces incredibly high levels of physical, emotional, and psychological harm, both among humans and non-humans, and in part because this relationship is central to the mind/body dichotomy that produces so much pain and suffering around the world.

Exactly how we are to achieve these outcomes is not clear to me. But I suspect that the best place to look for guidance are activist organizations, in particular those that are working to overcome intersectional inequalities, to develop new, inclusive, and more fluid ways of thinking about gender and humanity's place in the natural world, and to challenge specific forms of entrenched violence, such as sexual violence against women, police and political violence against African Americans, and violence against Indigenous groups, immigrants, and refugees. For it is exactly these organizations and activists that have thought the longest and hardest about how to overcome multiple injustices and inequalities and how to abolish the social divisions, social structures, discursive categories, and violence that produce inequality, alienation, oppression, and social order.

I defer to activist organizations on this particular issue because I am not a scholar of social change, and unlike activists, my expertise is not in producing social change but in analyzing and theorizing currently existing social structures, which is what I have done in this book. And what my analysis and book show is that we live in a world and society that depend fundamentally on violent harm being done to others and in many cases, to ourselves. They also show that violence is not solely or primarily a characteristic of subordinate groups and the deviant but is instead a key property of the US social system and, thus, that social scientists need to rethink their understanding of social order, make the study of violence a mainstream academic concern, and investigate the myriad ways in which violence throughout society benefits elites and dominant groups.

But most importantly, my analysis highlights the great moral obligation that so many of us have to stop this violence, which would greatly benefit the lives of all those who are directly harmed by it. But ending violence would also benefit the lives of many other people, because regardless of whether we perpetrate or benefit from violence, are its direct victims, or stand by and let it happen, violence alienates us from other people and from our own humanity, making us lesser people in the process. Those who benefit from violence or stand by and let it happen also become less morally worthy beings. Moreover, in alienating and separating us from ourselves and others, violence makes it exceedingly difficult for us to work with others to challenge elite interests and create a world that benefits all non-elites, thereby harming nearly every person on the planet. It is thus in the long-term interests of the vast majority of the world's people to eradicate violence and treat every person and group in the world as if they are what they truly are: fully and equally human, deserving of human rights and dignity, full and healthy lives, and the chance to develop their abilities, talents, and creativity to their fullest. Treating people in this way is, of course, also the morally correct thing to do. It is thus time that we start doing it.

ACKNOWLEDGMENTS

First and foremost, I would like to thank the graduate and undergraduate students who helped me conduct much of the research for this book: Juliana Kagan, Micah Pyles, Asa Iacobucci, Derek Lee, Kevin Adams, and Kate LaMair. Without their help, this book would not have been written, and I am especially indebted to Micah, Asa, and Derek for their assistance, friendship, and support. I would also like to thank my friends and colleagues at the University of Colorado–Boulder, in particular Matt Desan and Isaac Reed, who provided helpful advice as I developed my initial ideas into a more formal theoretical model and then into this book.

The years spent writing this book were particularly difficult ones for me due to medical issues that affected both me and my family. As a result, the support I received from friends and medical practitioners was critical to the completion of this project. Mark Arroyo and Dave Ross were especially important in this regard, getting together at my house every Friday evening to talk, laugh, and make some really good rock n' roll. Also critically important were Dr. Karen Andrews and Sarito Carroll. The medical care they gave me was top-notch, but just as important, they listened to my concerns and cared for me as a human being and not simply another patient. I cannot express how important that was to me and how much it helped me with the writing of this book.

My wife, Alessandra, and grown children, Maja, Natalie, and Dax, also supported me throughout my illness and the writing of this book. Their love for me and mine for them are the most important things in my life.

Finally, I cannot express how grateful I am for the enthusiastic support and advice of Ilene Kalish, executive editor for the social sciences at New York University Press, and for the assistance I received from Sonia Tsuruoka, Yasemin Torfilli, Alexia Traganas, and the production team at NYU. I would also like to thank the scholars who anonymously reviewed my manuscript and Rosalie Morales Kearns, who did the difficult work of correcting the many editing mistakes I made while writing this book. It is much better for their advice and suggestions.

NOTES

1 Some people might argue that it is morally acceptable for individuals, organizations, groups, and governments to use violence in response to other actors' prior violence and thus, that actors are not always morally obligated to help those harmed by their violent actions. While this is likely true in some cases, it is also true that very often what we perceive as prior violence is actually a response to violent actions we engaged in or violent structures we created at an even earlier date. Moreover, given the great degree of prior violence the United States has perpetrated around the world, this argument clearly justifies the use of extremely high levels of retaliatory violence against the United States, which the US government and most US citizens would not support or believe to be morally justified. Finally, those who are harmed when actors respond to prior violence are often not those who engaged in the prior violence.

2 As I discuss in detail in chapter 1, Gramsci, Foucault, and Bourdieu all recognized that violence continues to shape social order, and Bourdieu developed a concept he called symbolic violence. But violence played a less central role for these scholars than for previous scholars and their work led subsequent scholars to downplay violence in favor of other factors.

3 It makes us alien to ourselves because we are ignoring our experiences and alien to the world because we are ignoring both our experiences and empirical evidence in favor of a fantasy world based on a fantasy belief system.

CHAPTER 1. VIOLENCE AND SOCIAL ORDER

1 Natural resources do not have to be exported to the United States for the violence associated with their extraction (if there is any) to benefit US businesses and consumers. For such benefits to accrue to US businesses and consumers, these resources just need to (a) be exported to nations that use them to produce goods consumed by US consumers and businesses, (b) be used to transport consumer and business goods to the United States, or (c) reduce US consumer prices and business costs by increasing global supplies of the resource.

2 As I have discussed in great detail elsewhere (Downey 2020, 2015), the United States also relies on bilateral negotiations, coercive market mechanisms, international organizations such as the World Bank, International Monetary Fund, and World Trade Organization, and various other non-military organizations, institutions, and networks to achieve its resource-related goals.

3 The Israeli-Palestinian conflict has, of course, resulted in significant physical trauma and death among Israelis. However, this section of the chapter is concerned with violence perpetrated by governments that have received US military support, and the United States does not provide such support to the Palestinians. Israel is also able to unleash much greater violence than are the Palestinians. During the 2014 invasion of Gaza, for example, seventy-three Israelis were killed, six of them civilians, and "up to 1,600 Israelis were injured, including 270 children" (United Nations OCHA OPT 2015c). This is a very high level of violence, but much lower than that which Israel unleashed during the war.

4 Immigrants from South and Central American countries are also arrested and deported each year. But the majority of undocumented immigrants from the Americas are Mexican citizens (US Immigration and Customs Enforcement 2017).

5 Of course, not all uses of physical force are violent and not all physical harm results from violence.

6 Mary Jackman (1994, 2002) is one of the few sociologists who have thought extensively about multiple forms of violence operating in multiple social arenas and social relationships. But though her work is incredibly important, she does not link violence to overall social order. For instance, she seems more interested in violence and social control, which is clearly one important aspect of social order, and in why people behave violently than in violence and social order broadly conceived. This is not a criticism of her work. I wish more social scientists recognized, as she does, the centrality of violence to social life. Nevertheless, the link between violence and overall social order is not the focus of her work, leaving an important gap in the literature that needs to be filled.

7 As I argue in the next few paragraphs, Bourdieu did not so much reject this idea as fail to clearly and convincingly explain whether or how violence produces social order.

8 Though Foucault seems to equate violence with capillary power early in one of his lectures on psychiatric power, he quickly disavows this connection in the same lecture (Foucault 2006). In addition, in "The Subject and Power," he quite clearly defines violence in physical and destructive terms, arguing that it "acts upon a body or . . . things; it forces, it bends, it breaks on the wheel, it destroys, or it closes off all possibilities" (Foucault 1982, 789). What it most certainly does not do, according to Foucault, is productively shape and increase the capacities of those upon whom it is exercised. Thus, for Foucault, violence is not a productive power.

9 Two points. First, one can certainly understand why symbolic violence might be violent. But Bourdieu does not tell us why *he* thought it was violent or why symbolic structures are violent only when they are accepted by the dominated. Second, in *On the State*, Bourdieu (2014) defines the state as possessing a legitimate monopoly over the means of physical and symbolic violence. However, the book focuses virtually no attention on physical violence and in it, Bourdieu treats symbolic violence much as he does in his other writings, leaving readers

to wonder, once again, how symbolic violence differs from domination and why Bourdieu thought that symbolic violence is violent.

10 Two points. First, whether one agrees that maintaining a strong military is in the material interests of most US citizens depends on how one defines material interests. I, like many others, believe that US citizens' material interests would be better served if the United States had a much smaller and less aggressive military. However, consistent with dominant US ideology, many other people define material interests fairly narrowly as the ability to make profits and purchase goods in the market. Since this is the dominant definition of material interests in the United States, it is safe to argue that having a strong and aggressive US military is "to some degree" in the material interests of most US citizens. Second, I make other claims about group interests in this section of the chapter that I also disagree with but still think are legitimate given dominant US ideologies and discourses. For instance, though I do not believe that sexual violence is ultimately in anyone's best interests, I do believe that it helps promote men's consent to the patriarchal and overall social orders by providing many men with something they see as benefitting them.

11 In the first draft of this book manuscript, I did include a formal list of hypotheses. But the list was much too long, complicated, and confusing to include in the published book.

12 As should be clear by now, I am not arguing that social order is based solely on violence, only that one cannot fully explain social order without including violence in one's explanatory framework.

CHAPTER 2. SEXUALIZED VIOLENCE AGAINST WOMEN

1 This, of course, is not universally true. The *New York Times*, for example, has argued that workplace harassment can limit women's career advancement opportunities and reduce their wages. Nevertheless, it is fair to say that the *New York Times*, other mainstream media outlets, and public discourse have generally viewed workplace harassment and sexual violation in isolation from broader social forces, in particular from broad patterns and structures of gender inequality.

2 Many of the specific phrases in this paragraph are taken directly from Bordo (2003), chapter 1.

3 Research shows, for instance, that self-blame following traumatic events increases the likelihood of experiencing anxiety, shame, humiliation, post-traumatic stress disorder, depression, substance abuse, psychic numbing, emotional flatness, feelings of powerlessness and worthlessness, and suicidal ideation, all of which represent extreme psychological harms (Norman et al. 2019; Wilson, Drozdek, and Turkovic 2006).

CHAPTER 3. SEXUAL HARASSMENT AND RAPE

1 In this study, harassment was defined as "unwanted interactions in public spaces between strangers that are motivated by a person's actual or perceived gender,

sexual orientation, or gender expression and that make the harassee feel annoyed, angry, humiliated, or scared" (Kearl 2014, 5).

2 The data presented in Sharon Smith et al. (2018) do not allow me to provide a more precise estimate than this.

3 At the time of the interview, Caryn Datz was chief trial deputy of the Sex Assault Unit in the Boulder County, Colorado, district attorney's office (20th Judicial District).

4 Rape trials are not, of course, the only trials in which cultural myths and stereotypes affect jury verdicts. Racial and ethnic myths, for example, also play key roles in many trials, including in rape trials, where they sometimes prove more powerful than rape myths.

5 Wanting to call someone who she knew would probably be awake at that point in the evening and not wanting to call a family member or good friend hardly seem irrational to me. It's also difficult to understand how Bowman could have made a phone call (in 1991 and in a neighborhood that probably did not have a nearby payphone) without going into the Kennedy house. Moreover, as Matoesian (2001) points out, Bowman might have been crying when she said, "I've been raped" or might have said something before or afterward that showed she was not unemotional about what had happened. Bowman might also have been in shock immediately after the rape and for that reason sounded emotionless.

6 The rape of men and boys, who by virtue of being raped are feminized, also supports these discursive elements.

7 According to Caryn Datz (2017), some defense lawyers argue that their client was too drunk to accurately interpret the signals the woman was sending him and therefore that the alleged rape was not really rape.

8 Punishing members of the dominant group who are egregious rule breakers— such as men who violently and brutally rape complete strangers—also helps support the social order by showing that society will, in fact, punish dominant group members who violate serious social norms.

9 As noted earlier, the agency line acknowledges women's rationality and agency, but only to a very limited degree.

10 Many men and boys are disadvantaged by these discursive rules too, but to a lesser degree, in general, than are women and girls.

CHAPTER 4. POLICE VIOLENCE AGAINST BLACK PEOPLE

1 There have, of course, been many police killings of Black people since 2014. I focus on these killings, however, because they played an important role in Donald Trump's presidential election victory, which strengthened national cultural divisions that (a) shape US politics and (b) are an important focus of the following chapter.

2 Unless otherwise noted, my sources for these Supreme Court decisions are M. Alexander 2010; P. Butler 2017; A. Davis 2017; and Epp, Maynard-Moody, and Haider-Markel 2014.

3 Many African Americans living in high-crime neighborhoods want extra police protection. But they often complain that in their neighborhoods the police seem more interested in stopping and harassing innocent people than in investigating actual crimes that have occurred (Center for Constitutional Rights 2012; A. Davis 2017; Gau and Brunson 2010).

4 An initial analysis of 2011–2015 FIOFS data shows that during this period, Blacks represented nearly 60 percent of those who experienced a FIOFS encounter with the Boston police (Marcelo 2016).

5 Fear of being pulled over while driving leads many African Americans to avoid driving in certain areas or to allot extra time for driving so as to adjust for the fact that they are disproportionately likely to be pulled over by the police (Epp, Maynard-Moody, and Haider-Markel 2014).

6 Beck and Blumstein (2017) argue that Travis, Western, and Redburn's (2014) analysis is inaccurate, and present data that indicate that racial disparities in imprisonment rates relative to arrest rates have not worsened since the 1990s. Nevertheless, Beck and Blumstein still find that in 2011 Black/White disparities in arrest rates accounted for only 70 percent of the Black/White disparity in imprisonment rates for robbery, 68 percent of the disparity for burglary, 72 percent for public-order and other/unspecified offenses, 81 percent for rape and other sexual assaults, 88 percent for murder and nonnegligent manslaughter, 56 percent for aggravated assault, 62 percent for other violent offenses, 52 percent for drug trafficking, 52 percent for drug possession, and 53 percent for weapons offenses.

7 To maintain my friend's privacy, I am not providing her name. She approved what I have written about her experiences.

8 Misdemeanor offenses, such as drunk driving and domestic assault, can be quite serious. But very often they are relatively minor offenses such as loitering, spitting, jaywalking, possessing small amounts of marijuana, and shoplifting. Moreover, 97 percent of all misdemeanor convictions result from plea bargains rather than jury trials, with innocent people regularly pleading guilty to misdemeanor charges to avoid more serious charges for which they are also innocent.

9 People with misdemeanors can be jailed for failure to pay fines or fees tied to their arrest, plea deal, or conviction.

10 Because there is much more research available on the consequences of having a father rather than a mother in prison, my discussion focuses on the effects of having a father in prison.

11 Much attention has been paid in recent years to police shootings of African Americans. However, many Whites blame African Americans for these shootings, and most of the non-lethal consequences of the war on crime and drugs and mass incarceration are simply ignored or unknown by most Whites.

12 This is offset to some degree by the fact that prisoners sometimes produce market goods for extremely low wages while in prison.

13 In the quantitative data, respondents were primarily teenagers and young adults. The qualitative data included interviews with people ranging from age eighteen to more than fifty-five years old.

14 Two points. First, I am not arguing that mass incarceration, police violence, and the war on crime and drugs affect all poor, urban African Americans in this way, just a large and significant percentage of them. Second, the criminal justice system is not the only government institution that affects poor African Americans in this way. Government welfare agencies, for example, monitor and regulate poor people in ways that are violent and that make those subject to them distrust mainstream institutions and want to remain invisible.

15 It is not, of course, impossible for Blacks and Whites to work together to challenge the social order, as can be seen in the civil rights movement. But it is exceedingly difficult, and even when Blacks and Whites do work together to create social change, it can be very difficult for them to formulate goals that satisfy the members of each group.

16 This is not the first time I have discussed divergent subjectivities and identities in this chapter. Earlier, I discussed them in terms of the different norms, values, and behaviors held by ex-prisoners and people who have never been in prison. Earlier, I also discussed how biased policing and criminal justice can heighten the salience of race for African Americans, strengthening racial-identity differences between them and Whites. What I am discussing now is similar in that I am continuing to argue that divergent subjectivities and identities can strengthen overall social order by dividing non-elite groups that might otherwise work together to foster social change. But it is also different in several key respects. Most importantly, the point I am making now is that biased and violent policing and criminal justice, in addition to shaping divergent norms, values, and behaviors, also lead Blacks and Whites to have such fundamentally different understandings of the United States and of their own and each other's positions in the United States that it is as if they live in entirely different worlds, worlds that in many respects are unintelligible to each other.

17 A few years ago, a friend of mine told me that he had once received bad medical treatment because his doctors wanted to harm him. Based on my experiences, I thought that this was ridiculous, that the doctors might have been negligent but certainly did not want to harm him. Had he and I not been good friends, I likely would have insulted him by telling him this or I might have walked away because I thought he was living in a fantasy world. But because we were good friends we kept talking, and after an hour or two of additional conversation, I learned enough about his other experiences with doctors to understand not only why he believed this but why this explanation made the most sense given his prior medical treatment. Any pair of people could have had this conversation, including people organizing to change the way medical care is provided in this country. But such a conversation is very unlikely among people who do not know and trust each other well (my friend had to tell me very personal details about his life

before I could understand him) and who, except for the peculiar circumstances of his and my friendship, would be very unlikely to know or trust each other. The point is that his personal experiences and mine created completely different understandings of the world we live in. He lived in a world where doctors intentionally harm people and I did not, making communication and collective action extremely difficult for us. The other point is that it was this conversation that gave me the insight to make this argument. I cannot refer to my friend by name, but I would like to thank him for helping me understand this.

18 For instance, though neither the police nor the welfare system treats all African Americans the same way, the police do treat all African Americans poorly, whereas the welfare system does not. Similarly, though the police treat low-income African Americans and low-income Whites poorly, they treat poor African Americans much worse than they treat poor Whites.

CHAPTER 5. POLITICAL VIOLENCE AGAINST BLACK PEOPLE

1 Wallace, quoted in Carter (1996, 2). I include the n-word in this quote because I believe that it is important for readers to understand how Wallace and his supporters viewed Black people. I also include it, as I argue in the main text, because I believe that Democratic politicians such as Bill Clinton have made arguments so similar to the ones that Wallace made that they were implicitly using the n-word. However, because this word is so very offensive, I use the terms "n'ed" and "n-word" the few times it appears later in the text as either a verb or a noun.

2 Clinton, quoted in Mauer (2016).

3 In the late 1960s, official data showed that crime rates had increased sharply. But it is likely that much of this increase resulted from new and better data collection methods and not from liberal policies or a real increase in crime. Some of this increase also resulted from the growth of the youth population (M. Alexander 2010; Hinton 2016; Murakawa 2014).

4 Clinton, Bush, and Perot won 39 percent, 41 percent, and 20 percent of the White vote respectively.

5 Loo and Grimes (2004) show that in the 1960s, public anti-crime sentiment was also stirred up by the news media, with news media coverage producing rather than following public opinion.

6 Some people might argue that the Republican Party forced Obama to tighten the federal budget by forcing him to agree in 2011 to over $1 trillion in discretionary budget cuts over a ten-year period (as of 2012, Obama had also signed onto $590 billion in cuts to Medicare, Medicaid, and other mandatory programs). However, Obama made a tactical error that he did not have to make in agreeing to the Republican Party's budget ultimatums. More importantly, when Obama first ran for president in 2008, the securities and investment sector was one of his biggest campaign contributors, and when he became president, he chose Wall Street representatives as his key economic advisors. Since Wall Street bankers and investors typically demand government fiscal austerity, and since they provided 20 percent

of his campaign donations in 2008 and were his key economic advisors during his presidency, it is no accident that in addition to not punishing Wall Street for the 2008 financial crisis, Obama also made drastic budgetary cuts in 2011 (and other years) that greatly harmed average Americans (Davenport 2012; Kreitner 2011; Furman and Higginbottom 2012; Skidelsky 2018).

REFERENCES

ABC News. 2018. "5 Times Trump Was Accused of Making Racially Tinged Comments." January 12. www.abcnews.go.com.

Alexander, Jeffrey. 2004. "Cultural Pragmatics: Social Performance Between Ritual and Strategy." *Sociological Theory* 22:527–73.

———. 2016. "Performance and Politics: President Obama's Dramatic Reelection in 2012." *Drama Review* 60:130–42.

Alexander, Michelle. 2010. *The New Jim Crow: Mass Incarceration in the Age of Colorblindness*. New York: New Press.

Al Jazeera. 2019. "Death from Above." March 25. www.interactive.aljazeera.com.

American Civil Liberties Union. 2014. *Black, Brown and Targeted: A Report on Boston Police Department Street Encounters from 2007–2010*. Boston: ACLU Foundation of Massachusetts.

American Civil Liberties Union of Illinois. 2015. *Stop and Frisk in Chicago*. Chicago: American Civil Liberties Union of Illinois.

American Psychological Association. 2007. "Report of the APA Task Force on the Sexualization of Girls." American Psychological Association, Washington, DC.

American Society for Aesthetic Plastic-Surgery. 2014. "Quick Facts: Highlights of the ASAPS 2013 Statistics on Cosmetic Surgery." American Society for Aesthetic Plastic Surgery, Garden Grove, CA.

American Society of Plastic Surgeons. 2017. "2016 Cosmetic Plastic Surgery Statistics." American Society of Plastic Surgeons, Arlington Heights, IL.

American SPCC. 2022. "Child Maltreatment Statistics." April 8. americanspcc.org.

Amnesty International. 2012. "If You Resist, We'll Shoot You: The Democratic Republic of the Congo and the Case for an Effective Arms Trade Treaty." Amnesty International, London.

———. 2017. "Amnesty International Report 2016/17: The State of the World's Human Rights." Amnesty International, London.

Anderson, Irina, and Kathy Doherty. 2008. *Accounting for Rape: Psychology, Feminism and Discourse Analysis in the Study of Sexual Violence*. New York: Routledge.

Armstrong, Elizabeth, Laura Hamilton, and Paula England. 2010. "Is Hooking Up Bad for Young Women?" *Contexts* 9:22–27.

Armstrong, Ken. 2015. "How the Supreme Court Made It Legal for Cops to Pull You Over for Just About Anything—Even Hanging an Air Freshener." Marshall Project, August 3. www.themarshallproject.org.

Aronowitz, Teri, Cheryl Lambert, and Sara Davidoff. 2012. "The Role of Rape Myth Acceptance in the Social Norms Regarding Sexual Behavior among College Students." *Journal of Community Health Nursing* 29 (3): 173–82.

Ascherio, Alberto, Robert Chase, Tim Cote, Godelieave Dehaes, Eric Hoskins, Jilali Laaouej, Megan Passey, Saleh Qaderi, Saher Shuqaidef, Mary Smith, and Sarah Zaidi. 1992. "Effect of the Gulf War on Infant and Child Mortality in Iraq." *New England Journal of Medicine* 327:931–36.

Aubrey, Jennifer. 2006. "Effects of Sexually Objectifying Media on Self-Objectification and Body Surveillance in Undergraduates: Results of a 2-Year Panel Study." *Journal of Communication* 56:366–86.

Aubrey, Jennifer, and Cynthia Frisby. 2011. "Sexual Objectification in Music Videos: A Content Analysis Comparing Gender and Genre." *Mass Communication and Society* 14:475–501.

Ayo, Nike. 2012. "Understanding Health Promotion in a Neoliberal Climate and the Making of Health Conscious Citizens." *Critical Public Health* 22:99–105.

Bame, Yael. 2017. "Nearly a Third of Women Have Been Sexually Harassed at Work." YouGov, April 25. https://today.yougov.com.

Bartky, Sandra. 1988. "Foucault, Femininity, and the Modernization of Patriarchal Power." In *Feminism and Foucault: Reflections on Resistance*, edited by Irene Diamond and Lee Quinby, 61–86. Boston: Northeastern University Press.

———. 1990. *Femininity and Domination: Studies in the Phenomenology of Oppression.* New York: Routledge.

Baskerville, Stephen. 2004. *The Fatherhood Crisis: Time for a New Look?* Dallas: National Center for Policy Analysis.

Bass, Jack, and Walter DeVries. 1976. *The Transformation of Southern Politics: Social Change and Political Consequence since 1945.* New York: Basic Books.

Baumgartner, Frank, Derek Epp, and Kelsey Shoub. 2018. *Suspect Citizens: What 20 Million Traffic Stops Tell Us about Policing and Race.* New York: Cambridge University Press.

Bay-Cheng, Laina. 2012. "Recovering Empowerment: De-Personalizing and Re-Politicizing Adolescent Female Sexuality." *Sex Roles* 66:713–17.

———. 2015. "The Agency Line: A Neoliberal Metric for Appraising Young Women's Sexuality." *Sex Roles* 73:279–91.

Bay-Cheng, Laina, and Rebecca Eliseo-Arras. 2008. "The Making of Unwanted Sex: Gendered and Neoliberal Norms in College Women's Unwanted Sexual Experiences." *Journal of Sex Research* 45:386–97.

BBC News. 2003. "Flashback: 1991 Gulf War." March 20. http://news.bbc.co.uk.

Beck, Allen, and Alfred Blumstein. 2017. "Racial Disproportionality in US State Prisons: Accounting for the Effects of Racial and Ethnic Differences in Criminal Involvement, Arrests, Sentencing, and Time Served." *Journal of Quantitative Criminology.* DOI 10.1007/s10940-017-9357-6.

Beckett, Katherine. 1997. *Making Crime Pay: Law and Order in Contemporary American Politics.* New York: Oxford University Press.

Belknap, Joanne. 2010. "Rape: Too Hard to Report and Too Easy to Discredit Victims." *Violence Against Women* 16:1335–44.

Bener, Abdulbari, Suhaila Ghuloum, Abdulla Al-Hamaq, and Elnour Dafeeah. 2012. "Association between Psychological Distress and Gastrointestinal Symptoms in Diabetes Mellitus." *World Journal of Diabetes* 3 (6): 123–29.

Benston, Margaret. 1969. "The Political Economy of Women's Liberation." *Monthly Review* 21:13–27.

Bloustien, Gerry. 2003. *Girl Making: A Cross-Cultural Ethnography on the Processes of Growing Up Female*. New York: Berghahn Books.

Blum, William. 2014. *Killing Hope: US Military and CIA Interventions since World War II*. London: Zed Books.

Bobo, Lawrence, Camille Charles, Maria Krysan, and Alicia Simmons. 2012. "The Real Record on Racial Attitudes." In *Social Trends in American Life: Findings from the General Social Survey since 1972*, edited by Peter Marsden, 47–86. Princeton: Princeton University Press.

Bordo, Susan. 2003. *Unbearable Weight: Feminism, Western Culture, and the Body*. Berkeley: University of California Press.

Bourdieu, Pierre. 1977. *Outline of a Theory of Practice*. Cambridge: Cambridge University Press.

———. 1984. *Distinction*. New York: Routledge.

———. 1990. *The Logic of Practice*. Stanford: Stanford University Press.

———. 2001. *Masculine Domination*. Stanford: Stanford University Press.

———. 2014. *On the State: Lectures at the College de France, 1989–1992*. Cambridge, UK: Polity.

Bourdieu, Pierre, and Luc Boltanski. 1976. "La production de l'idéologie dominante." *Actes de la Recherche en Sciences Sociales* 2:4–73.

Bowley, Graham, and Richard Pérez-Peña. 2017a. "Cosby Lawyer Questions Accuser's Credibility during Second Day on Stand." *New York Times*, June 8, C15.

———. 2017b. "Cosby Accuser Takes the Stand for Nearly Four Grueling Hours." *New York Times*, June 7, A13.

Bradford, Ben, Jonathan Jackson, and Elizabeth Stanko. 2009. "Contact and Confidence: Revisiting the Impact of Public Encounters with the Police." *Policing and Society* 19 (1): 20–46.

Brah, Avtar, and Ann Phoenix. 2004. "Questions of Difference and International Feminism." *Journal of International Women's Studies* 5:75–86.

Braman, Donald. 2004. *Doing Time on the Outside: Incarceration and Family Life in Urban America*. Ann Arbor: University of Michigan Press.

Branch, Adam. 2011. *Displacing Human Rights: War and Intervention in Northern Uganda*. New York: Oxford University Press.

Breiding, Matthew, Sharon Smith, Kathleen Basile, Mikel Walters, Jieru Chen, and Melissa Merrick. 2014. "Prevalence and Characteristics of Sexual Violence, Stalking, and Intimate Partner Violence Victimization—National Intimate Partner and Sexual Violence Survey, United States, 2011." US Department of

Health and Human Services, Centers for Disease Control and Prevention, Washington, DC.

Breines, Juliana, Jennifer Crocker, and Julie Garcia. 2008. "Self-Objectification and Well-Being in Women's Daily Lives." *Personality and Social Psychology Bulletin* 34:583–98.

Breman, Jan. 2006. "Slumlands." *New Left Review* 40:141–48.

———. 2010. *Outcast Labor in Asia: Circulation and Informalization of the Workforce at the Bottom of the Economy.* New York: Oxford University Press.

Brison, Susan. 2002. *Aftermath: Violence and the Remaking of a Self.* Princeton: Princeton University Press.

Bronson, Brittany. 2017. "Where Are the Rape-Kit Nurses?" *New York Times*, June 20, A25.

Brooks, David. 2018. "Now Is the Time to Talk about the Power of Touch." *New York Times*, January 18. www.nytimes.com.

Brown, Brian, and Sally Baker. 2012. *Responsible Citizens: Individuals, Health, and Policy under Neoliberalism.* New York: Anthem.

Brown, Wendy. 2003. "Neo-Liberalism and the End of Liberal Democracy." *Theory and Event* 7:1–43.

Brunson, Rod. 2007. "Police Don't Like Black People: African-American Young Men's Accumulated Police Experiences." *Criminology and Public Policy* 6 (1): 71–102.

Brunson, Rod, and Jody Miller. 2006. "Gender, Race, and Urban Policing: The Experience of African American Youths." *Gender and Society* 20 (4): 531–52.

Bufacchi, Vittorio. 2007. *Violence and Social Justice.* New York: Palgrave Macmillan.

Bunker, Stephen, and Paul Ciccantell. 2005. *Globalization and the Race for Resources.* Baltimore: Johns Hopkins University Press.

Burawoy, Michael. 1979. *Manufacturing Consent: Changes in the Labor Process under Monopoly Capitalism.* Chicago: University of Chicago Press.

Burt, Callie, Gary Sweeten, and Ronald Simons. 2014. "Self-Control through Emerging Adulthood: Instability, Multidimensionality, and Criminological Significance." *Criminology* 52 (3): 450–87.

Burtman, Heather. 2017. "My Body Doesn't Belong to You." *New York Times*, June 18, Sunday Styles, 5.

Butler, Judith. 1990. *Gender Trouble.* New York: Routledge.

Butler, Paul. 2017. *Chokehold: Policing Black Men.* New York: New Press.

Cahill, Ann. 2011. *Overcoming Objectification: A Carnal Ethics.* New York: Routledge.

Cantor, David, Bonnie Fisher, Susan Chibnall, Reanne Townsend, Hyunshik Lee, Carol Bruce, and Gail Thomas. 2017. "Report on the AAU Campus Climate Survey on Sexual Assault and Sexual Misconduct." Association of American Universities, Washington, DC.

Carter, Dan. 1996. *From George Wallace to Newt Gingrich: Race in the Conservative Counterrevolution, 1963–1994.* Baton Rouge: Louisiana State University Press.

Center for Constitutional Rights. 2011. *2011 NYPD Stop and Frisk Statistics.* New York: Center for Constitutional Rights.

———. 2012. *Stop and Frisk: The Human Impact.* New York: Center for Constitutional Rights.

Centers for Disease Control. 2016. "About Behavioral Risk Factor Surveillance System ACE Data." February 16. www.cdc.gov.

Chakraborty, Jayajit, and Marc Armstrong. 2001. "Assessing the Impact of Airborne Toxic Releases on Populations with Special Needs." *Professional Geographer* 53 (1): 119–31.

Chamberlain, Alyssa, and John Hipp. 2015. "It's All Relative: Concentrated Disadvantage within and across Neighborhoods and Communities, and the Consequences for Neighborhood Crime." *Journal of Criminal Justice* 43 (6): 431–43.

Cheng, Yawen, Chun-Li Du, Juey-Jen Hwang, I-Shin Chen, Ming-Fong Chen, and Ta-Chen Su. 2014. "Working Hours, Sleep Duration and the Risk of Acute Coronary Heart Disease: A Case-Control Study of Middle-Aged Men in Taiwan." *International Journal of Cardiology* 171:419–22.

Chira, Susan. 2017. "Cosby Case Raises Issue of Legal Bias." *New York Times*, June 21, C1.

Chomsky, Noam, and Edward Herman. 1979. *The Political Economy of Human Rights.* Vols. 1 and 2. Boston: South End.

Clark, Ramsey. 1992. *The Fire This Time: US War Crimes in the Gulf.* New York: Thunder's Mouth.

Clegg, John, and Adaner Usmani. 2019. "The Economic Origins of Mass Incarceration." *Catalyst* 3 (3). catalyst-journal.com.

Clinton, Bill. 1993. "Remarks to the Community in Memphis." American Presidency Project, November 13. www.presidency.ucsb.edu.

———. 1994. "Remarks at the Democratic Leadership Council Gala." American Presidency Project, December 6. www.presidency.ucsb.edu.

———. 1995. "Remarks at the White House Conference on Character Building for a Civil and Democratic Society." American Presidency Project, May 20. www.presidency.ucsb.edu.

Cohen, Cathy. 2010. *Democracy Remixed: Black Youth and the Future of American Politics.* Oxford: Oxford University Press.

Cohn, Amy, Heidi Zinzow, Heidi Resnick, and Dean Kilpatrick. 2013. "Correlates of Reasons for Not Reporting Rape to Police: Results from a National Telephone Household Probability Sample of Women with Forcible or Drug-or-Alcohol Facilitated/Incapacitated Rape." *Journal of Interpersonal Violence* 28:455–73.

Coleman, Rebecca. 2009. *The Becoming of Bodies: Girls, Images, Experience.* Manchester, UK: Manchester University Press.

Collins, Angela, Scott Menard, and David Pyrooz. 2018. "Collective Behavior and the Generality of Integrated Theory: A National Study of Gang Fighting." *Deviant Behavior* 39 (7): 992–1005.

Collins, Randall. 2004. *Interaction Ritual Chains.* Princeton: Princeton University Press.

———. 2008. *Violence: A Micro-Sociological Theory.* Princeton: Princeton University Press.

Collins, Rebecca. 2011. "Content Analysis of Gender Roles in Media: Where Are We Now and Where Should We Go?" *Sex Roles* 64:290–98.

Connell, R. W. 2000. *The Men and the Boys.* Berkeley: University of California Press.

———. 2005. *Masculinities.* 2nd. ed. Berkeley: University of California Press.

Connors, Joanna. 2016. *I will Find You: A Reporter Investigates the Life of the Man Who Raped Her.* New York: Grove.

Conrad, Kate, Travis Dixon, and Yuanyuan Zhang. 2009. "Controversial Rap Themes, Gender Portrayals and Skin Tone Distortion: A Content Analysis of Rap Music Videos." *Journal of Broadcasting and Electronic Media* 53:134–56.

Corrigan, Rose. 2013. *Up against a Wall: Rape Reform and the Failure of Success.* New York: New York University Press.

Crenshaw, Kimberlé. 1989. "Demarginalizing the Intersection between Race and Sex: A Black Feminist Critique of Anti-Discrimination Doctrine, Feminist Theory and Anti-Racist Politics." *University of Chicago Legal Forum* 1989 (1): 139–67.

———. 1991. "Mapping the Margins: Identity, Politics, Intersectionality and Violence against Women." *Stanford Law Review* 43:1241–79.

Crossette, Barbara. 1995. "Iraq Sanctions Kill Children, U.N. Reports." *New York Times*, December 1. www.nytimes.com.

Cypher, James. 2016. "Hegemony, Military Power Projection and US Structural Economic Interests in the Periphery." *Third World Quarterly* 37:800–817.

Damasio, Antonio. 1994. *Descartes' Error: Emotion, Reason, and the Human Brain.* London: Penguin.

Datz, Caryn. 2017. Author's interview with Caryn Datz, chief trial deputy, Sex Assault Unit, Office of the District Attorney, 20th Judicial District, Boulder County, CO. July 21.

Davenport, Reid. 2012. "Wall Street Funds Down from Obama's Inaugural Run." OpenSecrets News, October 25. www.opensecrets.org.

Davis, Angela. 2014. *From Murder Capital to Police State: The Real Story behind Camden's Transition.* Scotts Valley, CA: CreateSpace.

———. 2017. *Policing the Black Man.* New York: Pantheon.

Davis, Mike. 2007. *Planet of Slums.* New York: Verso.

Dawson, Michael, and Lawrence Bobo. 2004. "The Reagan Legacy and the Racial Divide in the George W. Bush Era." *Du Bois Review* 1 (2): 209–12.

Dean, Mitchell. 1999. *Governmentality: Power and Rule in Modern Society.* Thousand Oaks, CA: Sage.

Decker, Scott, Natalie Ortiz, Cassia Spohn, and Eric Hedberg. 2015. "Criminal Stigma, Race, and Ethnicity: The Consequences of Imprisonment for Employment." *Journal of Criminal Justice* 43:108–21.

Defense Security Cooperation Agency. 2014. "Foreign Military Sales, Foreign Military Construction Sales and Other Security Cooperation Historical Facts as of September 30, 2014." Department of Defense, Washington, DC.

Democracy Now. 2016a. "US-Backed Saudi Forces Bomb Yemeni Funeral, Killing 140, Injuring 500 in Possible War Crime." October 11. www.democracynow.org.

———. 2016b. "Journalist Iona Craig: The US Could Stop Refueling Saudis and End Devastating War in Yemen Tomorrow." December 15. www.democracynow.org.

———. 2017. "Gaza on Verge of Collapse as Israel Sends 2.2M People 'Back to Middle Ages' in Electricity Crisis." July 19. www.democracynow.org.

Dhoest, Alexander, Koen Panis, and Steve Paulussen. 2020. "Women at the Table: Female Guests and Experts in Current Affairs Television." *Journalism Practice* 16 (4): 1–18. https://doi.org/10.1080/17512786.2020.1807392.

Dines, Gail. 2009. "Childified Women: How the Mainstream Porn Industry Sells Child Pornography to Men." In *The Sexualization of Childhood*, edited by Sharna Olfman, 121–42. London: Praeger.

Dittmar, Helga, Emma Halliwell, and Suzanne Ive. 2006. "Does Barbie Make Girls Want to Be Thin? The Effect of Experimental Exposure to Images of Dolls on the Body Image of 5- to 8-Year-Old Girls." *Developmental Psychology* 42:283–92.

Dohnt, Hayley, and Marika Tiggemann. 2006. "Body Image Concerns in Young Girls: The Role of Peers and Media Prior to Adolescence." *Journal of Youth and Adolescence* 35:141–51.

Domhoff, William. 1990. *The Power Elite and the State: How Policy Is Made in America.* New York: Aldine De Gruyter.

Downey, Liam. 2006. "Environmental Racial Inequality in Detroit." *Social Forces* 85 (2): 771–96.

———. 2015. *Inequality, Democracy, and the Environment.* New York: New York University Press.

———. 2020. "Power, Hegemony, and World Society Theory: A Critical Evaluation." *Socius: Sociological Research for a Dynamic World.* doi.org/10.1177/2378023120920.

Downey, Liam, Eric Bonds, and Katherine Clark. 2010. "Natural Resource Extraction, Armed Violence, and Environmental Degradation." *Organization and Environment* 23 (4): 417–45.

Downs, Edward, and Stacy Smith. 2010. "Keeping Abreast of Hypersexuality: A Video Game Character Content Analysis." *Sex Roles* 62:721–33.

Drake, Bruce. 2018. *Incarceration Gap Widens between Whites and Blacks.* Pew Research Center. www.pewresearch.org.

Dressner, Julie, and Edwin Martinez. 2012. "The Scars of Stop-and-Frisk." *New York Times*, June 12. www.nytimes.com.

Du Bois, W. E. B. 1935. *Black Reconstruction in America: An Essay toward a History of the Part Which Black Folk Played in the Attempt to Reconstruct Democracy in America, 1860–1880.* New York: Russell and Russell.

Durham, Brandy M. 2005. "Presidential Rhetoric and the Economy." *Journal of Politics* 67 (3): 627–45.

Dworkin, Andrea. 1981. *Pornography: Men Possessing Women.* New York: Putnam's.

Eberhardt, Jennifer, Phillip Goff, Valerie Purdie, and Paul Davies. 2004. "Seeing Black: Race, Crime, and Visual Processing." *Journal of Personality and Social Psychology* 47 (6): 876–93.

Edsall, Thomas, and Mary Edsall. 1991a. *Chain Reaction: The Impact of Race, Rights, and Taxes on American Politics*. New York: Norton.

———. 1991b. "When the Official Subject Is Presidential Politics, Taxes, Welfare, Crime, Rights, or Values . . . the Real Subject Is Race." *Atlantic*, May. www.theatlantic.com.

Ehrlichman, John. 1982. *Witness to Power: The Nixon Years*. New York: Simon and Schuster.

Enns, Diane. 2006. "At the Limit: Violence, Belonging and Self-Determination." In *Violence, Victims, Justifications: Philosophical Approaches*, edited by Felix O. Murchadha. Bern: Peter Lang.

Epp, Charles, Steven Maynard-Moody, and Donald Haider-Markel. 2014. *Pulled Over: How Police Stops Define Race and Citizenship*. Chicago: University of Chicago Press.

Evans, Adrienne, and Sarah Riley. 2014. *Technologies of Sexiness: Sex, Identity, and Consumer Culture*. New York: Oxford University Press.

Ezzell, Matthew. 2009. "Pornography, Lad Mags, Video Games, and Boys: Reviving the Canary in the Cultural Coal Mine." In *The Sexualization of Childhood*, edited by Sharna Olfman, 7–32. London: Praeger.

Fagan, Jeffrey. 2012. *Second Supplemental Report of Jeffrey Fagan, Ph.D.* US District Court, Southern District of New York.

Fairness and Accuracy in Reporting. 2010. "Taking the Public Out of Public TV: PBS Fare Differs Little from Commercial TV." October 19. fair.org.

Fan, Andrew. 2018. "Chicago Police Are 14 Times More Likely to Use Force against Young Black Men Than against Whites." *Intercept*, August 16. theintercept.com.

Fanon, Frantz. 1967. *Black Skin, White Masks*. New York: Grove.

Farber, David. 1994. *The Age of Great Dreams: America in the 1960s*. New York: Hill and Wang.

Faux, Jeff. 1993. "The Myth of the New Democrats." *American Prospect*, December 19. prospect.org.

Feldblum, Chai, and Victoria Lipnic. 2016. "Report of the Co-Chairs of the EEOC Select Task Force on Study of Harassment in the Workplace." US Equal Employment Opportunity Commission, Washington, DC.

Ferree, Myra. 2012. *Varieties of Feminism: German Gender Politics in Global Perspective*. Stanford: Stanford University Press.

Finkelhor, D., H. Turner, R. Ormrod, and S. L. Hamby. 2009. "Violence, Abuse, and Crime Exposure in a National Sample of Children and Youth." *Pediatrics* 124:1411–23.

Fligstein, Neil. 2001. *The Architecture of Markets: An Economic Sociology of Twenty-First-Century Capitalist Societies*. Princeton: Princeton University Press.

Fontana, Benedetto. 2008. "Hegemony and Power in Gramsci." In *Hegemony: Studies in Consensus and Coercion*, edited by Richard Howson and Kylie Smith. New York: Routledge.

Foster, John, Hannah Holleman, and Robert W. McChesney. 2008. "The US Imperial Triangle and Military Spending." *Monthly Review* 60:1–19.

Foucault, Michel. 1972. *The Archaeology of Knowledge*. New York: Routledge.

———. 1977. *Discipline and Punish: The Birth of the Prison*. London: Allen Lane.

———. 1981. "The Order of Discourse." In *Untying the Text: A Post-Structuralist Reader*, edited by Robert Young, 48–79. Boston: Routledge and Kegan Paul.

———. 1982. "The Subject and Power." *Critical Inquiry* 8:777–95.

———. 1990. *The History of Sexuality*. Vol. 1, *An Introduction*. New York: Vintage.

———. 2006. *Psychiatric Power: Lectures at the College de France*. New York: Palgrave Macmillan.

Francisco, Patricia. 1999. *Telling: A Memoir of Rape and Recovery*. New York: HarperCollins.

Freedman, Karyn. 2014. *One Hour in Paris: A True Story of Rape and Recovery*. Chicago: University of Chicago Press.

Freedman, Rita. 1986. *Beauty Bound*. Lexington, MA: Lexington Books.

Frewen, Paul, and Ruth Lanius. 2015. *Healing the Traumatized Self: Consciousness, Neuroscience, Treatment*. New York: Norton.

Frontline. n.d. "Iraqi Death Toll." PBS. Accessed May 18, 2017. www.pbs.org.

Fryer, Roland. 2016. *An Empirical Analysis of Racial Differences in Police Use of Force*. Cambridge, MA: National Bureau of Economic Research.

Furman, Jason, and Heather Higginbottom. 2012. "President Obama's Record and Proposals for Cutting Spending." White House, December 11. https://obamawhitehouse.archives.gov.

Galston, William, and Elaine Kamarck. 1989. *The Politics of Evasion: Democrats and the Presidency*. Washington, DC: Progressive Policy Institute.

Galtung, Johan. 1969. "Violence, Peace, and Peace Research." *Journal of Peace Research* 3:167–91.

———. 1990. "Cultural Violence." *Journal of Peace Research* 27:291–305.

Gau, Jacinta. 2010. "A Longitudinal Analysis of Citizens' Attitudes about Police." *Policing: An International Journal of Police Strategies and Management* 33 (2): 236–52.

Gau, Jacinta, and Rod Brunson. 2010. "Procedural Justice and Order Maintenance Policing: A Study of Inner-City Young Men's Perceptions of Police Legitimacy." *Justice Quarterly* 27 (2): 255–79.

Gavey, Nicola. 2012. "Beyond 'Empowerment'? Sexuality in a Sexist World." *Sex Roles* 66:718–24.

Germov, John, and Lauren Williams. 1999. "Dieting Women: Self-Surveillance and the Body Panopticon." In *Weighty Issues: Fatness and Thinness as Social Problems*, edited by Jeffrey Sobal and Donna Maurer, 117–32. Hawthorne, NY: De Gruyter.

Gibson, Chris, Samuel Walker, Wesley Jennings, and J. Mitchell Miller. 2010. "The Impact of Traffic Stops on Calling the Police for Help." *Criminal Justice Policy Review* 21 (2): 139–59.

Gill, Rosalind. 2007. "Critical Respect: The Difficulties and Dilemmas of Agency and 'Choice' for Feminism: A Reply to Duits and van Zoonen." *European Journal of Women's Studies* 14:65–76.

———. 2008. "Culture and Subjectivity in Neoliberal and Postfeminist Times." *Subjectivity* 25:432–45.

———. 2012. "Media, Empowerment, and the 'Sexualization of Culture' Debates." *Sex Roles* 66:736–45.

Gilman, Robert. 2014. "Foreign Military Sales." Defense Security Cooperation Agency, Department of Defense, Washington, DC.

Glick, Peter, Sadie Larsen, and Cathryn Johnson. 2005. "Evaluations of Sexy Women in Low- and High-Status Jobs." *Psychology of Women Quarterly* 29:389–95.

Global Witness. 2016. "On Dangerous Ground." Global Witness, London.

Goff, Phillip, Jennifer Eberhardt, Melissa Williams, and Matthew Jackson. 2008. "Not Yet Human: Implicit Knowledge, Historical Dehumanization, and Contemporary Consequences." *Journal of Personality and Social Psychology* 94 (2): 292–306.

Goff, Phillip, Matthew Jackson, Brooke Di Leone, Carmen Culotta, and Natalie DiTomasso. 2014. "The Essence of Innocence: Consequences of Dehumanizing Black Children." *Interpersonal Relations and Group Processes* 106 (4): 526–45.

Goffman, Erving. 1959. *The Presentation of Self in Everyday Life*. New York: Doubleday.

Goldwater, Barry. 1964. Acceptance Speech at the 28th Republican National Convention, San Francisco. www.washingtonpost.com.

Gonzales, Roberto. 2016. *Lives in Limbo: Undocumented and Coming of Age in America*. Oakland: University of California Press.

Gonzalez-Barrera, Ana, and Jens Krogstad. 2016. "US Immigrant Deportations Declined in 2014, but Remain Near Record High." Pew Research Center, August 31. www.pewresearch.org.

Gordon, David M., Richard Edwards, and Michael Reich. 1982. *Segmented Work, Divided Workers*. New York: Cambridge University Press.

Gotell, Lise. 2008. "Sexual Assault Law: Neoliberal Sexual Subjects and Risky Women." *Akron Law Review* 41:865–98.

———. 2010. "Canadian Sexual Assault Law: Neoliberalism and the Erosion of Feminist-Inspired Law Reforms." In *Rethinking Rape Law: International and Comparative Perspectives*, edited by Clare McGlynn and Vanessa E. Munro, 209–23. New York: Routledge.

Gottinger, Paul, and Ken Klippentstein. 2014. "US Provides Israel Weapons Used on Gaza." *CounterPunch*, August 1. www.counterpunch.org.

Grabe, Shelly, L. Monique Ward, and Janet Hyde. 2008. "The Role of the Media in Body Image Concerns among Women: A Meta-Analysis of Experimental and Correlational Studies." *Psychological Bulletin* 134:460–76.

Graf, Nikki. 2018. "Sexual Harassment at Work in the Era of #MeToo." Pew Research Center, April 4. www.pewresearch.org.

Graff, Kaitlin, Sarah Murnen, and Linda Smolak. 2012. "Too Sexualized to Be Taken Seriously? Perceptions of a Girl in Childlike vs. Sexualizing Clothing." *Sex Roles* 66:764–75.

Gramsci, Antonio. 1971. *Selections from the Prison Notebooks*. New York: International Publishers.

———. 1992a. *Prison Notebooks*. Vol. 1. New York: Columbia University Press.

———. 1992b. *Prison Notebooks*. Vol. 2. New York: Columbia University Press.

Gray, Eliza. 2014. "Why Victims of Rape in College Don't Report to the Police." *Time*, June 23. time.com.

Greenberg, Jon. 2015. "Trump's Pants on Fire Tweet That Blacks Killed 81% of White Homicide Victims." Politifact, November 23. www.politifact.com.

Greenberg, Stanley. 1985. *Democratic Defection: A Report*. New Haven: Analysis Group.

Grimmett, Richard, and Paul Kerr. 2012. "Conventional Arms Transfers to Developing Nations, 2004–2011." Congressional Research Service, Washington, DC.

Grosz, Elizabeth. 1994. *Volatile Bodies: Toward a Corporeal Feminism*. Bloomington: Indiana University Press.

Guilliard, Joachim, Luhr Henken, Knut Mellenthin, Tim Takaro, Robert Gould, Ali Fathollah-Nejad, and Jens Wagner. 2015. "Body Count of the War on Terror: Casualty Figures after 10 Years." International Physicians for the Prevention of Nuclear War, Washington, DC.

Gurung, Regan, and Carly Chrouser. 2007. "Predicting Objectification: Do Provocative Clothing and Observer Characteristics Matter?" *Sex Roles* 57:91–99.

Guthman, Julie, and Melanie DuPuis. 2006. "Embodying Neoliberalism: Economy, Culture, and the Politics of Fat." *Environment and Planning D: Society and Space* 24:427–48.

Hager, Eli, and Bill Keller. 2017. "Everything You Think You Know about Mass Incarceration Is Wrong." Marshall Project, February 9. www.themarshallproject.org.

Hale, Jon. 1995. "The Making of the New Democrats." *Political Science Quarterly* 110 (2): 207–32.

Halliwell, Emma, Helen Malson, and Irmgard Tischner. 2011. "Are Contemporary Media Images Which Seem to Display Woman as Sexually Empowered Actually Harmful to Women?" *Psychology of Women Quarterly* 35:38–45.

Hamilton, Jon. 2015. "Pain Really Is All in Your Head and Emotion Controls Intensity." NPR, February 18. www.npr.org.

Haney, Craig. 2001. "The Psychological Impact of Incarceration: Implications for Post-Prison Adjustment." US Department of Health and Human Services, November 30. aspe.hhs.gov.

———. 2003. "Mental Health Issues in Long-Term Solitary and 'Supermax' Confinement." *Crime and Delinquency* 49:124–56.

Haney López, Ian. 2014. *Dog Whistle Politics: How Coded Racial Appeals Have Reinvented Racism and Wrecked the Middle Class*. Oxford: Oxford University Press.

Hansen, Elise. 2017. "The Forgotten Minority in Police Shootings." CNN, November 10. www.cnn.com.

Harris, David. 1999. "The Stories, the Statistics, and the Law: Why 'Driving While Black' Matters." *Minnesota Law Review* 84: 265–326.

Harrison, Jill. 2014. "Neoliberal Environmental Justice: Mainstream Ideas of Justice in Political Conflict over Agricultural Pesticides in the United States." *Environmental Politics* 23:650–69.

———. 2015. "Coopted Environmental Justice? Activists' Roles in Shaping EJ Policy Implementation." *Environmental Sociology* 1:241–55.

Harrison, Kristen, and Veronica Hefner. 2006. "Media Exposure, Current and Future Body Ideals, and Disordered Eating among Preadolescent Girls: A Longitudinal Panel Study." *Journal of Youth and Adolescence* 35:153–63.

Hart, Peter. 2014. "Who Gets to Speak on Cable News? The Identity of the Whitest, Malest Show We Found May Surprise You." Fairness and Accuracy in Reporting, July. fair.org.

Hartmann, Heidi. 1976. "Capitalism, Patriarchy, and Job Segregation by Sex." *Signs* 1:137–69.

Harvey, David. 2014. *Seventeen Contradictions and the End of Capitalism.* New York: Oxford University Press.

Healthline. 2020. "Alienation." Accessed May 5, 2020. www.healthline.com.

Heberle, Renee. 1996. "Deconstructive Strategies and the Movement against Sexual Violence." *Hypatia* 11:63–76.

Heckman, Susan. 1994. "The Feminist Critique of Rationality." In *The Polity Reader in Gender Studies.* Cambridge, UK: Polity.

Heer, Eric de, Marloes Gerrits, Aartjan Beekman, Jack Dekker, Harm van Marwijk, Margot de Waal, Philip Spinhoven, Brenda Penninx, and Christina van der Feltz-Cornelis. 2014. "The Association of Depression and Anxiety with Pain: A Study from NESDA." *PLOS One* 9 (10): 1–11.

Hesse-Biber, Sharlene. 2007. *The Cult of Thinness.* New York: Oxford University Press.

Hessler, Peter. 2017. "Egypt's Failed Revolution." *New Yorker,* January 2. www.newyorker.com.

Hetey, Rebecca, and Jennifer Eberhardt. 2014. "Racial Disparities in Incarceration Increase Acceptance of Punitive Policies." *Psychological Science* 25 (10): 1949–54.

Hill, Catherine, and Holly Kearl. 2011. "Crossing the Line: Sexual Harassment at School." American Association of University Women, Washington, DC.

Hilmers, Angela, David Hilmers, and Jayna Dave. 2012. "Neighborhood Disparities in Access to Healthy Foods and Their Effects on Environmental Justice." *American Journal of Public Health* 102:1644–54.

Hilt, Lori, Christina Roberto, and Susan Nolen-Hoeksema. 2013. "Rumination Mediates the Relationship between Peer Alienation and Eating Pathology in Young Adolescent Girls." *Eating and Weight Disorders—Studies on Anorexia, Bulimia and Obesity* 18:263–67.

Hinshaw, Stephen. 2009. *The Triple Bind: Saving Our Teenage Girls from Today's Pressures.* New York: Ballantine.

Hinton, Elizabeth. 2016. *From the War on Poverty to the War on Crime: The Making of Mass Incarceration in America.* Cambridge: Harvard University Press.

Hixson, Walter. 2013. *American Settler Colonialism: A History.* New York: Palgrave Macmillan.

Hochschild, Adam. 2018. "American Devilry." *New York Review of Books,* October 25. www.nybooks.com.

Hoffman, Wilhelm, Bertram Gawronski, Tobias Gschwendner, Huy Le, and Manfred Schmitt. 2005. "A Meta-Analysis on the Correlation between the Implicit Association Test and Explicit Self-Report Measures." *Personality and Social Psychology Bulletin* 31 (10): 1369–85.

Holt, Richard, David Phillips, Karen Jameson, Cyrus Cooper, Elaine Dennison, Robert Peveler, and Hertfordshire Cohort Study Group. 2013. "The Relationship between Depression, Anxiety and Cardiovascular Disease: Findings from the Hertfordshire Cohort Study." *Journal of Affective Disorders* 150:84–90.

Holtzman, Linda, and Leon Sharpe. 2014. *Media Messages: What Film, Television, and Popular Music Teach Us about Race, Class, Gender, and Sexual Orientation.* New York: Routledge.

Hopper, James. 2015. "Why Many Rape Victims Don't Fight or Yell." *Washington Post,* June 23.

Hopper, James, and David Lisak. 2014. "Why Rape and Trauma Survivors Have Fragmented and Incomplete Memories." *Time,* December 9. time.com.

Horowitz, Jake, and Connie Utada. 2018. "Community Supervision Marked by Racial and Gender Disparities." Pew Charitable Trusts, December 6. www.pewtrusts.org.

Huddy, Leonie, and Stanley Feldman. 2009. "On Assessing the Political Effects of Racial Prejudice." *Annual Review of Political Science* 12:423–47.

Human Rights Watch. 2017. "Egypt: Consolidating Repression under al-Sisi." January 12. www.hrw.org.

Hurwitz, Jon, and Mark Peffley. 2005. "Explaining the Great Racial Divide: Perceptions of Fairness in the US Criminal Justice System." *Journal of Politics* 67 (3): 762–83.

Hutchings, Vincent, and Ashley Jardina. 2009. "Experiments on Racial Priming in Political Campaigns." *Annual Review of Political Science* 12:397–402.

Iadicola, Peter, and Anson Shupe. 2003. *Violence, Inequality, and Human Freedom.* New York: Rowman and Littlefield.

Ifeagwazi, Mike, John Chukwuorji, and Endurance Zacchaeus. 2014. "Alienation and Psychological Wellbeing: Moderation by Resilience." *Social Indicators Research* 120 (2): 525–44.

Institute for Palestine Studies. 2017. "Special Focus: Israeli Prison, Palestinian Lives." April. www.palestine-studies.org.

International Trade Union Confederation. 2015. *The 2015 ITUC Global Rights Index.* Brussels: International Trade Union Confederation.

IPPNW, Physicians for Social Responsibility, and Physicians for Global Survival. 2015. "Casualty Figures after 10 Years of the 'War on Terror': Iraq, Afghanistan, Pakistan." International Physicians for the Prevention of Nuclear War, Berlin.

Iraq Body Count. 2017. "Iraq Body Count." Accessed May 18, 2017. www.iraqbody-count.org.

Irigaray, Luce. 1985. *Speculum of the Other Woman.* Ithaca: Cornell University Press.

Jackman, Mary. 1994. *The Velvet Glove: Paternalism and Conflict in Gender, Class, and Race Relations.* Berkeley: University of California Press.

———. 2002. "Violence in Social Life." *Annual Review of Sociology* 28:387–415.

Jamail, Dahr. 2007. "Iraq's Forgotten Refugees." Alternet, April 23. www.alternet.org.

Jannetta, Jesse, Justin Breaux, and Helen Ho. 2014. *Examining Racial and Ethnic Disparities in Probation Revocation Summary Findings and Implications from a Multisite Study*. Washington, DC: Urban Institute.

Jarrett, Christian. 2018. "How Prison Changes People." BBC, April 30. www.bbc.com.

Jeffreys, Sheila. 2005. *Beauty and Misogyny: Harmful Cultural Practices in the West*. New York: Routledge.

Jenkins, Richard. 1992. *Pierre Bourdieu*. New York: Routledge.

Johnson, Lyndon Baines. 1965. "Howard University Commencement Address." Howard University, June 4. www.americanrhetoric.com.

———. 1967. "State of the Union Address." January 10. www.presidency.ucsb.edu.

Jones, Maggie. 2018. "When Porn Is Sex Ed." *New York Times Magazine*, February 11, 30–35, 48–49.

Jost, John, Laurie Rudman, Irene Blair, Dana Carney, Nilanjana Dasgupta, Jack Glaser, and Curtis Hardin. 2009. "The Existence of Implicit Bias Is beyond Reasonable Doubt: A Refutation of Ideological and Methodological Objections and Executive Summary of Ten Studies That No Manager Should Ignore." *Research in Organizational Behavior* 29:39–69.

Kaeble, Danielle, and Mary Cowhig. 2018. *Correctional Populations in the United States, 2016*. Washington, DC: US Department of Justice.

Kaiser, Joshua. 2016. "Revealing the Hidden Sentence: How to Add Transparency, Legitimacy, and Purpose to 'Collateral' Punishment Policy." *Harvard Law and Policy Review* 10:123–84.

Kamarck, Elaine, and William Galston. 1993. "A Progressive Family Policy for the 1990s." In *Mandate for Change, edited by* Will Marshall and Martin Schram, 153–78. New York: Berkley Books.

Kang-Brown, Jacob, Chase Montagnet, and Jasmine Heiss. 2021. *People in Jail and Prison in Spring 2021*. Brooklyn: Vera Institute of Justice.

Katz, Jennifer, and Monica Schneider. 2015. "(Herero)sexual Compliance with Unwanted Sex: Associations with Feelings about First Sex and Sexual Self-Perceptions." *Sex Roles* 72:451–61.

Katz, Jennifer, and Vanessa Tirone. 2015. "From the Agency Line to the Picket Line: Neoliberal Ideals, Sexual Realities, and Arguments about Abortion in the US." *Sex Roles* 73:311–18.

Keaney, Thomas, and Eliot Cohen. 1993. "Gulf War Air Power Survey Summary Report." US Air Force, Washington, DC.

Kearl, Holly. 2014. "Unsafe and Harassed in Public Spaces: A National Street Harassment Report." Stop Street Harassment, Reston, VA.

Keneally, Meghan. 2018. "5 Times Trump Was Accused of Making Racially Tinged Comments about Immigrants, People of Color." ABC News, January 12. abcnews.go.com.

Kenworthy, E. W. 1964. "Johnson Disputes Goldwater Views." *New York Times*, July 25, 1, 6.

Khalidi, Rashid. 2014. "Israel: A Carceral State." *Journal of Palestine Studies* 43 (4): 5–10.

Kilgore, Ed. 1993. "Safer Streets and Neighborhoods." In *Mandate for Change*, edited by Will Marshall and Martin Schram, 179–95. New York: Berkley Books.

———. 2010. "About Race." Progressive Policy Institute, April 1. www.progressivepolicy.org.

Kimeldorf, Howard. 1988. *Reds or Rackets? The Making of Radical and Conservative Unions on the Waterfront*. Berkeley: University of California Press.

King, Keith, Rebecca Lake, and Amy Bernard. 2006. "Do the Depictions of Sexual Attire and Sexual Behavior in Music Videos Differ Based on Video Network and Character Gender?" *American Journal of Health Education* 37: 146–53.

Kirker, Douglas. 1964. "Johnson Vows to Halt Street Violence Anywhere in Nation." *Boston Globe*, August 13, 6.

Kitossa, Tamari. 2020. "How to Understand Police Violence: Not a Case of Good Cop vs. Bad Cop." *Conversation*, June 8. theconversation.com.

Klare, Michael. 2001. *Resource Wars: The New Landscape of Global Conflict*. New York: Henry Holt.

———. 2004. *Blood and Oil: The Dangers and Consequences of America's Growing Dependency on Imported Petroleum*. New York: Henry Holt.

Klement, Kathryn, Brad Sagarin, and John Skowronski. 2018. "Accusers Lie and Other Myths: Rape Myth Acceptance Predicts Judgments Made about Accusers and Accused Perpetrators in a Rape Case." *Sex Roles* 81:16–33.

Kohler-Hausmann, Issa. 2018. *Misdemeanorland: Criminal Courts and Social Control in an Age of Broken Windows Policing*. Princeton: Princeton University Press.

Kojola, Erik, and David Pellow. 2020. "New Directions in Environmental Justice Studies: Examining the State and Violence." *Environmental Politics*. https://doi.org/10.10 80/09644016.2020.1836898.

Kozlowska, Kasia, Peter Walker, Loyola McLean, and Pascal Carrive. 2015. "Fear and the Defense Cascade: Clinical Implications and Management." *Harvard Review of Psychiatry* 23 (4): 263–87.

Kreitner, Ricky. 2011. "Wall Street Responsible for One-Third of Obama's Campaign Funds." *Business Insider*, July 22. www.businessinsider.com.

Krivo, Lauren, and Ruth Peterson. 2000. "The Structural Context of Homicide: Accounting for Racial Differences in Process." *American Sociological Review* 65 (4): 547–59.

Krivo, Lauren, Ruth Peterson, and Danielle Kuhl. 2009. "Segregation, Racial Structure, and Neighborhood Violent Crime." *American Journal of Sociology* 114 (6): 1765–1802.

Krugman, Paul. 2007. "Innocent Mistakes." *Krugman Blog, New York Times*, November 10. www.krugman.blogs.nytimes.com.

Kuzmarov, Jeremy. 2012. *Modernizing Repression: Police Training and Nation-Building in the American Century*. Amherst: University of Massachusetts Press.

Lamb, Sharon, and Zoe Peterson. 2012. "Adolescent Girls' Sexual Empowerment: Two Feminists Explore the Concept." *Sex Roles* 66:703–12.

Layton, Alexi, and Alicia Shepard. 2013. "Lack of Female Sources in NY Times Front-Page Stories Highlights Need for Change." Poynter Institute, St. Petersburg, FL.

LeBesco, Kathleen. 2011. "Neoliberalism, Public Health, and the Moral Perils of Fatness." *Critical Public Health* 21:153–64.

Lee, Ching Kwan. 2016. "Precarization or Empowerment? Reflections on Recent Labor Unrest in China." *Journal of Asian Studies* 75:317–33.

Lehrman, Karen. 1997. *The Lipstick Proviso.* New York: Anchor.

Lemke, Thomas. 2001. "'The Birth of Bio-Politics': Michel Foucault's Lecture at the Collège de France on Neo-Liberal Governmentality." *Economy and Society* 30:190–207.

Lerman, Amy, and Vesla Weaver. 2013. "Staying out of Sight: Concentrated Policing and Local Political Action." *Annals of the American Association of Political Science* 20:1–18.

———. 2014. *Arresting Citizenship: The Democratic Consequences of American Crime Control.* Chicago: University of Chicago Press.

Lessa, Iara. 2006. "Discursive Struggles within Social Welfare: Restaging Teen Motherhood." *British Journal of Social Work* 36:283–98.

Levien, Michael. 2012. "The Land Question: Special Economic Zones and the Political Economy of Dispossession in India." *Journal of Peasant Studies* 39 (3–4): 933–69.

———. 2013. "The Politics of Dispossession: Theorizing India's 'Land Wars.'" *Politics and Society* 41 (3): 351–94.

Levy, Ariel. 2005. *Female Chauvinist Pigs: Women and the Rise of Raunch Culture.* New York: Free Press.

Light, Michael, and Jeffrey Ulmer. 2016. "Explaining the Gaps in White, Black, and Hispanic Violence since 1990: Accounting for Immigration, Incarceration, and Inequality." *American Sociological Review* 81 (2): 290–315.

Liu, Y., H. Tanaka, and Fukuoka Heart Study Group. 2002. "Overtime Work, Insufficient Sleep, and Risk of Non-Fatal Acute Myocardial Infarction in Japanese Men." *Occupational and Environmental Medicine* 59:447–51.

Lloyd, Genevieve. 1984. *The Man of Reason.* Minneapolis: University of Minnesota Press.

———. 1993. *The Man of Reason: "Male" and "Female" in Western Philosophy.* 2nd ed. London: Routledge.

Loo, Dennis, and Ruth-Ellen Grimes. 2004. "Polls, Politics, and Crime: The 'Law and Order' Issue of the 1960s." *Western Criminology Review* 5 (1): 50–67.

Los Angeles Times. 1964. "Text of Johnson Statement on Harlem Riots." July 22, 17.

Lubell, Samuel. 1970. *The Hidden Crisis in American Politics.* New York: Norton.

Luna, Jessie. 2019. "The Ease of Hard Work: Embodied Neoliberalism among Rocky Mountain Fun Runners." *Qualitative Sociology* 42:251–71.

Lurie, Stephen. 2019. "There's No Such Thing as a Dangerous Neighborhood." Bloomberg, February 25. www.bloomberg.com.

Lynch, Annette. 2012. *Porn Chic: Exploring the Contours of Raunch Eroticism.* New York: Berg.

Lynch, Colum. 2010. "The Battle over the Cost of War." *Foreign Policy*, January 20. www.foreignpolicy.com.

MacKinnon, Catharine. 1982. "Feminism, Marxism, Method and the State." *Signs* 7:515–44.

———. 1989. *Toward a Feminist Theory of the State*. Cambridge: Harvard University Press.

Mager, John, and James Helgeson. 2011. "Fifty Years of Advertising Images: Some Changing Perspectives on Role Portrayals along with Enduring Consistencies." *Sex Roles* 64: 238–52.

Mann, Michael. 1986. *The Sources of Social Power: A History of Power from the Beginning to A.D. 1760*. Cambridge: Cambridge University Press.

Marcelo, Philip. 2016. "AP Finds Boston Police Inflate Progress on Searches, Frisks." *Washington Times*, March 7. www.washingtontimes.com.

Marcus, Sharon. 1992. "Fighting Bodies, Fighting Words: A Theory and Politics of Rape Prevention." In *Feminists Theorize the Political*, edited by Judith Butler and Joan W. Scott, 385–403. New York: Routledge.

Mardorossian, Carine. 2002. "Towards a New Feminist Theory of Rape." *Signs: Journal of Women in Culture and Society* 27:743–75.

———. 2014. *Framing the Rape Victim: Gender and Agency Reconsidered*. New Brunswick: Rutgers University Press.

Margolick, David. 1991. "Smith Lawyers Assail Accuser's Memory." *New York Times*, December 6, A16.

Marshall, Will, with reply by Jeff Faux. 1994. "The Evasion of Politics." *American Prospect*, December 19. prospect.org.

Marshall, Will, and Elaine Kamarck. 1993. "Replacing Welfare with Work." In *Mandate for Change*, edited by Will Marshall and Martin Schram, 217–36. New York: Berkley Books.

Marshall, Will, and Martin Schram, eds. 1993. *Mandate for Change*. New York: Berkley Books.

Marston, Cicely, and Ruth Lewis. 2014. "Anal Heterosex among Young People and Implications for Health Promotion: A Qualitative Study in the UK." *BMJ Open* 4:1–6.

Martínez, Daniel, Robin Reineke, Raquel Rubio-Goldsmith, and Bruce Parks. 2014. "Structural Violence and Migrant Deaths in Southern Arizona: Data from the Pima County Office of the Medical Examiner, 1990–2013." *Journal on Migration and Human Security* 2:257–86.

Massey, Douglas, and Nancy Denton. 1993. *American Apartheid: Segregation and the Making of the Underclass*. Cambridge: Harvard University Press.

Matoesian, Gregory. 2001. *Law and the Language of Identity: Discourse in the William Kennedy Smith Rape Trial*. New York: Oxford University Press.

Mauer, Marc. 2006. *Race to Incarcerate*. New York: New Press.

———. 2016. "Bill Clinton, 'Black Lives' and the Myths of the 1994 Crime Bill." Marshall Project, April 11. www.themarshallproject.org.

McDade-Montez, Elizabeth, Jan Wallander, and Linda Cameron. 2017. "Sexualization in US Latina and White Girls' Preferred Children's Television Programs." *Sex Roles* 77:1–15.

McKenney, Sarah, and Rebecca Bigler. 2016. "Internalized Sexualization and Its Relation to Sexualized Appearance, Body Surveillance, and Body Shame among Early Adolescent Girls." *Journal of Early Adolescence* 36:171–97.

McKernan, Patricia. 2017. "Homelessness and Prisoner Reentry: Examining Barriers to Housing Stability and Evidence-Based Strategies That Promote Improved Outcomes." *Journal of Community Corrections* 27 (1): 7–29.

McLeod, Melissa, Daliah Heller, Meredith Manze, and Sandra Echeverria. 2020. "Police Interactions and the Mental Health of Black Americans: A Systematic Review." *Journal of Racial and Ethnic Health Disparities* 7:10–27.

McMillan, Tracie. 2017. "The Cost of Raunchy Kitchen Talk." *New York Times*, October 31, A23.

Mendelberg, Tali. 2001. *The Race Card: Campaign Strategy, Implicit Messages, and the Norm of Equality*. Princeton: Princeton University Press.

Menjívar, Cecilia, and Leisy Abrego. 2012. "Legal Violence: Immigration Law and the Lives of Central American Immigrants." *American Journal of Sociology* 117 (5): 1380–1421.

Mepham, David. 2016. "Repression Unbound: Egypt Under Sisi." *Huffington Post*, November 4. www.huffingtonpost.com.

Mercurio, Andrea, and Laura Landry. 2008. "Self-Objectification and Well-Being: The Impact of Self-Objectification on Women's Overall Sense of Self-Worth and Life Satisfaction." *Sex Roles* 58:458–66.

Mikkola, Mari. 2022. "Feminist Perspectives on Sex and Gender." In *The Stanford Encyclopedia of Philosophy* (Summer 2022 edition), edited by Edward N. Zalta. https://plato.stanford.edu.

Millett, Kate. 1971. *Sexual Politics*. New York: Avon.

Mills, Sara. 2003. *Michel Foucault*. New York: Routledge.

Mohr, Charles. 1964. "Goldwater Links the Welfare State to Rise in Crime." *New York Times*, September 11, 1, 21.

Moodley, Kiran. 2015. "Donald Trump Says African-American Youths 'Have No Spirit.'" *Independent* (London), June 25. www.independent.co.uk.

Moradi, Bonnie, and Yu-Ping Huang. 2008. "Objectification Theory and Psychology of Women: A Decade of Advances and Future Directions." *Psychology of Women Quarterly* 32:377–98.

Morrison, Wayne. 2017. "China-US Trade Issues." Congressional Research Service, Washington, DC.

Morsy, Leila, and Richard Rothstein. 2016. *Mass Incarceration and Children's Outcomes: Criminal Justice Policy Is Education Policy*. Washington, DC: Economic Policy Institute.

Moynihan, Daniel Patrick. 1965a. *The Negro Family: The Case for National Action*. Washington, DC: Office of Policy Planning and Research, US Department of Labor.
———. 1965b. "A Family Policy for the Nation." *America*, September 18, 280–83.

Murakawa, Naomi. 2014. *The First Civil Right: How Liberals Built Prison America*. New York: Oxford University Press.

Murchadha, Felix O., ed. 2006. *Violence, Victims, Justifications: Philosophical Approaches*. Bern: Peter Lang.

Murnen, Sarah, and Linda Smolak. 2012. "Social Considerations Related to Adolescent Girls' Sexual Empowerment: A Response to Lamb and Peterson." *Sex Roles* 66:725–35.

Myrdal, Gunnar. 1944. *An American Dilemma: The Negro Problem and Modern Democracy*. New York: Harper and Brothers.

Natapoff, Alexandra. 2018. *Punishment without Crime: How Our Massive Misdemeanor System Traps the Innocent and Makes America More Unequal*. New York: Basic Books.

National Women's Law Center. 2016. "Workplace Justice: Sexual Harassment in the Workplace." National Women's Law Center, Washington, DC.

Nealon, Jeffrey. 2008. *Foucault beyond Foucault: Power and Its Intensifications since 1984*. Stanford: Stanford University Press.

Newell, Jim. 2019. "When Joe Biden Was the Candidate of the Young." *Slate*, June 11. slate.com.

Newton, Creede. 2018. "Trump's America: A War on Police, or Their Detractors?" Al Jazeera, January 20. www.aljazeera.com.

New York Times. 1964. "Goldwater Has Had a Virtual Monopoly on the Morality Issue in the Campaign." October 29, 21.

———. 1965. "Hot Summer." August 15, E1.

New York Times Editorial Board. 2016. "American Complicity in Yemen's War." *New York Times*, August 17, A18.

———. 2017. "Will President Trump Help Save Yemen?" *New York Times*, May 25, A26.

Nibert, David. 2013. *Animal Oppression and Human Violence: Domesecration, Capitalism, and Global Conflict*. New York: Columbia University Press.

Nixon, Richard. 1968a. "Toward Freedom from Fear." *Congressional Record*, 114: 936–39.

———. 1968b. "A Commitment to Order." NBC Radio Network, March 7. www.presidency.ucsb.edu.

Nordstrom, Carolyn. 2004. *Shadows of War: Violence, Power, and International Profiteering in the Twenty-First Century*. Berkeley: University of California Press.

Norman, Sonya, Carolyn Allard, Kendall Browne, Christy Capone, Brittany Davis, and Edward Kubany. 2019. *Trauma Informed Guilt Reduction Therapy: Treating Guilt and Shame Resulting from Trauma and Moral Injury*. Cambridge: Academic Press.

O'Connor, Alice. 2001. *Poverty Knowledge: Social Science, Social Policy, and the Poor in Twentieth-Century US History*. Princeton: Princeton University Press.

O'Connor, James. 1973. *The Fiscal Crisis of the State*. New York: St. Martin's.

———. 1996. "The Second Contradiction of Capitalism." In *The Greening of Marxism*, edited by Ted Benton, 197–221. New York: Guilford.

Oksala, Johanna. 2012. *Foucault, Politics, and Violence*. Evanston: Northwestern University Press.

O'Mara, Shane. 2015. *Why Torture Doesn't Work: The Neuroscience of Interrogation*. Cambridge: Harvard University Press.

Oppliger, Patrice. 2008. *Girls Gone Skank: The Sexualization of Girls in American Culture*. London: McFarland.

O'Reilly, Kenneth. 1995. *Nixon's Piano: Presidents and Racial Politics from Washington to Clinton*. New York: Free Press.

Pager, Devah. 2003. "The Mark of a Criminal Record." *American Journal of Sociology* 108 (5): 937–75.

Pager, Devah, Bruce Western, and Bart Bonikowski. 2009. "Discrimination in a Low Wage Labor Market: A Field Experiment." *American Sociological Review* 74 (5): 777–99.

Paschel, Tianna. 2016. *Becoming Black Political Subjects: Movements and Ethno-Racial Rights in Colombia and Brazil*. Princeton: Princeton University Press.

Pascoe, C. J. 2012. *Dude, You're a Fag: Masculinity and Sexuality in High School*. Berkeley: University of California Press.

Payne, B. Keith, Jon Krosnick, Josh Pasek, Yphtack Lelkes, Omair Akhtar, and Trevor Tompson. 2010. "Implicit and Explicit Prejudice in the 2008 American Presidential Election." *Journal of Experimental Social Psychology* 46:367–74.

Payne, Diana, Kimberly Lonsway, and Louise Fitzgerald. 1999. "Rape Myth Acceptance: Exploration of Its Structure and Its Measurement Using the Illinois Rape Myth Acceptance Scale." *Journal of Research in Personality* 33:27–68.

Pellow, David. 2014. *The Power and Promise of Animal Rights and the Radical Earth Movement*. Minneapolis: University of Minnesota Press.

Penner, Andrew, and Aliya Saperstein. 2008. "How Social Status Shapes Race." *Proceedings of the National Academy of Sciences* 105 (50): 19628–30.

Pérez-Peña, Richard. 2015. "1 in 4 Women Experience Sex Assault on Campus." *New York Times*, September 22. www.nytimes.com.

Perloff, Richard. 2014. "Social Media Effects on Young Women's Body Image Concerns: Theoretical Perspectives and an Agenda for Research." *Sex Roles* 71:363–77.

Perlo-Freeman, Sam, Aude Fleurant, Pieter Wezeman, and Siemon Wezeman. 2015. "Trends in World Military Expenditure, 2014." Stockholm International Peace Research Institute, Solna, Sweden.

Peterson, Zoe, and Charlene Muehlenhard. 2004. "Was It Rape? The Function of Women's Rape Myth Acceptance and Definitions of Sex in Labeling Their Own Experiences." *Sex Roles* 51:129–44.

Petrella, Christopher. 2016. "On Stone Mountain: White Supremacy and the Birth of the Modern Democratic Party." *Boston Review*, March 30. bostonreview.net.

Pettit, Becky. 2012. *Invisible Men: Mass Incarceration and the Myth of Black Progress*. New York: Russell Sage Foundation.

Pew Center on the States. 2009. *One in 31: The Long Reach of American Corrections*. www.pewtrusts.org.

Pfaff, John. 2017. *Locked In: The True Causes of Mass Incarceration and How to Achieve Real Reform*. New York: Basic Books.

Phillips, Kevin. 1969. *The Emerging Republican Majority*. New Rochelle, NY: Arlington House.

Pilger, John. 2000. "Squeezed to Death." *Guardian*, March 4. www.theguardian.com.

Ponterotto, Diane. 2007. "The Repertoire of Complicity vs. Coercion: The Discursive Trap of the Rape Trial Protocol." In *The Language of Sexual Crime*, edited by Janet Cotterill. New York: Palgrave Macmillan.

Potter, Hillary. 2008. *Battle Cries: Black Women and Intimate Partner Abuse*. New York: New York University Press.

President's Commission on Law Enforcement and Administration of Justice. 1967. *The Challenge of Crime in a Free Society*. Washington, DC: US Government Printing Office.

President's Committee on Civil Rights. 1947. *To Secure These Rights: The Report of the President's Committee on Civil Rights*. Washington, DC: US Government Printing Office.

Prokhovnik, Raia. 1999. *Rational Woman*. London: Routledge.

Przeworski, Adam. 1985. *Capitalism and Social Democracy*. Cambridge: Cambridge University Press.

Pujols, Yassica, Cindy Meston, and Brooke Seal. 2009. "The Association between Sexual Satisfaction and Body Image in Women." *Journal of Sexual Medicine* 7:905–16.

Pulido, Laura. 2017. "Geographies of Race and Ethnicity II: Environmental Racism, Racial Capitalism and State-Sanctioned Violence." *Progress in Human Geography* 41 (4): 524–33.

Pyrooz, David, and Scott Decker. 2019. *Competing for Control: Gangs and the Social Order of Prisons*. New York: Cambridge University Press.

Qiu, Linda. 2016. "Donald Trump's False Claim That Oakland, Ferguson Are 'Among the Most Dangerous in the World.'" Politifact, May 25. www.politifact.com.

Rape, Abuse, and Incest National Network. 2016. "The Criminal Justice System: Statistics." Rape, Abuse, and Incest National Network, Washington, DC.

Raspberry, William. 1990. "Common Sense about the Family." *Washington Post*, October 13. www.washingtonpost.com.

Rattan, Aneeta, and Jennifer Eberhardt. 2010. "The Role of Social Meaning in Inattentional Blindness: When the Gorillas in Our Midst Do Not Go Unseen." *Journal of Experimental Social Psychology* 46:1085–88.

Rattan, Aneeta, Cynthia Levine, Carol Dweck, and Jennifer Eberhardt. 2012. "Race and the Fragility of the Legal Distinction between Juveniles and Adults." *PLOS One* 7 (5).

Reed, Isaac. 2013. "Power: Relational, Discursive, and Performative Dimensions." *Sociological Theory* 31 (3): 193–218.

Reed, Isaac, and Julia Adams. 2011. "Culture in the Transition to Modernity: Seven Pillars of a New Research Agenda." *Theory and Society* 40:247–72.

Reiff, David. 2003. "Were Sanctions Right?" *New York Times Magazine*, July 27. www.nytimes.com.

Reinarman, Craig, and Harry Levine. 1995. "The Crack Attack: America's Latest Drug Scare, 1986–1992." In *Images of Issues: Typifying Contemporary Social Problems*, edited by Joel Best, 147–90. New York: Aldine De Gruyter.

Restaurant Opportunities Centers United Forward Together. 2014. "The Glass Floor: Sexual Harassment in the Restaurant Industry." Restaurant Opportunities Centers United, New York.

Rice, Carla. 2014. *Becoming Women: The Embodied Self in Image Culture*. Toronto: University of Toronto Press.

Rich, Adrienne. 1980. "Compulsory Heterosexuality and Lesbian Existence." *Signs* 5:631–60.

Rich, Motoko. 2017. "She Reported It. And Her Country Ignored Her." *New York Times*, December 30, A1, A8.

Richardson, Lynne, and Marlaina Norris. 2010. "Access to Health and Health Care: How Race and Ethnicity Matter." *Mount Sinai Journal of Medicine* 77:166–77.

Right Web. 2011. "Democratic Leadership Council." February 15. rightweb.irc-online.org.

Robinson, Cedric. 2000. *Black Marxism: The Making of the Black Radical Tradition*. Chapel Hill: University of North Carolina Press.

Robinson, Nathan. 2016. "Bill Clinton's Stone Mountain Moment." *Jacobin*, September 16. www.jacobinmag.com.

Roediger, David. 1991. *The Wages of Whiteness: Race and the Making of the American Working Class* New York: Verso.

Roiphe, Katie. 1993. *The Morning After: Sex, Fear, and Feminism on Campus*. Boston: Little, Brown.

Rose, Nikolas, and Peter Miller. 1992. "Political Power beyond the State: Problematics of Government." *British Journal of Sociology* 43:173–205.

Ross, Catherine, and John Mirowsky. 2009. "Neighborhood Disorder, Subjective Alienation, and Distress." *Journal of Health and Social Behavior* 50 (1): 49–64.

Ross, Cody. 2015. "A Multi-Level Bayesian Analysis of Racial Bias in Police Shootings at the County-Level in the United States, 2011–2014." *PLOS One* 10 (11): 1–34.

Rothwell, Jonathon. 2014. "How the War on Drugs Damages Black Social Mobility." Brookings Institution, September 30. www.brookings.edu.

Rovere, Richard. 1964. "The Campaign: Goldwater." *New Yorker*, October 3. www.newyorker.com.

Safipour, Jalal, Donald Schopflocher, Gina Higginbottom, and Aziat Amami. 2011. "The Mediating Role of Alienation in Self-Reported Health among Swedish Adolescents." *Vulnerable Groups and Inclusion* 2 (1): 1–11.

Saif, Atef. 2015. *The Drone Eats with Me: A Gaza Diary*. Boston: Beacon.

Salmi, Jamil. 1993. *Violence and Democratic Society*. London: Zed Books.

Sampson, Robert, William Julius Wilson, and Hanna Katz. 2018. "Reassessing 'Toward a Theory of Race, Crime, and Urban Inequality.'" *Du Bois Review* 15 (1): 13–34.

Scaer, Robert. 2014. *The Body Bears the Burden: Trauma, Dissociation, and Disease*. New York: Routledge.

Scammon, Richard, and Ben Wattenberg. 1970. *The Real Majority*. New York: Coward-McCann.

Schippers, Mimi. 2007. "Recovering the Feminine Other: Masculinity, Femininity, and Gender Hegemony." *Theory and Society* 36:85–102.

Schwartz, Martin. 2010. "National Institute of Justice Visiting Fellowship: Police Investigation of Rape—Roadblocks and Solutions." US Department of Justice, Washington, DC.

Schwartzapfel, Beth, and Bill Keller. 2015. "Willie Horton Revisited." Marshall Project, May 13. www.themarshallproject.org.

Scott, James. 1998. *Seeing Like a State: How Certain Schemes to Improve the Human Condition Have Failed*. New Haven: Yale University Press.

Sentencing Project. 2013. *Report of the Sentencing Project to the United Nations Human Rights Committee Regarding Racial Disparities in the United States Criminal Justice System*. Washington, DC: Sentencing Project.

———. 2020. *Incarcerated Women and Girls*. Washington, DC: Sentencing Project.

Shenker, Jack. 2016. "State Repression in Egypt Worst in Decades, Says Activist." *Guardian*, January 24. www.theguardian.com.

Shihadeh, Edward, and Wesley Shrum. 2004. "Serious Crime in Urban Neighborhoods: Is There a Race Effect?" *Sociological Spectrum* 24 (4): 507–33.

Sinton, Meghan, and Leann Birch. 2006. "Individual and Sociocultural Influences on Pre-Adolescent Girls' Appearance Schemas and Body Dissatisfaction." *Journal of Youth and Adolescence* 35:165–75.

Skidelsky, Robert. 2018. *Money and Government: The Past and Future of Economics*. New Haven: Yale University Press.

Skogan, Wesley. 2005. "Citizen Satisfaction with Police Encounters." *Police Quarterly* 8 (3): 298–321.

———. 2006. "Asymmetry in the Impact of Encounters with Police." *Policing and Society* 16 (2): 99–126.

Slotkin, Richard. 1973. *Regeneration through Violence: The Mythology of the American Frontier, 1600–1860*. Middletown: Wesleyan University Press.

Smith, Andrea. 2005. *Conquest: Sexual Violence and American Indian Genocide*. Cambridge, MA: South End.

Smith, Kylie. 2008. "Hegemony, Subalternity, and Subjectivity in Early Industrial Sydney." In *Hegemony: Studies in Consensus and Coercion*, edited by Richard Howson and Kylie Smith. New York: Routledge.

Smith, Sharon, Xinjian Zhang, Kathleen Basile, Melissa Merrick, Jing Wang, Marciejo Kresnow, and Jieur Chen. 2018. *National Intimate Partner and Sexual Violence Survey: 2015 Data Brief—Updated Release*. Atlanta: National Center for Injury Prevention and Control, Centers for Disease Control and Prevention.

Smith, Stacy, Marc Choueiti, Katherine Pieper, Ariana Case, Kevin Yao, and Angel Choi. 2017. "Inequality in 900 Popular Films: Examining Portrayals of Gender, Race/Ethnicity, LGBT, and Disability from 2007–2016." Media, Diversity, and Social Change Initiative, Los Angeles.

Smith, Stacy, Marc Choueiti, Ashley Prescott, and Katherine Pieper. 2013. "Gender Roles and Occupations: A Look at Character Attributes and Job-Related Aspirations in Film and Television." Geena Davis Institute on Gender in Media, Los Angeles.

Solnit, Rebecca. 2017. *The Mother of All Questions*. Chicago: Haymarket Books.

Stankiewicz, Julie, and Francine Rosselli. 2008. "Women as Sex Objects and Victims in Print Advertisements." *Sex Roles* 58:579–89.

Stannard, David. 1992. *American Holocaust: Columbus and the Conquest of the New World*. New York: Oxford University Press.

Starr, Christine, and Gail Ferguson. 2012. "Sexy Dolls, Sexy Grade-Schoolers? Media and Maternal Influences on Young Girls' Self-Sexualization." *Sex Roles* 67:463–76.

Stearns, Jason, Judith Verweijen, and Maria Baaz. 2012. "The National Army and Armed Groups in the Eastern Congo: Untangling the Gordian Knot of Insecurity." Usalama Project, Rift Valley Institute, Nairobi.

Steffensmeier, Darrell, Jeffrey Ulmer, Ben Feldmeyer, and Casey Harris. 2010. "Scope and Conceptual Issues in Testing the Race-Crime Invariance Thesis: Black, White, and Hispanic Comparisons." *Criminology* 48 (4): 1133–69.

Steger, Manfred. 2003. *Judging Nonviolence: The Dispute between Realists and Idealists*. New York: Routledge.

Stein, David. 2019. "The Untold Story: Joe Biden Pushed Ronald Reagan to Ramp Up Incarceration—Not the Other Way Around." *Intercept*, September 17. theintercept.com.

Steinberg, Stephen. 2001. *The Ethnic Myth: Race, Ethnicity, and Class in America*. Boston: Beacon.

Stermer, S. Paul, and Melissa Burkley. 2012. "Xbox or Sexbox? An Examination of Sexualized Content in Video Games." *Social and Personality Psychology Compass* 6/7:525–35.

Stolberg, Sheryl, and Astead Herndon. 2019. "'Lock the S.O.B.s Up': Joe Biden and the Era of Mass Incarceration." *New York Times*, June 25. www.nytimes.com.

Stringer, Rebecca. 2013. "Vulnerability after Wounding: Feminism, Rape Law, and the Differend." *Substance* 42:148–68.

Suarez, Eliana, and Tahany Gadalla. 2010. "Stop Blaming the Victim: A Meta-Analysis on Rape Myths." *Journal of Interpersonal Violence* 25 (11): 2010–35.

Summers, Alicia, and Monica Miller. 2014. "From Damsels in Distress to Sexy Super-heroes." *Feminist Media Studies* 14:1028–40.

Swaine, Jon, Oliver Laughland, Jamiles Lartey, and Ciara McCarthy. 2015. "Young Black Men Killed by US Police at Highest Rate in Year of 1,134 Deaths." *Guardian*, December 31. www.theguardian.com.

Szymanski, Dawn, and Stacy Henning. 2007. "The Role of Self-Objectification in Women's Depression: A Test of Objectification Theory." *Sex Roles* 56:45–53.

Takaki, Ronald. 1993. *A Different Mirror: A History of Multicultural America*. Boston: Little, Brown.

Taslitz, Andrew. 1999. *Rape and the Culture of the Courtroom*. New York: New York University Press.

Taylor, Keeanga-Yamahtta. 2017. *How We Get Free: Black Feminism and the Combahee River Collective*. Chicago: Haymarket Books.

Tiggemann, Marika, and Amy Slater. 2013. "NetGirls: The Internet, Facebook, and Body Image Concern in Adolescent Girls." *International Journal of Eating Disorders* 46:630–33.

———. 2017. "Facebook and Body Image Concern in Adolescent Girls: A Prospective Study." *International Journal of Eating Disorders* 50:80–83.

Tolman, Deborah. 2013. "It's Bad for Us Too: How the Sexualization of Girls Impacts the Sexuality of Boys, Men, and Women." In *The Sexualization of Girls and Girlhood*, edited by Eileen L. Zurbriggen and Tomi-Ann Roberts. Oxford: Oxford University Press.

Travis, Jeremy, Bruce Western, and Steve Redburn. 2014. *The Growth of Incarceration in the United States: Exploring Causes and Consequences*. Washington, DC: National Research Council.

Tuttle, Ross, and Erin Schneider. 2012. "Stopped-and-Frisked: 'For Being a F**king Mutt.'" *Nation*, October 8. www.thenation.com.

Tyler, Tom, and Yuen Huo. 2002. *Trust in the Law: Encouraging Public Cooperation with the Police and Courts*. New York: Russell Sage Foundation.

Tyler, Tom, and Cheryl Wakslak. 2004. "Profiling and Police Legitimacy: Procedural Justice, Attributions of Motive, and Acceptance of Police Authority." *Criminology* 42 (2): 253–81.

Uggen, Christopher, Ryan Larson, and Sarah Shannon. 2016. *6 Million Lost Voters: State-Level Estimates of Felony Disenfranchisement, 2016*. Washington, DC: Sentencing Project.

United Nations Human Rights Council. 2015. *Human Rights Situation in Palestine and Other Occupied Arab Territories: Report of the Independent Commission of Inquiry Established Pursuant to Human Rights Council Resolution S-21/1*. New York: United Nations.

United Nations OCHA OPT. 2014. "Fragmented Lives: Humanitarian Overview 2013." United Nations Office for the Coordination of Humanitarian Affairs Occupied Palestinian Territory, East Jerusalem.

US Department of Agriculture. 2016. "Background." Accessed May 18, 2017. www.ers.usda.gov.

US Department of Justice. 2016. *Investigation of the Baltimore City Police Department*. Washington, DC: US Department of Justice.

US Equal Employment Opportunity Commission. 2017. "Sexual Harassment." Accessed November 21, 2017. www.eeoc.gov.

US Immigration and Customs Enforcement. 2017. "Fiscal Year 2016 ICE Enforcement and Removal Operations Report." Washington, DC.

US Trade Representative's Office. 2022. "Countries and Regions." Accessed April 8, 2022. ustr.gov.

Vagianos, Alanna. 2015. "1 in 3 Women Has Been Sexually Harassed at Work, According to Survey." *Huffington Post*, February 19. www.huffingtonpost.com.

Valenti, Jessica. 2016a. *Sex Object: A Memoir*. New York: Harper Collins.

———. 2016b. "What Does a Lifetime of Leers Do to Us?" *New York Times*, June 4, Week in Review, 7.

Valentino, Nicholas, Vincent Hutchings, and Ismail White. 2002. "Cues That Matter: How Political Ads Prime Racial Attitudes during Campaigns." *American Political Science Review* 96 (1): 75–90.

Valentino, Nicholas, Kosuke Imai, L. Matthew Vandenbroek, and Teppei Yamamoto. 2013. "Obama and the End of Racial Priming." Unpublished paper.

Van der Kolk, Bessel. 2014. *The Body Keeps the Score: Brain, Mind, and Body in the Healing of Trauma*. New York: Penguin.

Vargas, Joao. 2008. *Never Meant to Survive: Genocide and Utopias in Black Diaspora Communities*. New York: Rowman and Littlefield.

Veracini, Lorenzo. 2010. *Settler Colonialism: A Theoretical Overview*. New York: Palgrave Macmillan.

Verité Research. 2004. "Excessive Overtime in Chinese Supplier Factories: Causes, Impacts, and Recommendations for Action." Verité, Amherst, MA.

Wade, Lisa. 2017. *American Hookup: The New Culture of Sex on Campus*. New York: Norton.

Wakefield, Sara, and Christopher Wildeman. 2013. *Children of the Prison Boom: Mass Incarceration and the Future of American Inequality*. Oxford: Oxford University Press.

Walby, Sylvia. 1986. *Patriarchy at Work: Patriarchal and Capitalist Relations in Employment*. Cambridge: Polity.

Wallace, George. 1963. "The Inaugural Address of Governor George C. Wallace." Montgomery, AL, January 14. digital.archives.alabama.gov.

Wallis, Cara. 2011. "Performing Gender: A Content Analysis of Gender Display in Music Videos." *Sex Roles* 64:160–72.

Wall Street Journal. 1965. "Behind the Riots: Family Life Breakdown in Negro Slums Sows Seeds of Race Violence—Husbandless Homes Spawn Young Hoodlums, Impede Reforms, Sociologists Say." August 16, 1.

Walmsley, Roy. 2013. "World Prison Population List." International Centre for Prison Studies, London.

Walsh, Declan, and Eric Schmitt. 2018. "Arms Sales to Saudis Leave American Fingerprints on Yemen's Carnage." *New York Times*, December 25. www.nytimes.com.

Walsh, Kimberly, Elfriede Fursich, and Bonnie Jefferson. 2008. "Beauty and the Patriarchal Beast: Gender Role Portrayals in Sitcoms Featuring Mismatched Couples." *Journal of Popular Film and Television* 36:123–32.

Walter, S. A., M. P. Jones, N. J. Talley, L. Kjellstrom, H. Nyhlin, A. N. Andreasson, and L. Agreus. 2013. "Abdominal Pain Is Associated with Anxiety and Depression Scores in a Sample of the General Adult Population with No Signs of Organic Gastrointestinal Disease." *Neurogastroenterology and Motility* 25 (9): 741-e576.

Washington Post. 2022. "Fatal Force: 1,024 People Have Been Shot and Killed by the Police in the Past Year." April 19. www.washingtonpost.com.

Watts, Michael. 2008. "Economies of Violence: More Oil, More Blood." In *Contested Grounds: Essays on Nature, Culture, and Power*, edited by Amita Baviskar. New York: Oxford University Press.

Weaver, Vesla. 2007. "Frontlash: Race and the Development of Punitive Crime Policy." *Studies in American Political Development* 21:230–65.

Weedon, Chris. 1997. *Feminist Practice and Poststructuralist Theory*. 2nd ed. Cambridge, MA: Blackwell.

Weiner, Jennifer. 2017. "The Women I'm Thankful For." *New York Times*, November 21, A25.

Weitzer, Ronald, and Steven Tuch. 2006. *Race and Policing in America: Conflict and Reform*. New York: Cambridge University Press.

Western, Bruce, and Becky Pettit. 2010. *Collateral Costs: Incarceration's Effect on Economic Mobility*. Pew Charitable Trusts. www.pewtrusts.org.

Western, Bruce, and Catherine Sirois. 2017. *Racial Inequality in Employment and Earnings after Incarceration*. Working Paper. Cambridge: Harvard University.

Western Washington Medical Group. 2020. "Depression and Its Mental and Physical Effects." Accessed May 1, 2020. www.wwmedgroup.com.

Whyte, Kyle. 2017. "The Dakota Access Pipeline, Environmental Injustice, and US Colonialism." *RED INK: An International Journal of Indigenous Literature, Arts, and Humanities* 19:154–69.

———. 2018. "Settler Colonialism, Ecology, and Environmental Injustice." *Environment and Society: Advances in Research* 9:125–44.

Williams, David, and Selina Mohammed. 2009. "Discrimination and Racial Disparities in Health: Evidence and Needed Research." *Journal of Behavioral Medicine* 32:20–47.

Williams, Kristian. 2007. *Our Enemies in Blue: Police and Power in America*. Cambridge: South End.

Wilson, John, Boris Drozdek, and Silvana Turkovic. 2006. "Posttraumatic Shame and Guilt." *Trauma, Violence and Abuse* 7 (2): 122–41.

Wolf, Naomi. 1993. *Fire with Fire: The New Female Power and How It Will Change the 21st Century*. New York: Random House.

Wolfe, Patrick. 1999. *Settler Colonialism and the Transformation of Anthropology: The Politics and Poetics of an Ethnographic Event*. New York: Cassell.

Wolitzky-Taylor, Kate, Heidi Resnick, Jenna McCauley, Ananda Amstadter, Dean Kilpatrick, and Kenneth Ruggiero. 2011. "Is Reporting of Rape on the Rise? A Comparison of Women with Reported versus Unreported Rape Experiences in the National Women's Study-Replication." *Journal of Interpersonal Violence* 26:807–32.

World Without Genocide. 2016. "Democratic Republic of Congo." Accessed January 23, 2017. worldwithoutgenocide.org.

Worrell, Judith. 2001. *Encyclopedia of Women and Gender: Sex Similarities and Differences and the Impact of Society on Gender*. Vol. 1. San Diego: Academic Press.

Yung, Corey. 2013–2014. "How to Lie with Rape Statistics: America's Hidden Rape Crisis." *Iowa Law Review* 99:1197–1256.

Yuval-Davis, Nira. 2006. "Intersectionality and Feminist Politics." *European Journal of Women's Studies* 13:193–209.

Zhou, Yixue. 2011. *Contempt and Self-Esteem: The Effect of the Contempt Expression on Self-Enhancing Behaviors*. Philadelphia: Wharton School, University of Pennsylvania.

Zinn, Howard. 1980. *A People's History of the United States*. New York: Harper and Row.

Zurbriggen, Eileen L., and Tomi-Ann Roberts, eds. 2013. *The Sexualization of Girls and Girlhood*. New York: Oxford University Press.

INDEX

abuse, 20, 24, 28, 88
activist organizations, 256–57
Adams, Julia, 55–56
advertisements, 80, 126–27
affirmative action, Reagan opposing, 218
African Americans, 154–55, 218, 267n18; associated with crime, 189, 200–201, 205, 225–26, 230, 233–34; blame toward, 174; civil rights for, 192–94, 197; criminal justice system relation to, 157–58, 179, 266n14; defined as poor people, 231; families of, 194–96, 197, 206, 217–18; mass incarceration of, 9–10, 143, 156, 171; police stopping of, 149–50, 152–53, 178; police violence against, 20, 52, 53, 54, 58, 63, 137–40, 143–44, 189, 247, 251, 252, 256, 264n1, 265n11; public defenders representing, 157; racial discourses relation to, 70–71, 175; state violence against, 172, 235–36; US view of, 181–82; war on crime and drugs effect on, 159, 217, 239; Whites relation to, 52, 54, 100, 141, 142, 188, 189, 239–40, 241, 242–43, 265n11, 266n15
agency: aggression relation to, 93–94; in bodily practices, 92; gender differences in, 66–67; hookup culture relation to, 88–89; of subordinate groups, 67, 85; of victims, 68; of women and girls, 68, 69, 83–85, 87–88, 90–91
aggression, 55–56, 98, 116; agency relation to, 93–94; in US courtroom culture, 106
agribusiness industry, 15, 19

agriculture industry, 19
Alabama, 187–88
Alexander, Michelle, 137, 166; on war on drugs, 236–37
alienation, 91, 261n3; of inmates families, 170–71; psyches affected by, 7; violence relation to, 6, 253, 257
American Independent Party, 208
animals, institutionalized violence against, 33
anti-crime rhetoric, of Democratic Party, 234
anti-crime sentiment, media stirring, 267n5
Anti-Drug Abuse Act (1986), 222, 223
Anti-Drug Abuse Act (1988), 222
anti-drug rhetoric, 221–22
anti-Indigenous violence, colonialism relation to, 33
armed violence: against protests, 52; by US, 50–51; against workers, 49
arrest rates, 265n6
Atlantic Monthly (magazine), 225
authoritarian governments, social engineering projects of, 33
avoidability, 29, 30

Baltimore, stop and search in, 151
Barnes, Cliff, 219, 220
Bay-Cheng, Laina, 87–88, 93
beauty practices, patriarchy effect on, 21, 54
Biden, Joe, 215, 226, 234; election of, 250; racist rhetoric of, 222–24

ABOUT THE AUTHOR

LIAM DOWNEY is Associate Professor of Sociology at the University of Colorado–Boulder. He has published numerous journal articles and a prize-winning book, *Inequality, Democracy, and the Environment*, with New York University Press.